The Power to Legislate

A Reference Guide to the United States Constitution

Richard E. Levy

Foreword by RICHARD A. POSNER

REFERENCE GUIDES TO THE
UNITED STATES CONSTITUTION, NUMBER 17
Jack Stark, *Series Editor*

PRAEGER

**Westport, Connecticut
London**

Library of Congress Cataloging-in-Publication Data

Levy, Richard E., 1956–
    The power to legislate : a guide to the United States
Constitution / Richard E. Levy; foreword by Richard A.
Posner
        p.   cm. — (Reference guides to the United States
Constitution, ISSN 1539-8986 ; no. 17)
    Includes bibliographical references and index.
    ISBN 0-313-32284-8 (alk. paper)
    1. United States. Congress—Powers and duties.   2. United
States. Congress—Powers and duties—History.   3.
Constitutional law—United States.   I. Title.   II. Series.
    KF4940.L48 2006
        328.73'074—dc22   2006015117

British Library Cataloguing in Publication Data is available.

Library of Congress Catalog Card Number: 2006015117
ISBN: 0-313-32284-8
ISSN: 1539-8986

First published in 2006

Praeger Publishers, 88 Post Road West, Westport, CT 06881
An imprint of Greenwood Publishing Group, Inc.
www.praeger.com

Printed in the United States of America

∞™

The paper used in this book complies with the
Permanent Paper Standard issued by the National
Information Standards Organization (Z39.48–1984).

10 9 8 7 6 5 4 3 2 1

To Kathleen, Ben, and Erin

Contents

Series Foreword

JACK STARK

One can conceive of the United States Constitution in many ways. For example, noting the reverence in which it has been held, one can think of it as equivalent to a sacred text. Unfortunately, most of its devotees have had less knowledge and even less understanding of the document than they have had reverence for it. Sometimes it is treated as primarily a political document and on that basis has been subjected to analysis, such as Charles Beard's *An Economic Interpretation of the Constitution of the United States.* One can plausibly argue that the Constitution seems most astounding when it is seen in the light of the intellectual effort that has been associated with it. Three brief but highly intense bursts of intellectual energy produced, and established as organic law, most of the Constitution as it now exists. Two of these efforts, sustained over a long period of time, have enabled us better to understand that document.

The first burst of energy occurred at the Constitutional Convention. Although some of the delegates' business, such as the struggle between populous and nonpopulous states about their representation in Congress, was political, much of it was about fundamental issues of political theory. A few of the delegates had or later achieved international eminence for their intellects. Among them were Benjamin Franklin, Alexander Hamilton, and James Madison. Others, although less well known, had first-rate minds. That group includes George Mason and George Wythe. Many of the delegates contributed intelligently. Although the Convention's records are less than satisfactory, they indicate clearly enough that the delegates worked mightily to constitute not merely a polity but a rational polity—one that would rise to the standards envisioned by the delegates' intellectual ancestors. Their product, though brief, is amazing. William Gladstone called it "the most wonderful work ever struck off."

Despite the delegates' eminence and the Constitution's excellence as seen from our place in history, its ratification was far from certain. That state of affairs necessitated the second burst of intellectual energy associated with that document: the debate over ratification. Soon after the Convention adjourned, articles and speeches—some supporting the Constitution and some attacking it—began to proliferate. A national debate commenced, not only about the document itself, but also about the nature of the polity that ought to exist in this country. Both sides included many writers and speakers who were verbally adroit and steeped in the relevant political and philosophical literature. The result was an accumulation of material that is remarkable for both its quantity and its quality. At its apex is *The Federalist Papers*, a production of Alexander Hamilton, James Madison, and John Jay that deserves a place among the great books of Western culture.

Another burst, not as impressive as the first two but highly respectable, occurred when the Bill of Rights was proposed. Some delegates to the Constitutional Convention had vigorously asserted that such guarantees should be included in the original document. George Mason, the principal drafter of the Virginia Declaration of Rights, so held, and he walked out of the Convention when he failed to achieve his purpose. Even those who had argued that the rights in question were implicit recognized the value of adding protection of them to the Constitution. The debate was thus focused on the rights that were to be explicitly granted, not on whether any rights *ought* to be explicitly granted. Again many writers and speakers entered the fray, and again the debate was solidly grounded in theory and was conducted on a high intellectual level.

Thus, within a few years a statement of organic law and a vital coda to it had been produced. However, the meaning and effect of many of that document's provisions were far from certain; the debates on ratification of the Constitution and the Bill of Rights had demonstrated that. In addition, the document existed in a vacuum, because statutes and actions had not been assessed by its standards. The attempt to resolve these problems began after Chief Justice John Marshall, in Marbury v. Madison, asserted the right of the U.S. Supreme Court to interpret and apply the Constitution. Judicial interpretation and application of the Constitution, beginning with the first constitutional case and persisting until the most recent, is one of the sustained exertions of intellectual energy associated with the Constitution. The framers would be surprised by some of the results of those activities. References in the document to "due process," which seems to refer only to procedures, have been held also to have a substantive dimension. A right to privacy has been found lurking among the penumbras of various parts of the text. A requirement that states grant the same "privileges and immunities" to citizens of other states that they granted to their own citizens, which seemed to guarantee important rights, was held not to be particularly important. The corpus of judicial interpretations of the Constitution is now as voluminous as that document is terse.

As the judicial interpretations multiplied, another layer—interpretations of interpretations—appeared, and also multiplied. This layer, the other sustained intellectual effort associated with the Constitution, consists of articles, most of them published in law reviews, and books on the Constitution. This material varies in quality and significance. Some of these works of scholarship result from meticulous examination and incisive thought. Others repeat earlier work, or apply a fine-tooth comb to matters that are too minute even for such a comb. Somewhere in that welter of tertiary material is the answer to almost every question that one could ask about constitutional law. The problem is finding the answer that one wants. The difficulty of locating useful guidance is exacerbated by the bifurcation of most constitutional scholarship into two kinds. In "Two Styles of Social Science Research," C. Wright Mills delineates macroscopic and molecular research. The former deals with huge issues, the latter with tiny issues. Virtually all of the scholarship on the Constitution is of one of those two types. Little of it is macroscopic, but that category does include some first-rate syntheses such as Jack Rakove's *Original Meanings*. Most constitutional scholarship is molecular and, again, some fine work is included in that category.

In his essay, Mills bemoans the inability of social scientists to combine the two kinds of research that he describes to create a third category that will be more generally useful. This series of books is an attempt to do for constitutional law the intellectual work that Mills proposed for social science. The author of each book has dealt carefully and at reasonable length with a topic that lies in the middle range of generality. Upon completion, this series will consist of thirty-seven books, each on a constitutional law topic. Some of the books, such as the book on freedom of the press, explicate one portion of the Constitution's text. Others, such as the volume on federalism, treat a topic that has several anchors in the Constitution. The books on constitutional history and constitutional interpretation range over the entire document, but each does so from one perspective. Except for a very few of the books, for which special circumstances dictate minor changes in format, each book includes the same components: a brief history of the topic, a lengthy and sophisticated analysis of the current state of the law on that topic, a bibliographical essay that organizes and evaluates scholarly material in order to facilitate further research, a table of cases, and an index. The books are intellectually rigorous—in fact, authorities have written them—but, due to their clarity and to brief definitions of terms that are unfamiliar to laypersons, each is comprehensible and useful to a wide audience, one that ranges from other experts on the book's subject to intelligent nonlawyers.

In short, this series provides an extremely valuable service to the legal community and to others who are interested in constitutional law, as every citizen should be. Each book is a map of part of the U.S. Constitution. Together they map all of that document's territory that is worth mapping. When this series is complete, each book will be a third kind of scholarly work that combines the macroscopic and the molecular. Together they will explicate all of the important constitutional topics. Anyone who wants assistance in understanding either a topic in constitutional law or the Constitution as a whole can easily find it in these books.

Foreword

Richard A. Posner

Richard Levy's book on the federal legislative power is a distinguished addition to a highly worthwhile series of books on constitutional law. Levy addresses the vexed subject of the separation of powers. The Constitution famously created a tripartite system of government, consisting of a legislative branch (Congress) (Article I), an executive branch (the President) (Article II), and the judicial branch (the Supreme Court, and other federal courts at the option of Congress) (Article III). Although some cases describe the branches as separate—and indeed they are distinct—they overlap to a considerable degree; they also overlap with the powers of state government. Sorting out this tangle, determining the actual powers (and the limits on those powers) of each branch, is a task that has stumped the Supreme Court, to which has fallen the ultimate responsibility for defining those powers and those limitations.

Levy has chosen to focus on one aspect of the separation of powers, namely the extent of the power of Congress; and within that large subject to concentrate on three issues that he shows to be related and that, once resolved, are seen to define Congress's power. One issue is the scope of legislative authority conferred by the "necessary and proper clause" of Article I; another is the power of Congress to augment the legislative power by delegating power to courts and executive agencies, because its power to legislate directly is limited by the difficulty (transaction costs) of forging majority agreement in each of the two houses of Congress and (a usual though not invariable necessity, because a veto can be overridden, although with difficulty) getting the President to go along. The third issue Levy discusses is the set of powers that Congress exercises, often in committees rather than in each house as a whole, without explicit authorization in Article I or elsewhere in the Constitution, such as the power to investigate.

I had not realized what subtle questions each of these issues presents. Especially the first—"necessary and proper" seems such a straightforward formula—but, as Levy shows, it can be understood either as adding to the powers of Congress specifically listed in Article I (hence regulation of local commerce as "necessary and proper" to effective regulation of interstate commerce), or merely as providing means for the enforcement of an enumerated power.

The matters that the book discusses may seem abstract and esoteric, of interest to lawyers only and, perhaps, to few of them. Actually they are of considerable moment. The reason is that Congress—besieged by lobbyists, distracted by the demands of fund-raising, baffled by the growing complexity of government, but awash in committees and bolstered by huge staffs—has taken to legislating in minute detail, and to harrowing officials of the executive branch with investigations and demands for information, exercising oversight that is at times perfunctory and at times inquisitorial. Increasingly, it has cast itself in a managerial role, in which it faces off against a highly aggressive Supreme Court bent on vigorously policing the limits of the legislative power. It is important to know what those limits are, and Professor Levy's book will help in determining them.

Acknowledgments

I would like to acknowledge the help I received from three groups of people in completing this book.

First, I am grateful to friends and colleagues at the University of Kansas and elsewhere who provided financial and intellectual support for this project. This includes Deans Stephen R. McAllister and Michael J. Davis, who provided financial support; Chris Drahozal, Rob Glicksman, Flip Kissam, Sid Shapiro, Tom Stacy, and Steve Ware, who provided comments on drafts of some or all of the book; and participants at faculty workshops at the University of Kansas Law School, the University of Iowa College of Law, and the University of San Diego Law School. In addition, I appreciate the valuable research assistance of Diana Lee, Larkin Evans, and Ivery Goldstein, and the help of the library staff, particularly Rob Mead and Chris Steadham. I also owe a special note of thanks to Judge Richard Posner for writing the foreword.

Second, I am grateful to those involved in the production of the book, including Jack Stark, who conceptualized the series, put it together, and invited me to be an author. I appreciate the support of the people at Praeger/Greenwood Press and Cadmus Communications who have assisted with the "nuts and bolts" of preparing the book for publication.

Third, but by no means last, I want to thank my family and friends for all that they have done for me over the years. My parents provided me with the foundations on which I could build a rewarding life of academic inquiry into the law. My children have inspired me and put up with (or perhaps rejoiced in) my preoccupation with this project over several years. Finally, my wife Kathleen has given me love and support, created the space for me to complete the book, and diligently read multiple drafts.

Introduction: Triangulating the Federal Legislative Power

This book offers an historical and doctrinal analysis of three distinct, yet related, aspects of the federal legislative power: (1) the power of Congress to enact "necessary and proper" laws;[1] (2) the delegation of authority by Congress to the executive and judicial branches or other institutions; and (3) what I shall call the "deliberative powers" of Congress to conduct investigations, compel testimony and the production of documents, and punish for contempt. Each of these topics presents important and difficult constitutional issues that warrant careful analysis. At the same time, however, they share important commonalities that have seldom been explored.[2] The enactment of necessary and proper laws, legislative delegations, and deliberative powers do not operate as independent bases of legislative power, but rather each arises only as an incident to the exercise of the enumerated powers of Congress. These aspects of the legislative power therefore derive from some core understanding of what it means to "legislate" with respect to a given subject. By exploring these powers and their common core, we can gain a deeper appreciation of the federal legislative power itself.[3]

THE "OTHER" POWERS OF CONGRESS

Judicial and scholarly analysis of necessary and proper legislation, legislative delegations, and deliberative powers typically treats these issues as separate constitutional problems, each with a distinct focus. The jurisprudence of the Necessary and Proper Clause is dominated by the need to reconcile its sweeping grant of authority with the preservation of state power. Legislative delegations are analyzed in terms of the so-called nondelegation doctrine, under which Congress may delegate considerable discretionary authority to executive and judicial actors but may not delegate the legislative power itself. Congressional authority to investigate, subpoena, and sanction for contempt have been accepted as a matter of institutional necessity whose relationship to the broader legislative power is implicit but largely unexplored.

The power to enact necessary and proper laws is the essence of the federal legislative power. Indeed, in the Federalist Papers, both Hamilton and Madison defended the Necessary and Proper Clause as simply confirming explicitly what was implicit in the legislative power itself: the authority to enact appropriate laws to carry into effect the exercise of the enumerated powers.[4] This reasoning was echoed by Chief Justice Marshall in McCulloch v. Maryland (1819),[5] which adopted the seminal test for evaluating whether a given law is necessary and proper to an enumerated power: "Let the end be legitimate, let it be within the scope of the constitution, and all means which are appropriate, which are plainly adapted to that end, which are not prohibited, but consist with the letter and spirit of the constitution, are constitutional."

Notwithstanding its central role in the Framers' understanding of the legislative power and the attention it received at the founding, the Necessary and Proper Clause has largely disappeared as a separate element of the Court's analysis of the federal legislative power.[6] More recent cases addressing the scope of federal legislative power have tended to focus on the content of specific enumerated powers, such as the commerce power[7] or the power to enforce the Reconstruction Amendments.[8] To be sure, the *McCulloch* test provides the framework for analyzing the scope of these enumerated powers, but it has been subsumed into specific and somewhat divergent tests that have evolved for each of the enumerated powers.[9]

These cases, moreover, do not approach the question in terms of what it means to legislate with respect to the enumerated powers. Instead, the cases are dominated by the Court's effort to balance federal and state authority in accordance with some underlying conception of federalism. Thus, during periods in which the Court has read the scope of federal legislative power narrowly, as in the pre–New Deal period or in more recent cases reinvigorating states' rights, its analysis has typically proceeded from the premise that certain powers are reserved to the states and that these reserved powers operate as an external limit on federal authority.[10] As a result, the cases do not articulate a coherent conception of the federal legislative power; they define that power in terms of what it is not (e.g., the state police power), rather than in terms of what it is.[11]

Legislative delegation is implicit in a system of separation of powers, for although the legislative power includes the power to make laws, it does not include the power to execute those laws or to adjudicate cases arising under them. Congress must delegate that authority, by means of a statute, to officials within the executive and judicial branches, respectively, and this sort of delegation is necessary and proper to the exercise of any enumerated power. Conversely, neither the executive branch nor the judiciary may exercise the legislative power, whether on the assertion of its own constitutional authority or by virtue of a legislative delegation. Thus, the legislative delegation of authority, or the lack of delegated authority, is an important aspect of many separation of powers questions that require the Court to distinguish between legislative power and executive or judicial powers.

The leading decision in this area is the *Steel Seizure Case* (1952),[12] which invalidated President Truman's seizure of steel mills notwithstanding his assertion that the seizure was necessary to ensure continued steel production for the Korean War in the face of labor unrest. Of critical significance for present purposes was the Court's rejection of the President's contention that, even without a statutory delegation, he had independent constitutional authority to take this action pursuant to Article II, section 1 (vesting of executive power in the President). Justice Black's opinion for the Court reasoned that the President's order was a legislative rather than executive act: "The President's order does not direct that a congressional policy be executed in a manner prescribed by Congress—it directs that a presidential policy be executed in a manner prescribed by the President." This reasoning reflects a basic concept of the legislative power as the power to make the antecedent policy choice (from within the range of legitimate policy objectives) and prescribe the means for its implementation. Nonetheless, the Court's analysis was primarily concerned with the limits of the executive power.

Similarly, the nondelegation doctrine also requires the Court to draw a line between legislative and executive power. The underlying premise of the doctrine is that, because the legislative power is vested in Congress, Congress may not delegate that power to anyone else.[13] To determine whether a particular statutory delegation confers executive or legislative power, the Court asks whether Congress has provided an "intelligible principle," or standard, to guide and control administrative discretion. The requirement of an intelligible principle ensures that Congress has made the antecedent decision concerning the ends and means of federal policy,[14] and thus rests on the same underlying conception of the legislative power as the *Steel Seizure Case.*

Unlike the cases concerning the scope of the federal legislative power, the delegation cases offer an understanding of the legislative power unaffected by federalism concerns. At the same time, however, they too tend to define that power by reference to what it is not—in this instance, the executive (or judicial) power. Thus, while the delegation cases confirm *McCulloch's* basic conception of the federal legislative power as the power to determine the ends of public policy and the means to achieve it, they do not go much further.

Since the earliest sessions of Congress, both chambers have exercised the deliberative powers to conduct investigations, subpoena witnesses and documents, and punish for contempt. These actions have met with little resistance from the Court, notwithstanding several fundamental constitutional problems with their exercise. First, these powers are nowhere explicitly granted in the Constitution itself. They are not contained in the provisions concerning the composition and operation of Congress, although other powers of internal governance are explicitly granted.[15] Second, these powers are exercised by either chamber of Congress, or even by congressional committees, without bicameralism and presentment.[16] Finally, these actions closely resemble functions that are quintessentially executive and judicial in character. Despite these concerns, the Court has had little difficulty concluding that these deliberative powers are inherent in a legislative body and implicitly vested in Congress.[17]

Thus, deliberative powers derive from the Framers' historical expectations concerning the inherent powers of a legislative body and from the practical needs of Congress as it conducts its business. Later cases have made clear, however, that the powers to investigate, subpoena, and punish for noncompliance are not free-standing powers to be exercised whenever and however Congress may choose, but rather must be related to some congressional end within federal legislative authority.[18] In this sense, these powers are also a manifestation of the legislative power itself, and the Court's analysis of which deliberative powers are inherent in the exercise of legislative power also offers insight into the meaning of that power.[19] Once again, however, while this analysis incorporates basic assumptions about the nature of federal legislative power, it has not been developed as part of any comprehensive conception of that power.

IN SEARCH OF THE FEDERAL LEGISLATIVE POWER

Article I, section 1 of the U.S. Constitution provides that "[a]ll legislative Powers herein granted shall be vested in a Congress of the United States. . . ." The place-ment of the Vesting Clause as the first substantive provision of the Constitution reflects the preeminent role of the federal legislative power in the constitutional scheme of government. In a representative democracy that operates under the rule of law, the sovereign authority of the people is exercised in the first instance by the legislature, which has the power to prescribe binding rules to govern society. Thus, the valid legislative enactments of Congress are the "Supreme Law of the Land" (Art. VI, cl. 2) that bind private parties, the executive and judicial branches, and the states. As the foregoing discussion suggests, however, the federal legislative power has been the subject of surprisingly little systematic analysis.

The limits of our understanding of the legislative power are well illustrated by the opinion in INS v. Chadha (1983), in which the Supreme Court invalidated the leg-islative veto, a statutory device permitting either or both houses to veto administra-tive action by resolution. The Court reasoned that the use of the legislative veto constituted the exercise of legislative power and concluded that this exercise of leg-islative power was unconstitutional, because it did not comply with the Article I requirements of bicameralism and presentment (Art. I, §7, cls. 2–3). The character-ization of the legislative veto as a legislative act was thus central to the majority's analysis and one might expect a careful explanation of why it was so.[20] Nonetheless, the opinion by Chief Justice Burger did not offer any convincing rationale for this characterization.

The Court began with the presumption that because the veto was exercised by one of the chambers of Congress, it was legislative in character, based on a broader presumption that "[w]hen any branch acts, it is presumptively exercising the power the Constitution has delegated to it." Starting with this presumption, the Court turned to the question of whether the veto was legislative in purpose and effect so that the bicameralism and presentment requirements applied. First, the veto was legislative because it had the "purpose and effect of altering the legal rights, duties, and relations of persons . . . outside the Legislative Branch." Second, the veto was legislative because of the "character of the congressional action it supplant[ed]"; in the absence of a veto provision, Congress could have overruled the INS or the attorney general, "if at all, only by legislation requiring deportation." Finally, the veto was legislative in character because it reversed Congress's original decision to delegate the power of granting asylum to the attorney general, a delegation that could only be "legislatively altered or revoked." None of these rationales, however, tells us much about the nature of legislation or effectively distinguishes legislative action from other exercises of government authority.

The presumption that congressional action is legislative in character, however justified as a starting point, is circular and therefore unhelpful in understanding the nature of the federal legislative power. If the presumption is applied literally, anything Congress does is legislative in character, and there is no limit to its ability to exercise functions assigned to the other branches, so long as the requirements of bicameralism and presentment are followed. Of course, the Court has rejected such a sweeping view of the legislative power in other contexts. For example, in Bowsher v. Synar (1986), the Court held that Congress could not control the removal of officers exercising executive power (except by impeachment). In any event, this presumption offers no insight into what features of the legislative veto or any other congressional action might be relevant to supporting or rebutting the presumption that it is legislative in character.

The argument that the veto changed the legal rights, duties, and relations of people outside the legislative branch does not distinguish it from executive or judicial action, both of which frequently alter legal rights and duties. A legislative act affected legal rights by establishing that aliens without valid visas are deportable and that the attorney general—acting through the INS—may suspend deportation and grant asylum, but legal rights and duties were also affected by executive and judicial actions. Chadha's legal rights and duties were altered by executive actors (the INS and the attorney general) through the decision to grant asylum. In the same way, the judicial decision of the Supreme Court in Chadha itself clearly had the effect of altering the legal rights, duties, and relations of the attorney general, the INS, and Chadha. Thus, the fact that the veto altered legal rights, duties, and relations did not distinguish it from either executive or judicial action and cannot be the defining characteristic of the legislative power.

That Congress, in the absence of the veto, would have been required to legislate to effect Chadha's deportation is equally unhelpful. This is also true of any exercise of delegated authority by either the executive or judicial branches. If Congress had not delegated the authority to the attorney general and INS to suspend deportation, it would have had to legislate to grant asylum, but it does not follow that the attorney general and INS were exercising legislative authority. While there are important differences between executive and judicial action pursuant to statutory delegations and the exercise of the legislative veto—which will be discussed shortly—the character of the congressional action supplanted is not one of them.

Finally, the suggestion that the veto was the functional equivalent of legislation revoking the original delegation of authority is unpersuasive on the facts. It is certainly true that delegation of authority to implement a statutory scheme is ordinarily a legislative act and that once power has been so delegated it requires another legislative act to revoke the delegation.[21] But that is not what happened in *Chadha*. The delegation of authority and the legislative veto provision were part of the same statute, so the power delegated was always limited by the veto. Thus, the exercise of the veto did not rescind a delegated power, but rather involved the exercise of a built-in condition on the delegated power. Such an action is not inherently legislative in character.

The point here is not that the Court was wrong to conclude that the veto was a legislative act, but rather that the Court's conclusion was not explained in terms of any workable conception of what made it so. The closest the Court came to identifying a distinctive feature of the legislative veto that rendered it legislative in character—aside from the fact that it emanated from one chamber of Congress—was in a footnote responding to the argument that, if the veto was legislative then so was the attorney general's authority to grant or withhold asylum. In this footnote, the Court reasoned that, unlike the legislative veto, the attorney general's decision was subject to statutory constraints and potentially subject to judicial review for compliance with those constraints. This sort of statutory implementation pursuant to standards and procedures is an executive act. This distinction is significant and points in the direction of one essential characteristic of legislative power; it is the plenary authority to make policy choices that are legally constrained only by the Constitution. Even as to this essential point, however, the Court in *Chadha* defined legislative power in terms of what it was not, rather than in terms of any articulated conception of the legislative power.

As this discussion suggests, there is a basic concept of the legislative power that underlies both *Chadha* and the various doctrinal fields analyzed in this book. The legislative power is the antecedent power to determine and prescribe through binding rules (laws) the ends of public policy and the means to implement them, constrained only by political structures and processes and constitutional limits. This conception is in one form or another reflected in the jurisprudence of necessary and proper legislation, legislative delegations, and deliberative powers. Nonetheless, the power to legislate remains a basic, intuitive conception that has not been fleshed out in any detail so as to provide a basis for analyzing diverse legislative power questions. Instead, the powers to enact necessary and proper laws, to delegate authority, and to investigate, subpoena, and sanction for contempt have been analyzed as distinct constitutional issues from distinct constitutional perspectives.

Like the proverbial blindfolded men, each of whom touches a different part of the elephant and reaches a different conclusion about what sort of animal it is, these partial doctrinal portraits leave us with an incomplete picture of the federal legislative power. In addition to exploring the distinct constitutional issues raised by necessary and proper legislation, legislative delegation, and deliberative powers, an overarching aim of this book is to integrate the analysis of these related issues and, by working backward from each power toward their common core, gain a better understanding of the federal legislative power itself. In other words, I hope to "triangulate" the federal legislative power.

The book proceeds in two parts. Part I takes an historical and evolutionary perspective. It reviews early constitutional sources and important historical decisions in chronological order, highlighting recurrent themes and key doctrinal developments. This historical background in turn provides the raw material for Part II, which engages in a detailed doctrinal analysis, informed by collective action theory, of these three aspects of the federal legislative power. The purpose of this analysis is not only to provide a clear exposition of the current law, but also to synthesize the diverse elements of this doctrine into a more comprehensive conception of the federal legislative power. A concluding section summarizes the implications of the analysis for our understanding of the federal power to legislate.

NOTES

1. U.S. Const., Art. I, § 8, cl. 18.

2. One notable exception is Gary Lawson, who has addressed the delegation of legislative power and the nondelegation doctrine as an issue of "necessary and proper" legislation implementing the enumerated powers. See Gary Lawson, "Discretion as Delegation: the "Proper" Understanding of the Nondelegation Doctrine," 73 *Geo. Wash. L. Rev.* 235 (2005); Gary Lawson, "Delegation and Original Meaning," 88 *Va. L. Rev.* 327 (2002).

3. When I was contacted to write this installment of the Praeger Series, A Reference Guide to the U.S. Constitution, the project was proposed as a book on the "other" powers of Congress, designed to cover miscellaneous issues not covered in other volumes. One thing that intrigued me about the project was the challenge of developing a common theme that would unify the seemingly disparate issues to be addressed. In that respect, the project has not disappointed.

4. See Federalist No. 33 (Hamilton); Federalist No. 44 (Madison). This defense of the Clause is discussed further in Part I.

5. *McCulloch* was the culmination of an ongoing controversy over the constitutionality of the Bank of the United States, which had been the focal point of arguments about the permissible scope of federal power and which divided Madison and Hamilton. The bank controversy is discussed in some detail in Part I.

6. A recent exception is Justice Scalia's concurring opinion in Gonzales v. Raich, 235 S. Ct. 2195 (2005).

7. This was true both during the pre–New Deal Period, see, e.g., Carter v. Carter Coal Co., 298 U.S. 238 (1936) (holding that the commerce power did not extend to the regulation of mining); Hammer v. Dagenhart (The Child Labor Case), 247 U.S. 251 (1918) (holding that Congress could not prohibit the interstate shipment of goods made with child labor); The Shreveport Rate Case (Houston E. & W. Texas Ry. v. United States), 234 U.S. 342 (1914) (holding that the Interstate Commerce Commission could extend its jurisdiction to intrastate rates that diverted shipping from interstate commerce); United States v. E.C. Knight Co., 156 U.S. 1 (1895) (holding that the Sherman Antitrust Act could not be extended to bar a monopoly in sugar refining), and in more recent decisions, see, e.g., United States v. Morrison, 529 U.S. 598 (2000) (holding that the Federal Violence Against Women Act was beyond the scope of congressional authority under the commerce power and the Fourteenth Amendment); United States v. Lopez, 514 U.S. 549 (1995) (holding that the Federal Gun-Free School Zones Act exceeded the scope of the commerce power).

8. In Katzenbach v. Morgan, 384 U.S. 641 (1966) (upholding section 4(e) of the Voting Rights Act), the Court held that section 5 of the Fourteenth Amendment, which authorizes Congress to enforce the Amendment's substantive provision by "appropriate" legislation, incorporates the Necessary and Proper Clause, and adopted a variation of the *McCulloch* test as the test for the exercise of that power. More recently, in City of Boerne v. Flores, 521 U.S. 507 (1997) (holding that the Religious Freedom Restoration Act of 1993 was not congruent and proportional to any underlying Fourteenth Amendment violation), the Court has adopted a distinctive "congruence and proportionality" test for this power. See also Board of Trustees of University of Alabama v. Garrett, 531 U.S. 356 (2001) (holding that Americans with Disabilities Act provisions authorizing suit against states exceeded the scope of congressional authority under the Fourteenth Amendment); Kimel v. Florida Board of Regents, 528 U.S. 62 (2000) (holding that Age Discrimination in Employment Act's provisions authorizing suits against states exceeded the scope of congressional authority under the Fourteenth Amendment).

9. See David E. Engdahl, "The Necessary and Proper Clause as an Intrinsic Restraint on Federal Lawmaking Power," 22 *Harv. J.L. & Pub. Pol'y* 107 (1998) (criticizing *Lopez* for its failure to analyze the issue from the perspective of the Necessary and Proper Clause and advocating the development of this analysis). For a detailed discussion of the various tests, see infra in Part II.

10. This sort of reasoning is most obvious in cases like Alden v. Maine, 527 U.S. 706 (1999), which held that state sovereign immunity was an implied limit on federal legislative authority and New York v. United States, 505 U.S. 144 (1992), which held that Congress may not commandeer the states to implement federal policies. In cases like *Lopez* and *Morrison*, the Court also relied on the notion of reserved state powers to reject broad readings of the commerce power and the power to enforce the Fourteenth Amendment. Interestingly, in some of the state sovereignty cases, the Court has relied on the *McCulloch* test to support implied restrictions on permissible means. See J. Randy Beck, "The New Jurisprudence of the Necessary and Proper Clause," 2002 *U. Ill. L. Rev.* 581 (2002) (arguing that the history of the Clause supports implied limits on the substantive scope of federal powers but not implied restrictions based on state sovereignty).

11. In the same vein, there has been some renewed scholarly interest in the Necessary and Proper Clause, but much of it is directed at challenging *McCulloch* in defense of states' rights rather than at understanding the federal legislative power. See, e.g., Randy Barnett, "Necessary and Proper," 44 *U.C.L.A. L. Rev.* 745 (1995); Gary Lawson & Patricia B. Granger, "The 'Proper' Scope of Federal Power: A Jurisdictional Interpretation of the Sweeping Clause," 43 *Duke L.J.* 267 (1993).

12. Youngstown Sheet & Tube Co. v. Sawyer, 343 U.S. 579 (1952).

13. See Whitman v. American Trucking Associations, 531 U.S. 457, 472 (2001) ("Article I, § 1, of the Constitution vests '[a]ll legislative Powers herein granted . . . in a Congress of the United States.' This text permits no delegation of those powers . . .").

14. The clearest articulation of this reasoning comes in (then) Justice Rehnquist's concurring opinion in Industrial Union Dept., AFL-CIO v. American Petroleum Institute (The Benzene Case), 448 U.S. 607 (1980) (reasoning that OSHA's authority to set exposure levels for workplace chemicals violated the nondelegation doctrine because Congress did not resolve the fundamental question of how much value to place on a human life).

15. See U.S. Const. Art. I, § 2, cl. 5 and § 3, cls. 4 & 5 (authorizing each house to choose its officers); § 5 (providing for, inter alia, each house to be the sole judge of the elections and qualifications of its members, to make rules governing its internal operation and punishment of it members, and to maintain and publish an official journal).

16. Thus, while the adoption of legislation serving similar purposes, such as the federal bribery statute, can be defended as authorized by the Necessary and Proper Clause, the exercise of these functions by subunits of Congress cannot.

17. See Anderson v. Dunn, 19 U.S. (6 Wheat.) 204 (1821) (relying in part on *McCulloch* to find an inherent power of each House to punish for contempt).

18. See Kilbourn v. Thompson, 103 U.S. 168 (1881) (invalidating issuance of contempt citation for refusing to cooperate with an investigation on the ground that the investigation was not connected to any valid legislative action and thus exceeded the scope of congressional authority). Under *Anderson*, however, congressional authority to sanction for contempt extends beyond enforcing subpoenas and includes the power to punish for acts that undermine Congress as an institution, such as bribery or libel, and this exercise of the contempt power need not be linked to any particular legislative action within the scope of congressional authority.

19. As will be discussed further, infra Part I, the recognition of these deliberative powers also reflects the Framers' understanding that Congress was to be a true legislative body with the sorts of powers and authorities historically accorded to Parliament.

20. The characterization of the veto as a legislative act was not, however, necessary to the result. Justice Powell concurred on the ground that, in the particular case, the veto reflected the exercise of the judicial power. A similar result would likely obtain if the veto were characterized as an executive act, insofar as Congress cannot execute the laws. Thus, whether the veto was a legislative, executive, or judicial act, its exercise by a house of Congress would be unconstitutional. See Metropolitan Washington Airports Authority v. Citizens for Abatement of Aircraft Noise, Inc., 501 U.S. 252 (1991).

21. This reflects the general principle that a statute can normally be repealed only by another statute. See Clinton v. City of New York, 524 U.S. 417 (1998) (invalidating federal Line Item Veto Act because it delegated authority to the President to repeal legislation).

Part I

History of the Federal Legislative Power

One of the primary functions of a constitution is to establish essential government institutions and allocate authority among them. To prevent the abuse of power and protect individual liberties, the U.S. Constitution divides governmental authority among the institutions of government according to two principles: federalism and separation of powers. Federalism divides authority between the national government and the states, largely according to subject matter. Separation of powers divides federal authority among the legislative, executive, and judicial branches according to the form and nature of the power exercised. The federal legislative power represents that portion of government authority that the Constitution allocates to the federal government that is legislative in character. Each topic covered in this book concerns the federal legislative power. Collectively, their history provides important insights into our understanding of that power.

The history of the Necessary and Proper Clause has been one of tension and accommodation between two competing principles. Under the "plenary power" principle, the legislative power of Congress with respect to each enumerated power is complete. It is the supreme expression of sovereign law-making authority delegated by the people to their government that includes the power to choose both the ends of public policy and the means to achieve them. While specific laws may violate constitutional limitations, the legislative power is plenary in the sense that legislative discretion over both ends and means is unconstrained. Under the "enumerated powers" principle, however, this plenary federal legislative power is confined to constitutionally specified subjects, while the states retain the residual sovereign legislative authority. The enumerated powers principle implies that some subjects that would otherwise be within the legislative authority of government fall within the exclusive legislative authority of the states. As Justice Kennedy put it in his concurring opinion in U.S. Term Limits, Inc. v. Thornton (1995), "[t]he Framers split the atom of sovereignty." This unprecedented division of sovereign authority created the fundamental dilemma of federalism. Insofar as virtually any law can be justified as a means to accomplish ends within one of the enumerated powers, how can federal legislative authority be at once plenary and at the same time limited to enumerated powers? As a result, while the power to enact necessary and proper laws describes the essential nature of legislative power from a separation of powers perspective, our understanding of that power has been heavily influenced by the need to preserve the substantive division of authority contemplated by federalism.

Issues surrounding legislative delegation and deliberative powers are more narrowly focused on separation of powers and consequently on the form and nature of the legislative power. Legislative delegations require that the power to legislate—that is, to make laws—be distinguished from the power to execute those laws and from the power to resolve cases and controversies arising under them. While Congress can, indeed *must*, delegate power to execute and adjudicate pursuant to legislation, it cannot delegate the legislative power itself. Deliberative powers, however, confound the separation of powers because their exercise, while perhaps essential to the making of laws, need not follow the process or take the form of enacting legislation. Instead, the deliberative powers partake of executive and judicial components and can be exercised without compliance with the normal requirements of bicameralism and presentment. Deliberative powers therefore require special justification in terms of separation of powers.

The federal legislative power has experienced phenomenal growth since the adoption of the Constitution. The substantive enumerated powers and the power to enact necessary and proper laws to carry them into effect have both been construed broadly and federal legislation is now ubiquitous, with few areas of even traditional state authority completely free of federal laws. Pursuant to these laws, a massive federal bureaucracy with broad authority implements a host of federal regulatory regimes and benefit programs, and the federal judiciary correspondingly resolves an ever-increasing range and number of cases and controversies arising under federal laws. Likewise, the institutional bureaucracy and activity of Congress has grown, as legislative committees are increasingly active in investigation of legislative issues and oversight of administrative activity pursuant to statutes.

This growth has strained both federalism and separation of powers, as reflected in the following historical overview of the federal legislative power, which traces the evolution of the power to enact necessary and proper laws, the problem of legislative delegation, and the exercise of deliberative powers. For convenience, this history is divided into a number of key stages. First, the adoption of the Constitution effected the transformation of Congress, which under the Articles of Confederation was more akin to an international organization, into a true legislative body. Second, early political and Supreme Court precedents established the federal legislative power in the constitutional order. Third, during the antebellum era, a theory of dual sovereignty gained ascendency and challenged the plenary character of the federal legislative power. Fourth, the Civil War and reconstruction saw both the assertion of federal sovereignty as dominant over states and the expansion of federal legislative power, which prompted the judicial endorsement of dual sovereignty theory to constrain the impact of these changes. Fifth, in the period leading up to the New Deal, the Supreme Court used dual sovereignty theory and other constitutional doctrines to support a program of laissez faire constitutionalism, ultimately provoking a constitutional crisis. Sixth, in the post–New Deal period, the Court rejected dual sovereignty theory and embraced the principle of plenary federal legislative authority, imposing few, if any, separation of powers or federalism-based limitations on Congress's choice of public policy ends or means. Finally, in the late-twentieth century, the Court began to impose some structural limits on federal legislative authority, resurrecting a somewhat more moderate form of dual sovereignty theory to protect the interests of states.

THE CONSTITUTIONAL TRANSFORMATION OF CONGRESS

In the broadest sense, the Congress of the United States established by Article I of the Constitution is a continuation of the Continental Congress of the American Revolution and the Congress that operated under the Articles of Confederation, but its form and function are radically different. Before the Constitution, Congress was not a legislative body and the powers it exercised could not be characterized as legislative. It was more akin to an international confederation of sovereign states than to a constitutional government. After the adoption of the Constitution, Congress became a true legislative body with substantial, albeit enumerated, legislative powers as part of a comprehensive national government with separate executive and judicial branches. Examination of the constitutional transformation of Congress is therefore the starting point for understanding the federal legislative power and the related phenomena of necessary and proper legislation, legislative delegation, and deliberative powers.

Congress Under the Articles of Confederation

Under the Articles of Confederation, Congress was not the legislative branch of a national government; it was the United States. The Articles refer repeatedly to "the United States in Congress assembled," reflecting the fact that there was no government of the United States, except as a body of diplomatic representatives sent by independent states. Under Article IX of the Articles, this body operated essentially by consensus and exercised only limited powers, most of which related to foreign and interstate relations. In the realm of foreign relations, Article IX granted "the United States in Congress assembled" the "sole and exclusive right and power" of determining war and peace, entering into international treaties and alliances, appointing officers of and regulating the land and naval forces of the United States, and regulating and providing for adjudication of the capture and disposition of vessels and cargo. As to internal matters, "the United States in Congress assembled" was granted the power to (1) resolve disputes between states and controversies over land that arose out of competing grants from different states, (2) regulate the value of "coin struck by their own authority or that of the respective States," (3) fix the standards of weights and measures, (4) regulate trade and manage all affairs with Indians, and (5) establish and manage a postal system.

More generally, Congress was also authorized to borrow money, create a committee to function while in recess, and "appoint such other committees and civil officers as may be necessary for managing the general affairs of the United States under their direction."

While these powers are substantial, critical omissions created a number of well-known difficulties. The lack of any national authority to assess and collect taxes made the United States dependent on contributions from the states. When states proved reluctant to meet their obligations, the United States lacked the power to enforce them. The absence of any national authority to regulate interstate commerce left the United States powerless to control the proliferation of internal trade barriers and retaliatory actions by the states. Even in situations in which the Articles granted power to the United States, most major decisions required the consent of nine states, including the powers to engage in war, grant letters of marque and reprisal, enter into treaties and alliances, coin money or regulate its value, borrow money, and make certain military decisions. The limitations of the substantive authority of the United States and the difficulties in exercising it are critical defects of the Articles but, for purposes of this discussion, it is the character of the powers exercised by Congress under the Articles that is most important.

At one level, Congress did not exercise legislative power at all, because it lacked the authority to make laws that bound those within the jurisdiction of the United States. Sovereignty remained with the individual states and congressional action applied only to the states in their corporate capacity. As Article II proclaimed, "[e]ach state retains its sovereignty, freedom, and independence, and every power, jurisdiction and right, which is not by this Confederation expressly delegated to the United States, in Congress assembled." Likewise, because individual states were responsible for the maintenance of their representatives and could recall them at will, members of Congress acted as representatives of independent states rather than as part of a national government (see Article V). The Articles relied on the states themselves to implement the decisions of Congress. There was no federal executive or judicial power, and enforcement operated "horizontally" through the ability of other states to exert pressure on those who shirked their obligation rather than vertically through a coercive authority and enforcement apparatus. The lack of any effective enforcement authority meant that states could effectively ignore their obligations with impunity and was a more serious defect than the lack of any specific substantive power.

In short, under the Articles of Confederation, the interaction among states was more analogous to international relations than to a federal nation state. The Articles created a kind of supranational organization whose powers were quite limited in practice. As Professor Edward Corwin put it in 1925, "The essential defect of the Articles of Confederation . . . consisted in the fact that the government established by them operated not upon the individual citizens of the United States but upon the states in their corporate capacity—that, in brief, it was not a government at all, but rather the central agency of an alliance."[1] Indeed, under the Articles, the United States had less governmental authority than many current supranational authorities, such as the European Union. It is therefore not surprising that the structure envisioned by the

Articles proved inadequate to manage the relations among the states, whose interdependence necessitated a far more powerful central authority.

While the powers exercised by Congress under the Articles were, in this sense, something less than the legislative power, at another level congressional power under the Articles went beyond the legislative power and included authority to take actions and make decisions that more properly would be characterized as executive or judicial. The Articles made no pretense of separation of powers, perhaps because the powers vested in Congress were so limited. As George Ticknor Curtis put it over one hundred years ago, "[t]he government established by the Articles of Confederation consisted of a single representative body, called a General Congress. In this body were vested all the powers, executive, legislative, and judicial, granted to the United States."[2] For example, Congress eventually created "departments" to handle foreign affairs, war, naval, and treasury matters, which were the precursors to the executive departments established by the first Congress under the Constitution.[3] Likewise, Congress was empowered to exercise judicial functions, such as the resolution of disputes between states. These rudimentary executive and judicial functions, however, fell far short of the full range of executive and judicial powers and institutions necessary for a functional government.

Congress Under the Constitution

It is unnecessary to recount here in full the various defects in the Articles of Confederation and the resulting difficulties that arose during the preconstitutional period and led to the framing of a new Constitution. The critical point in this context is that one of those defects was the absence of any true legislative powers, in response to which the Framers found it necessary in the new Constitution to fashion a legislative body and vest it with legislative power. The Framers self-consciously changed the character of the new government from a confederation of sovereign states operating on the plane of international law to a national government with the sovereign capacity to enact generally applicable laws that directly bound its people. This change is evident in both the composition and powers of Congress.

Under the Constitution, members of Congress were not diplomatic representatives of their respective states, but rather officials of the national government. To this end, the Constitution took various steps to insulate senators and representatives from the control of states. Although senators were initially selected by the state legislatures and thus by the states in their governmental capacity (until the Seventeenth Amendment was adopted in 1913), representatives were elected by direct popular vote to represent their respective districts. Under Article I, section 6, of the Constitution, moreover, senators and representatives receive their compensation from the federal government and enjoy privileges and immunities that operate against their own states (as well as the national government). Finally, unlike the Articles, the Constitution does not authorize states to recall their senators or representatives. Thus, while members of Congress may represent the peoples of their respective states, they do not represent the governments of those states.

More fundamentally, the legislative power vested in the new Congress was the power to make directly binding federal laws and that power extended to an expanded field of substantive authority, including the power to tax and to regulate commerce among the states, with foreign countries, and with Indian tribes. Of greater importance, however, was a critical change in the operation of federal authority. Whereas congressional action under the Articles bound the states in their corporate or governmental capacities and relied on them for implementation within their respective territories, federal law under the Constitution applies directly to individuals. In addition to its obvious practical significance in creating an effective national government, this change was the key to the establishment of a true federal legislative power. Conversely, and consistently with the separation of powers principles that animated the structure of the Constitution, the Constitution also removed most executive and judicial functions from Congress and vested them instead in a federal executive with power to implement and enforce the laws and a federal judiciary with power to interpret and apply them.

A central component of the legislative power vested in Congress was the power under the Necessary and Proper Clause (Art. I, § 8, cl. 18) to make "necessary and proper" laws to carry into effect the enumerated powers. This Clause, like the other enumerated powers, was the product of the "Committee on Detail," which was charged by the convention with writing a draft constitution based on principles previously agreed to by the delegates.[4] Before the work of the committee, the Convention had agreed on the scope of the federal legislative power in general terms. For example, the Virginia Resolutions provided that Congress was to have power "to legislate in all cases for the general interests of the union, and also in those to which the States are separately incompetent, or in which the harmony of the United States may be interrupted by the exercise of individual legislation."[5] Whether because it was the shared understanding of the Convention or because the committee preferred it, the committee's draft defined the legislative power not in general terms, but rather in terms of the now-familiar list of enumerated federal legislative powers contained in Article I, section 8. Nonetheless, the enumerated powers reflect the Framers' understanding of fields in which the "general interests of the union" are engaged. The Necessary and Proper Clause was the final enumerated power and generated no discussion or debate before the Convention as whole.[6] It has been suggested that the phrase "necessary and proper" was borrowed from agency law and was used to denote both the broad powers of Congress as an agent of the people and its fiduciary responsibility to them.[7]

The Necessary and Proper Clause not only confirmed that Congress was vested with a true legislative power, but also implied a generous interpretation of the enumerated powers, especially when contrasted with the Articles' requirement that federal power be "expressly" granted. The significance of the Clause did not go unnoticed by opponents of broad national authority during the ratification debates, who referred to the Necessary and Proper Clause as the "Sweeping" or "Elastic" Clause. They argued that the Necessary and Proper Clause, taken together with the Supremacy Clause, granted essentially unlimited authority to the national government and posed a great danger to states.[8] This criticism was colorfully described by Alexander Hamilton in the Federalist No. 33[9]:

These two clauses have been the source of much virulent invective and petulant declamation against the proposed Constitution. They have been held up to the people in all the exaggerated colors of misrepresentation as the pernicious engines by which their local governments were to be destroyed and their liberties exterminated; as the hideous monster whose devouring jaws would spare neither sex nor age, nor high nor low, nor sacred nor profane; . . .

Both Hamilton (in the Federalist No. 33) and James Madison (in the Federalist No. 44) responded to these criticisms. Their arguments rested on the basic proposition that the Necessary and Proper Clause merely confirmed what was implicit or inherent in the grant of legislative power itself. Thus, their reasoning tells us a good deal about their understanding of the federal legislative power.

Hamilton's response came as part of a broader discussion addressing the anti-Federalist complaint that the combination of the taxing power, the Necessary and Proper Clause, and the Supremacy Clause would permit pernicious federal legislation. Contrary to these assertions, Hamilton argued, the Necessary and Proper and Supremacy Clauses "are only declaratory of a truth which would have resulted by necessary and unavoidable implication from the very act of constituting a federal government, and vesting it with certain specified powers." This conclusion followed from the nature of the legislative power:

What is a power, but the ability or faculty of doing a thing? What is the ability to do a thing, but the power of employing the MEANS necessary to its execution? What is a LEGISLATIVE power, but a power of making LAWS? What are the MEANS to execute a LEGISLATIVE power but LAWS? What is the power of laying and collecting taxes, but a LEGISLATIVE POWER, or a power of MAKING LAWS, to lay and collect taxes? What are the proper means of executing such a power, but NECESSARY and PROPER laws?

Thus, Hamilton conceived of the legislative power as the power to make laws that are the means to the execution of a valid legislative end.

Madison's argument for the Necessary and Proper Clause, which came as part of a discussion of several provisions establishing federal authority or limiting that of the states, reflected similar reasoning. He began with the premise that "without the SUBSTANCE of this power, the whole Constitution would be a dead letter." Thus, the only question was what form the expression of this power should take, and Madison proceeded to demonstrate that alternatives to the Necessary and Proper Clause either would be ineffective or would not avoid the problems asserted by opponents. As part of this demonstration Madison reasoned:

Had the Constitution been silent on this head, there can be no doubt that all the particular powers requisite as means of executing the general powers would have resulted to the government, by unavoidable implication. No axiom is more clearly established in law, or in reason, than that wherever the end is required, the means are authorized; wherever a general power to do a thing is given, every particular power necessary for doing it is included.

Thus, Madison concluded, even without the Necessary and Proper Clause, "every objection" now raised against the scope of federal legislative power "would remain in all its plausibility." The real "inconveniency" would be that the absence of the Necessary and Proper Clause could be used as a pretext for objecting to the use of essential powers.

Hamilton and Madison also offered similar responses to the anti-Federalists' argument that Congress might rely on a broad construction of the Clause to justify outrageous laws. The ultimate control over such abuses rested in the structure of government, including political accountability and the separation of powers. As Hamilton put it, "[i]f the federal government should overpass the just bounds of its authority and make a tyrannical use of its powers, the people, whose creature it is, must appeal to the standard they have formed, and take such measures to redress injury done to the Constitution as the exigency may suggest and prudence justify." Hamilton also observed that laws that were not necessary and proper to an enumerated power would not have been adopted "pursuant" to the Constitution; they would therefore not be the supreme law of the land, but rather ultra vires and void. Likewise, Madison reasoned that "the success of [such a] usurpation will depend on the executive and judiciary departments, which are to expound and give effect to the legislative acts" and that "in the last resort a remedy must be obtained from the people who can, by the election of more faithful representatives, annul the acts of the usurpers."

The debate surrounding the Necessary and Proper Clause revealed the fundamental tension between plenary and limited legislative authority that is inherent in federalism. In a unitary system, the legislative power is the ultimate expression of the sovereign will of the people; its objects and means are plenary, subject only to limitations based on separation of powers and individual rights (i.e., rights reserved to the people). In a federal system, however, sovereign authority over different aspects of human activity has been divided between the state and national governments. Thus, the legislative power of the national government is at once plenary and limited. The problem is that if the power to legislate with respect to the enumerated powers is construed broadly enough, the enumeration of powers becomes meaningless because any action can always be justified by reference to one of the enumerated powers. Conversely, to the extent that the choice of ends and means available to Congress is limited for purposes of preserving the principle of enumerated powers, Congress does not possess full plenary authority even as to those enumerated powers. Over the years, this inherent contradiction has permitted no easy accommodation.

Conclusion

The Constitution effected fundamental changes in the nature of Congress, converting it into a true legislative body vested with the power to make laws.

Critically, and in contrast to the Articles of Confederation, these laws are directly binding on individuals within the jurisdiction of the United States, as opposed to binding on the states in their corporate capacities at the level of international law. Through the Necessary and Proper Clause, moreover, the Constitution confirmed that although Congress possessed only certain enumerated powers, with respect to those powers it was nonetheless vested with the full measure of legislative power to determine the ends of public policy and make "necessary and proper" laws to accomplish those ends. Notwithstanding the tension between the plenary and enumerated federal powers principles, these basic propositions provided the foundations for federal legislative power under the Constitution.

FEDERAL LEGISLATIVE POWER IN THE CONSTITUTIONAL ORDER

While the Constitution transformed the federal legislative power, much remained to be resolved through the practical implementation of the new government, and the formative decades following ratification are rich with important historical and judicial precedents. The early Congress actively went about the business of establishing the new government and providing for the exercise of its powers.[10] It created key executive departments—the Departments of State, of War, and of the Treasury—as well as other important offices under the authority of the United States, such as the Postmaster General. Likewise, it provided for the structure and jurisdiction of the court system in the Judiciary Act of 1789. Congress employed its fiscal powers to provide for the operation of government, imposing taxes to raise revenue (mostly tariffs and other taxes on commerce with foreign nations, much of which was consciously designed to protect domestic industry), appropriating funds for various projects, and providing for full payment of the debts owed by the United States under the Articles of Confederation. In addition, although there was not a great deal of regulatory activity by modern standards, Congress also enacted significant legislation designed to promote development and commerce.

Much of this early legislative activity was set against the backdrop of political turmoil. The Federalists, who favored a strong national government, gained power initially and asserted federal authority aggressively. They were opposed by Republicans (or anti-Federalists), who favored a narrower conception of national power and the preservation of states' rights. These differences divided former allies (most notably, Hamilton and Madison), produced bitter disagreements, and led to tactics of dubious constitutional validity, such as the Federalists' adoption of the Alien and Sedition Acts and the Republicans' later use of impeachment. Over time, the Republicans gained ascendancy and the Federalist party faded into history, but once in power, the Republicans also showed a willingness to use federal power aggressively in some circumstances. Legislative and executive actions during the late-eighteenth and early nineteenth centuries, informed by political disagreements and differences over the meaning of the Constitution, established important precedents concerning a variety of constitutional issues surrounding the new government. Indeed, as Professor David Currie has suggested, "[i]t was in the legislative and executive branches, not in the courts, that the original understanding of the Constitution was forged."[11]

These early legislative and executive precedents—many of which eventually found their way to the Supreme Court—touch on all three aspects of the federal legislative power that are the focus of this study. First, the controversy surrounding the creation of a national bank was the occasion for seminal debates concerning the meaning of the Necessary and Proper Clause and eventually led to the Supreme Court's landmark McCulloch v. Maryland (1819) decision.[12] Second, legislative practice and judicial decisions established the necessity for and delimitations of legislative delegations to executive officials and the courts. Finally, Congress exercised the inherent deliberative powers of a legislative body to investigate and to sanction by contempt, and the Supreme Court recognized these powers. Thus, notwithstanding the political turmoil and the later ascendency of the Republicans, the early precedents confirmed the creation of a new constitutional order in which the Congress exercised sovereign legislative authority as a true legislative body.

The Bank Controversy and the Meaning of the Necessary and Proper Clause

Although Hamilton and Madison were united in their defense of the Necessary and Proper Clause during the ratification debates, they soon parted company concerning its interpretation and application. In his capacity as Secretary of the Treasury, Hamilton developed and promoted in Congress an aggressive plan to address the national debt and secure financial stability.[13] The centerpiece of Hamilton's plan was the incorporation and capitalization of a Bank of the United States. Madison, as a member of the House of Representatives, vigorously opposed the bank bill, and argued in a speech delivered on the floor that the incorporation of a bank was beyond the scope of federal power.[14] Notwithstanding Madison's opposition, Congress approved the bill and presented it to President Washington, who sought advice concerning its constitutionality from Secretary of State Thomas Jefferson and Attorney General Edmund Randolph, both of whom agreed with Madison.[15] Their written opinions prompted a lengthy and spirited defense of the constitutionality of the bank from Hamilton,[16] who eventually prevailed when Washington signed the bill and the bank was formed.

Madison, Randolph, and Jefferson argued that the incorporation of a national bank was neither among the enumerated powers nor "necessary and proper" to one of those powers. They advanced both textual and federalism-based arguments for a narrow construction of the legislative power under which Congress could only make laws that are clearly incident to or absolutely necessary for the execution of an enumerated power. They reasoned that the power to charter corporations was a great, sovereign power, which had been specifically denied to the federal government when the delegates to the Constitutional Convention rejected a proposal to include it in the enumerated powers of Congress. They argued further that federal legislative power under the Necessary and Proper Clause, "according to the natural and obvious force of the terms and context, [must] be limited to means necessary to the end, and incident to the nature of the specified powers."[17] Under this view, it was not enough that the bank was a convenient means of carrying into effect the enumerated powers said to sustain it, because "they can all be carried into execution without a bank," which was therefore "not '*necessary*.'"[18]

Both Madison and Jefferson emphasized that reading the Clause as sufficiently broad to sustain the incorporation of a bank would effectively obliterate the premise of enumerated federal powers. As Madison put it:

Mark the reasoning on which the validity of the bill depends. To borrow money is made the end and the accumulation of capitals, implied as the means. The accumulation of capitals is then the end, and a bank implied as the means. The Bank is then the end, and a charter of incorporation, a monopoly, capital punishments, &c implied as the means. If implications, thus remote and multiplied, can be linked together, a chain may be formed that will reach every object of legislation, every object within the whole compass of political economy.[19]

This argument, of course, echoes that of the anti-Federalists, even if it is used as a justification for a narrow construction of federal legislative power rather than as an argument against the Constitution. That a leading architect of the Constitution would take this position underscores the fundamental tension inherent in a federal system in which legislative power is at once plenary and limited.

While the bank's opponents emphasized the principle of enumerated powers, Hamilton's response proclaimed the plenary character of federal legislative power. Because "every power vested in a government is in its nature sovereign," the United States possessed the full measure of sovereignty with respect to the enumerated objects of its authority.[20] The division of authority between the national and state governments did not diminish the sovereignty of the national government with respect to its enumerated powers, for to deny the sovereignty of the United States by virtue of its incomplete authority would be to deny the sovereignty of the states as well, for their authority also would be incomplete. This result "would furnish the singular spectacle of a political society without sovereignty, or of a people governed, without a government." Thus, viewed in the abstract, "the United States have the power to erect a corporation, [because] it is unquestionably an incident of sovereign power to erect corporations." This power, however, was limited to the fields of authority enumerated in the Constitution.

Hamilton also argued vehemently against Madison's construction of the Necessary and Proper Clause, declaring it "essential to the being of the national government that so erroneous a conception of the meaning of the word necessary should be exploded." From a textual perspective, "neither the grammatical nor popular sense of the term" required that a particular means be absolutely necessary, but rather "necessary often means no more than needful, requisite, incidental, useful or conducive to." Hamilton further contended that this broad interpretation reflected the intent of the Convention. On the practical level, Hamilton argued that a requirement that laws be "absolutely necessary" to the exercise of a given power would be unworkable, because "[t]here are few measures of any government which would stand so severe a test." To Hamilton, the complaint that a broad construction of the Necessary and Proper Clause was "calculated to extend the power of the government through the entire sphere of State legislation" did not justify a narrow construction because "difficulties on this point are inherent in the nature of the Federal Constitution; they result inevitably from a division of the legislative power." Thus, the proper test for the validity of federal legislation was its relationship as a means to an end within the scope of the enumerated powers. "If the end be clearly comprehended within any of the specified powers, and if the measure have an obvious relation to that end, and it is not forbidden by any particular provision of the Constitution, it may safely be deemed to come within the compass of the national authority."

In the end, Hamilton's view prevailed, although the matter was not finally resolved until much later. Washington signed the bill creating the bank, but the bill provided that the bank's charter would expire in 1811. By then, the political winds had shifted and Congress declined to renew it, which soon proved to be imprudent when the lack of a national bank caused difficulties for the United States during the War of 1812. By the time Madison, as president, confronted the issue again, he was convinced of the constitutionality of the bank. Although he vetoed legislation to incorporate a second bank in 1815, Madison signed similar legislation a year later. Even when vetoing the 1815 bill, Madison no longer objected to the bank on constitutional grounds, because he regarded the matter settled by the recognition of the legitimacy of the first bank.

These events, however, did not finally resolve the issue, as the second bank soon became embroiled in a different sort of controversy—one that is all too familiar to many readers. Financial scandal erupted as economic depression exposed imprudent and improper loans and fraudulent practices at many branches of the national bank, which therefore became a political target in many states. Riding on popular resentment against the bank, the State of Maryland imposed a tax on all banks not chartered by the state, which effectively applied only to the Baltimore branch of the Bank of the United States. It was against this backdrop that the great case of McCulloch v. Maryland (1819) arose. The ensuing litigation, in which the bank challenged the constitutionality of the tax, required the Supreme Court to determine whether the creation of the bank was a valid exercise of federal legislative power and whether the bank, if valid, was immune from state taxation under the Supremacy Clause.

Chief Justice Marshall's analysis of the constitutional validity of the bank reflected his familiarity with its history and generally followed Hamilton's argument, which Marshall had previously read.[21] Marshall's opinion for the Court began with a reference to that history:

The power now contested was exercised by the first congress elected under the present constitution. The bill for incorporating the Bank of the United States did not steal upon an unsuspecting legislature, and pass unobserved. Its principle was completely understood, and was opposed with equal zeal and ability. After being resisted, first, in the fair and open field of debate, and afterwards, in the executive cabinet, with as much persevering talent as any measure has ever experienced, and being supported by arguments which convinced minds as pure and as intelligent as this country can boast, it became a law. The original act was permitted to expire; but a short experience of the embarrassments to which the refusal to revive it exposed the government, convinced those who were most prejudiced against the measure of its necessity, and induced the passage of the present law. It would require no ordinary share of intrepidity, to assert that a measure adopted under these circumstances, was a bold and plain usurpation, to which the constitution gave no countenance.

While Marshall, like Madison, thus believed that the history of the bank provided precedent for its validity, the bulk of Marshall's opinion addressed the constitutionality of the bank as a matter of first principle and his reasoning embraced the plenary power of Congress.

Marshall's analysis proceeded from the initial premise that, although federal authority was limited to the enumerated powers, as to these powers, the national government possessed the full measure of sovereign authority. To establish this premise, Marshall rejected the state's contention that the Constitution (like the Articles of Confederation) derived its authority from the acts of sovereign and independent states. Under this "compact" theory of the Constitution, which has appeared in various forms to undergird states' rights arguments, the United States remains a confederation of sovereign states and the powers of the national government are derivative of state sovereignty. Marshall rejected this theory, emphasizing that the Constitution had been ratified through special conventions and not by the ordinary apparatus of state governments and concluding that the powers of the United States derived directly from the people of the states rather than from the states in their sovereign capacity. The people, in whom sovereignty originally vested, had divided sovereignty between the national government and state governments and, with respect to the enumerated powers, had given to the national government the full measure of sovereign authority to make laws. The supremacy of these laws, and hence the sovereignty of the United States with respect to them, was confirmed by the Supremacy Clause.

Marshall then reasoned that the sovereign authority of the United States within the sphere of enumerated powers implied that Congress possessed implied or incidental powers to use appropriate means to effectuate valid legislative ends. These powers included the power to establish a bank or to charter a corporation, even if such a power was not expressly granted, provided it was the means to an end within the enumerated powers. Marshall supported these conclusions with both textual arguments and arguments from practical necessity. Textually, Marshall reasoned that, unlike the Articles of Confederation, which required that federal powers be "expressly" granted, the Constitution did not specify that federal powers must be express. Moreover, because it would have been impossible for the framers to enumerate expressly "an accurate detail of all the subdivisions of which its great powers will admit, and of all the means by which they may be carried into execution," it followed that, having vested the national government with "great and sovereign powers," the Constitution must have contemplated the means to effectuate them. As Marshall put it:

[A] government, entrusted with such ample powers, on the due execution of which the happiness and prosperity of the nation so vitally depends, must also be entrusted with the means of their execution. The power being given, it is in the interest of the nation to facilitate its execution. It can never be their interest, and cannot be presumed to have been their intention, to clog and embarrass its execution, by withholding the most appropriate means.

Thus, a fair construction of the Constitution required the recognition of implied powers, and the only question was the scope of those powers.

On this point, Marshall rejected the state's argument that, although the enumerated powers carried with them the ordinary means of execution, the incorporation of a bank was excluded because that power "is one appertaining to sovereignty, and is not expressly conferred on congress." The problem with this argument, Marshall reasoned, is that the same was true of all legislative powers, for "[t]he original power of giving law on any subject is a sovereign power." Thus, the argument proved too much; it would effectively deny Congress the power to legislate except as expressly provided. Marshall acknowledged that the powers to make war, levy taxes, or regulate commerce were "great substantive and independent powers" and could not be implied as the means to implement some other power. But the power of incorporation was not such a power, because incorporation was "never the end for which other powers are exercised, but a means by which other objects are accomplished." The power of incorporation was therefore an inherent implied power of the national government when used as a means to implement the enumerated powers.

Only after having established that the enumerated legislative powers inherently incorporated the implied power to use appropriate means to implement them did Marshall turn to the Necessary and Proper Clause. Like Hamilton and Madison, Marshall viewed the Clause as confirming the character of the legislative power, stating that "the constitution of the United States has not left the right of congress to employ the necessary means, for the execution of the powers conferred on the government to general reasoning." Thus, Marshall's discussion of the Clause was aimed primarily at refuting the state's argument for a Madisonian construction of the Clause, which would confine Congress to those means that were "most direct and simple." Again drawing on Hamilton's defense of the bank, Marshall reasoned that the word "necessary" did not mean absolutely indispensable, but rather "frequently imports no more than that one thing is convenient, or useful, or essential to another." Thus, he continued, "[t]o employ the means necessary to an end, is generally understood as employing any means calculated to produce the end, and not as being confined to those single means, without which the end would be unattainable." This understanding of "necessary and proper" was supported by contrasting it with the language of Article I, section 10, which prohibits states from imposing import duties except as "absolutely necessary" to the execution of its inspection laws.[22]

Marshall then argued on practical grounds that the state's narrow interpretation was inconsistent with the intention of the Framers. In granting Congress broad powers to legislate, he reasoned, "[i]t must have been the intention of those who gave these powers to insure, so far as human prudence could insure, their beneficial execution." This intention could not be attained by strictly circumscribing Congress's choice of means. Likewise, it would have been impossible to list each necessary means explicitly, especially because the Constitution was meant to endure and would need to adapt to unforeseeable circumstances. Adopting either approach "would have been to deprive the legislature of its capacity to avail itself of experience, to exercise its reason, and to accommodate its legislation to the circumstances." Marshall then gave a variety of examples of legislative acts that clearly were within the scope of federal power but that would be difficult to distinguish from the chartering of a bank under the state's narrow test.

Marshall concluded his interpretative analysis by adopting Hamilton's test for the scope of federal power:

We admit, as all must admit, that the powers of the government are limited, and that its limits are not to be transcended. But we think the sound construction of the constitution must allow to the national legislature that discretion, with respect to the means by which the powers it confers are to be carried into execution, which will enable that body to perform the high duties assigned to it, in the manner most beneficial to the people. Let the end be legitimate, let it be within the scope of the constitution, and all means which are appropriate, which are plainly adapted to that end, which are not prohibited, but consist with the letter and spirit of the constitution, are constitutional.[23]

Under this test, which would form the foundations for subsequent development of the federal legislative power, Marshall had little difficulty concluding that the bank was an appropriate means to implement legitimate ends of Congress within the taxing and spending powers, among other things.[24]

The history of the Bank of the United States offers important lessons regarding the federal legislative power. First and foremost, it establishes that Congress is vested with sovereign legislative authority to make binding laws respecting the enumerated subjects of its legislative power and provide for their implementation by the executive and judicial branches. In particular, the limitation of Congress to enumerated powers does not alter the character of the legislative power it may exercise respecting those fields. Second, the history of the bank solidified Hamilton and Madison's position in the Federalist that the Necessary and Proper Clause is not an independent source of substantive legislative authority, but rather it confirms the character of the legislative power vested in Congress to use the necessary means to accomplish valid public policy ends.

The history of the bank also reflects the inherent tension between the plenary power and enumerated powers principles, as is evident in Hamilton and Madison's parting of the ways. Plenary legislative power is nearly impossible to confine within enumerated substantive fields. As Madison and Jefferson pointed out, if federal legislative authority is truly plenary, it is simple enough to conjure up arguments that would justify virtually any legislative means as related to an end within one of the enumerated powers. Conversely, as Hamilton and Marshall argued, to narrowly confine Congress in its choice of means to accomplish valid ends is to undermine the federal legislative power itself. *McCulloch* adopted a Hamiltonian conception of plenary federal legislative power, but neither the underlying problem nor the debate over the scope of federal legislative power ended there.

One critical feature of this debate that complicates analysis of the federal legislative power as such is the role of reserved state powers as an argument against a broad reading of the federal legislative power. To the extent that reserved state powers enter into the debate, analysis is no longer focused on what the federal legislative power *is*. Instead, the debate turns to what the federal legislative power *is not*. Thus, the argument against the bank turned less on any underlying conception of the federal legislative power than on the argument that incorporation was a power reserved to the states or that the creation of the bank itself would interfere with state prerogatives. While this is a powerful argument in terms of federalism, it does not bring us any closer to understanding the character of the federal legislative power. As we shall see, however, the idea of reserved state powers as a limit on federal legislative authority would soon emerge as a counterweight to the plenary power principle.

Legislative Delegation

Early congressional activity also set important precedents for the federal legislative power in relation to the delegation of authority to the executive and judicial branches. In a government characterized by separation of powers, the legislature must delegate authority both as a matter of principle and practical necessity. From the perspective of separation of powers, the legislative power vested in Congress is the power to make laws, not the power to execute them or to adjudicate cases arising under them. Thus, to make the exercise of legislative power effective, Congress must authorize the executive to administer and enforce the law and authorize the judiciary to decide cases arising under it. At a more practical level, it simply was not humanly possible—even in the early days of the federal system when the national government was relatively small and the field of federal legislation fairly narrow—for Congress to do everything. Early congressional action creating executive departments and providing for the judiciary reflect congressional recognition of this reality.

The First Congress's treatment of patents and copyrights provides an interesting early example of legislative delegation.[25] Initially, patent and copyright applications were submitted directly to Congress as requests for private bills. Although there seemed to be little doubt about congressional authority to enact private bills relating to patents and copyrights, none of these requests passed. Instead, Congress adopted legislation authorizing the attorney general, the secretary of state, and the secretary of war, acting as an early administrative agency, to grant patents for inventions or discoveries they considered to be "sufficiently useful or important."[26] This choice reflected the practical recognition that Congress could not pass individually on every patent or copyright request. It also indicates that the First Congress assumed it could delegate to executive branch officials authority to perform functions that would otherwise be within the legislative power. A similar pattern emerged in addressing disability and survivors benefits for veterans of the war, with respect to which Congress initially acted through private bills, but soon found it necessary to create an administrative and judicial structure to distribute benefits.[27]

While early Congresses apparently assumed the necessity and permissibility of delegations, a proposal during the Second Congress to delegate authority to the President to establish post offices and determine postal routes provoked a constitutional objection that sheds light on early views of the permissible scope of legislative delegation.[28] Objections to the proposal did not challenge the general practice of delegation, but rather they focused on the fact that the power to be delegated was one expressly included in the enumerated powers (Art. I, § 8, cl. 7). Thus, opponents of the proposal argued that the great legislative powers enumerated in Article I could not be delegated, even if incidental powers to implement laws passed pursuant to them could. During deliberations on the bill, the provision delegating authority to the President was deleted and, after further debate on the issue, efforts to restore it failed. Instead, Congress eventually enacted a statute incorporating detailed provisions for the establishment of specific post offices and designating specific postal routes. As is often the case for congressional precedents, the inferences that can be drawn from the rejection of this delegation are not entirely clear. While constitutional arguments figured into the debate, other factors, such as local politics or partisan positioning, may have fueled the result as much as constitutional objections. Nonetheless, the debate suggested that while Congress may delegate substantial authority to the executive or judicial branch, there are constitutional limits on legislative delegations. The Supreme Court soon endorsed this proposition.

The first nondelegation challenge to reach the Supreme Court was The Brig Aurora v. United States (1813), which arose from the condemnation of British cargo illegally imported into the United States. The Non-Intercourse Act of 1809 prohibited the importation of goods from France or Great Britain and provided for their forfeiture, but it contained a sunset provision and had expired by the time the goods in question were imported. Under a subsequent statute, however, if the President found by proclamation that one of those countries had ceased to violate the neutral commerce of the United States and the other had failed to follow suit, the Act would be revived against the offending country. On appeal, the cargo's owner advanced a number of arguments against the forfeiture, one of which was that Congress had impermissibly transferred the legislative power to the President: "To make the revival of a law dependent upon the President's proclamation, is to give to that proclamation the force of a law." Opposing counsel apparently accepted the premise that Congress could not delegate the legislative power, but denied that such an improper delegation had taken place, reasoning that Congress had "only prescribed the evidence which should be admitted of a fact, upon which the law should go into effect."

The Court affirmed the condemnation and approved the statutory mechanism for reviving the Non-Intercourse Act by proclamation. Justice Johnson's opinion (one of the few opinions for the Court that Chief Justice Marshall did not write during his tenure) was very brief and did not discuss extensively any of the issues raised by the claimant. As to the delegation issue, the Court said simply that "we can see no sufficient reason, why the legislature should not exercise its discretion in reviving the [Non-Intercourse Act], either expressly or conditionally, as their judgment should direct." While the *Brig Aurora* thus upheld the delegation in question, it offers little insight into the line between permissible delegations and the impermissible delegation of legislative power. At a minimum, the case approves delegations under which a statutory prohibition becomes effective only upon an executive finding of fact, at least regarding matters involving commerce with foreign countries.[29]

Chief Justice Marshall engaged in a more extensive discussion of the delegation issue in the second relevant case to reach the Court, Wayman v. Southard (1825), which concerned authority delegated to the federal courts to establish rules of procedure. The plaintiff, who had won a judgment in federal court, relied on a writ of execution issued by the court to enforce the judgment, while the defendants argued that the process of executing judgments was controlled by state law. The issue turned on the Judiciary Act of 1789 and related statutes, which established the federal courts, defined their jurisdiction, and authorized them to issue various writs. In particular, section 17 of the Judiciary Act authorized the Supreme Court to make necessary rules for the orderly conduct of business. Nonetheless, Congress also provided in the Process Act of 1789 that the forms of process in effect in the respective states (at the time of the enactment) would govern in federal courts, with later versions of that statute also authorizing federal courts to vary these processes by rule. The critical issue for present purposes was raised by the defendants' argument that the federal writ of execution was improper because Congress had impermissibly delegated legislative power to the federal courts.

In rejecting this argument, Chief Justice Marshall accepted the premise that Congress could not "delegate to the Courts, or to any other tribunals, powers which are strictly and exclusively legislative." Nonetheless, Marshall continued, "Congress may certainly delegate to others powers which it may rightfully exercise itself." Thus, Marshall recognized that there was an inevitable overlap between the legislative and judicial (as well as executive) powers:

The line has not been precisely drawn which separates those important subjects, which must be entirely regulated by the legislature itself, from those of less interest, in which a general provision may be made, and power given to those who are to act under such general provisions to fill up the details.

It is worth noting that Marshall regarded the line between permissible and impermissible delegations to turn on the importance of the subject, which in some respects echoes the argument raised in Congress against delegation of authority to determine post offices and routes. This approach may be contrasted with the modern nondelegation doctrine, under which the subject matter being regulated does not have a direct bearing on the permissibility of legislative delegations.[30]

Marshall then examined the power delegated to courts, which he characterized as a power to supervise officers in the execution of the courts' judgments. While Marshall observed that this power "seems to be properly within the judicial province, and has been always so considered," he did not definitely resolve the delegation issue. Instead, he rejected the defendants' nondelegation argument on the ground that, even if successful, it would not entitle the defendants, who relied on state law, to relief. Marshall reasoned that if Congress could not delegate this power to the federal courts, neither could it delegate that power to state legislatures, which had no independent authority to regulate the procedures of federal courts. This resolution of the case was to be preferred because "in the mode of observing the mandate of a writ issuing from a Court, so much of that which may be done by the judiciary, under the authority of the legislature, seems to be blended with that for which the legislature must expressly and directly decide, that there is some difficulty in discerning the exact limits within which the legislature may avail itself of the agency of the Courts." Thus, Marshall cautioned, "[t]he difference between the departments undoubtedly is, that the legislature makes, the executive executes and the judiciary construes the law; but the maker of the law may commit something to the discretion of the other departments, and the precise boundary of this power is a subject of delicate and difficult inquiry, into which a Court will not enter unnecessarily." Marshall also emphasized that Congress's decision to adopt the forms of process in effect in the states at the time, subject to variation by federal rules, was an expedient compromise at the outset of the new judicial system.

The Brig Aurora and *Wayman* decisions present a fascinating contrast in styles, yet they share certain basic features. Both leave considerable uncertainty surrounding legislative delegations—*The Brig Aurora* because of its brevity and lack of explanation and *Wayman* because of its extensive yet ultimately inconclusive discussion. Nonetheless, the cases establish certain key propositions. Both cases, like the early congressional precedent concerning patents, accept a delegation of authority to resolve a matter that could have been resolved directly by Congress and that therefore was at least potentially within the legislative power. At the same time, *Wayman* expressly states and *The Brig Aurora* might be read to imply that Congress may not delegate the legislative power itself to any other body. Thus, the cases reflect a broad recognition that the legislative, executive, and judicial powers overlap, with the result that many governmental acts are potentially within the sphere of more than one branch. The question remains, however, how to define the core of the legislative power that cannot be delegated.

The two cases also reflect different types of legislative delegations that would give rise to two lines of nondelegation decisions over time. *The Brig Aurora* involved what we may call the contingency model. Congress exercised its power to make a law, but specified that the law would go into effect only if a specified contingency arose and delegated to the President the authority to determine whether the contingency had arisen. *Wayman* involved what we may call the subsidiary rulemaking model. Congress provided a general framework and delegated the authority to make subsidiary rules so as to "fill in the details." Neither case offers a very clear conception of the legislative power to explain why contingent legislation or subsidiary rulemaking do not violate the rule against delegating legislative authority. In subsequent cases, legislation employing the contingency model presented few difficulties for the Court, but subsidiary rulemaking has given rise to somewhat more significant problems, particularly during the New Deal crisis, even if it is now broadly accepted.

Internal Operations of Congress and Inherent Legislative Authority

A third type of early congressional activity with important implications for the federal legislative power was the assertion of deliberative powers to facilitate and protect the law-making process itself. Some mechanism through which a legislative body considers proposed legislation—procedures to gather and assess information, debate the merits of proposed bills, and compromise among competing views—is essential to any legislative process. The Constitution provides greater detail on the structure and operation of Congress than of either the executive or judicial branch, but only a few provisions deal with the deliberative process and much is left unspecified. Thus, Congress had to adopt and refine rules to govern legislative deliberations and develop procedures for making informed decisions. In so doing, Congress asserted not only express constitutional powers to regulate its internal operations, but also inherent powers to command and sanction private parties as necessary to facilitate and protect the legislative function.

Article I specifies certain features of the deliberative process. The most important requirements are bicameralism and presentment: legislation must pass both houses of Congress and must be signed by the President, or his veto must be overridden (Art. I, § 7, cls. 2 & 3). The requirement that three separate government entities with different constituencies must concur in legislative action forces extensive deliberations on most legislation. Aside from bicameralism and presentment, however, Article I does not incorporate many specific procedural requirements for legislative deliberations. Revenue bills must originate in the House of Representatives (Art. I, § 7, cl. 1) and relatively detailed provisions govern deliberations to override a presidential veto (Art. I., § 7, cl. 2), but the Constitution omits many deliberation-reinforcing provisions common in state constitutions, such as single subject and title requirements, requirements of committee consideration, or minimum deliberation requirements.[31]

The Constitution does, however, contain several provisions concerning the conduct of business generally in the House and Senate. Congress must assemble at least once per year (Art. I, § 4, cl. 2) and neither house may adjourn without the consent of the other (Art. I, § 5, cl. 4). A majority is specified as the quorum for conducting business (Art. I, § 5, cl. 1) and each house is required to keep a journal of its proceedings (Art. I, § 5, cl. 3). Article I also explicitly authorizes each house to "chuse" its officers, except that the Vice President is designated as president of the Senate (Art. I, § 2, cl. 5 & § 3, cls. 4 & 5). Each house is the sole judge of the "Elections, Returns, and Qualifications" of its members (Art. I, § 5, cl. 1.) More broadly, "[e]ach House may determine the rules of its proceedings, punish its members for disorderly behavior, and, with the Concurrence of two thirds, expel a Member" (Art. I., § 5, cl. 2.)

Thus, it is clear that the Framers expected Congress to govern its own internal affairs, including the establishment of rules for the deliberative process. Nonetheless, the Constitution does not specify the scope of congressional authority to conduct business and leaves some significant questions unanswered, particularly when the deliberative powers of Congress affect private parties. As in other areas, the early actions of Congress concerning the legislative process set important precedents for the subsequent development of the legislative power and confirmed the Framers' intent to establish Congress as a true legislative body with plenary legislative authority.

Both the House and the Senate quickly adopted rules to govern their procedures. Each required bills to be read three times before passage and provided for bills to be referred to committees, embracing legislative practices that were common at the time and required by some state constitutions. The House also adopted rules requiring permission to speak more than twice on an issue and prohibiting representatives from voting on matters in which they had an immediate and particular interest. The creation of committees, which was not expressly authorized in Article I but would seem to fall within the general power to establish rules, is an important practical feature of the legislative process that enables the legislature to gather information on and process more than one bill at a time. Over time, the committee system also permitted individual legislators to specialize in areas of particular interest and develop expertise that could improve the quality of legislation.

These actions were generally noncontroversial and seem to fall squarely within the constitutional authority of Congress to govern its internal operations, but Congress also asserted inherent powers to investigate and to punish for contempt. Unlike the regulation of internal operations and the imposition of sanctions against members, these actions apply externally to private individuals. The power to investigate includes the power to compel the presence and testimony of witnesses and the production of documents, with the threat of sanctions to back them up. The power to punish for contempt includes potential imprisonment and fines for private actions, such as attempted bribery, libel or slander, or other forms of disrespect to Congress (including noncompliance with its subpoenas). From a separation of powers perspective, the assertion of these powers is all the more problematic because they are not expressly authorized, do not follow bicameralism and presentment, and seem to partake of executive and judicial functions. Nonetheless, early congresses repeatedly asserted investigatory and contempt powers notwithstanding constitutional objections, which were eventually brushed aside by the Supreme Court.[32]

The First Congress provided for at least two investigations, both with some-what inconclusive results. In response to a challenge to the New Jersey congres-sional delegation based on alleged irregularities in the elections, the House of Representatives formed an investigative committee. The committee reported that it could not adequately investigate without the testimony of absent witnesses, and the House debated a proposal to commission New Jersey state court judges to take testimony and report back to the House. Opponents of the proposal did not contest the power of the House to take this action, but rather argued that it would deny the right of cross-examination and that the House had a duty to hear the evi-dence itself. The session was adjourned for the day and the record does not reveal how the issue was resolved, but the committee eventually made findings of fact and the House voted to seat the challenged representatives.

The question of congressional investigatory powers also arose in connection with Senator Robert Morris's request that his conduct as superintendent of finance under the Articles of Confederation be investigated, apparently to quell allega-tions of malfeasance. The Senate requested the President to appoint commis-sioners to investigate, but the House appointed its own investigatory committee, notwithstanding constitutional objections from some members on the ground that Congress possessed no power to supervise executive conduct. Madison's argument that the House had the authority to gather information to do justice "to the coun-try and to public officers" carried the day and a committee was appointed, but its investigation proved inconclusive. A variety of other investigations followed on these incidents and tend to indicate that the authority of either house to create investigatory committees with the power to subpoena witnesses and papers was well accepted.[33]

These incidents established that Congress has inherent authority to conduct investigations, a premise that seems to be supported by the practices of Parliament, colonial legislatures, and the state legislatures of the time. Nonetheless, the inci-dents also raise questions about the scope of this authority. The investigation of the New Jersey election was directly connected with an explicit legislative function—each House's authority to judge the elections of its members. The same cannot be said of the investigation of Senator Morris, which was not attached to any partic-ular legislative action. Indeed, Madison asserted a general congressional investiga-tory power in the interest of justice. This seems a particularly extravagant assertion of power given Madison's narrow view of the Necessary and Proper Clause.[34]

Congress also asserted the power to punish for contempt in relation to bribery, libel, and failure to appear before committees. One of the earliest examples of the assertion of this power came in 1795, when the House determined that Robert Randall and Charles Whitney had committed contempt by attempting to bribe several members and directed the sergeant-at-arms to take them into custody.[35] Both men were reprimanded and confined for some period of time. This action apparently generated internal debate over the proper procedure for finding con-tempt, but not over the power to do so.[36] Five years later the Senate asserted a sim-ilar power against William Duane, who was accused of libel against the Senate in his capacity as editor of an anti-Federalist newspaper. Duane declined to appear before the Senate, which then found him in contempt and ordered him taken into custody by the sergeant-at-arms. It does not appear that Duane was actually arrested pursuant to this order, but before adjournment, the Senate passed another resolution requesting the President to order his prosecution in court.

Unlike the House, the Senate debated at some length its power to punish for contempt. Thomas Jefferson presided over the debate as Vice President and ably summarized the competing arguments in his "Manual of Parliamentary Practice: For the Use of the Senate."[37] According to Jefferson, the argument in favor of such a power rested on the inherent authority of public bodies "to do all acts necessary to keep themselves in a condition to discharge the trusts confided in them." This inherent authority was reflected in the historical practices of the British Parliament, state legislatures, and courts. As Jefferson summarized the argument on the other side, the power of Congress to protect itself was not to be doubted, but, under separation of powers principles, Congress must exercise that power through enactment of necessary and proper *laws* pursuant to Article I. Moreover, the historical precedents cited by proponents were inapt because Parliament, state legislatures, and courts all possessed the contempt power by virtue of positive law rather than an inherent power to act.

It is especially relevant to this study that (according to Jefferson's summary) opponents of a congressional contempt power attempted to distinguish the historical practice of state legislatures, "because their powers are plenary; they represent their constituents completely, and possess all their powers, except such as their constitutions have expressly denied them. . . ." This assertion would necessarily imply that the federal legislative power is less than plenary; indeed, if the states possess all sovereignty vested in them by their citizens, it would follow that the national government possesses none. This argument thus reflected the compact theory's premise that federal power is derivative of and subordinate to the states and was inconsistent with the plenary power principle advanced by Hamilton and embraced by Chief Justice Marshall in *McCulloch*. Insofar as the majority of the Senate approved the contempt resolution, the incident might be read as an early congressional rejection of the compact theory, but the matter was a highly partisan one and the extent to which the principle, as opposed to political considerations, prompted the vote cannot be determined.

Constitutional doubts about the power of Congress to punish for contempt were soon removed in the case of Anderson v. Dunn (1821). Anderson, the plaintiff, had been found in contempt of the House as the result of an attempted bribe, and the House issued an order to Dunn, the sergeant-at-arms of the House of Representatives, directing him to arrest Anderson. After Dunn executed the order, Anderson sued him for false imprisonment and assault and battery and Dunn asserted the order as a defense. Anderson responded by challenging the authority of the House to issue the order. In an opinion by Justice Johnson, the Court upheld the order. Although the Court recognized that "there is no power given by the constitution to either House to punish for contempts, except when committed by their own members," it nonetheless concluded that such a power was necessarily implied for the self-protection of Congress. In support of this conclusion, Johnson emphasized "that the public functionaries must be left at liberty to exercise the powers which the people have intrusted to them. The interests and dignity of those who created them, require the exertion of the powers indispensable to the attainment of the ends of their creation." Johnson also reasoned that the denial of any power of the House to protect itself against contempt "leaves it exposed to every indignity and interruption that rudeness, caprice, or even conspiracy, may mediate against it," an absurd result.

Perhaps recognizing the strength of the argument for an inherent power of self-preservation and echoing those in Congress who had opposed earlier exercises of the contempt power, Anderson did not challenge the power to punish contempts, but rather argued that Congress was required to establish a statutory sanction to ensure that punishment was not indefinite, at least when acting on contempt committed outside its presence. In responding to this argument, Justice Johnson indicated that there were inherent limits to the contempt power. First, the power to punish contempts was limited to " '*the least possible power adequate to the end proposed*;' which is the power of imprisonment." Although other sanctions, such as monetary penalties, might be used, imprisonment remained the ultimate sanction for those who refused to comply. Second, the length of any imprisonment was also limited by the purpose of the contempt power, which is to protect the legislative body, not the legislative power in the abstract. Thus, because "the legislative body ceases to exist on the moment of its adjournment or periodical dissolution, . . . imprisonment must terminate with that adjournment."

Justice Johnson also responded to the plaintiff's argument that the express power granted each house to punish its members should give rise to the negative inference that neither has any power to punish anyone else. He noted first that the argument proved too much because Congress must be able to provide for punishment of those who violate its laws. More fundamentally, however, Johnson reasoned that an express power to punish members was necessary because members were delegates from states and the power to punish them "was of such a delicate nature, that a constitutional provision became necessary to assert or communicate it." Given the need to expressly confirm the power to punish members, no negative inference should arise. This reasoning reinforces the conclusion that the Constitution transformed Congress from a collection of representatives of independent states to a legislative body for the national government.

While *Anderson* upheld the power of either house to punish nonmembers for contempt, Justice Johnson never came to grips with some fundamental problems raised by that power. Most important, even if the power to punish contempt is a necessary inference for the self-preservation of the legislature, it is unclear why each House, acting alone and without a statute, should be able to order such a punishment. The legislative power is generally the power to "make laws" and the making of laws requires bicameralism and presentment. Not only are these checks circumvented when either House acts alone, but the exercise of the contempt power also includes prosecutorial and judicial components. Indeed, in these incidents, Congress is the victim, prosecutor, and judge of alleged violations of unwritten rules. Such a procedure hardly seems consistent with either separation of powers or fundamental fairness. Subsequent experience would show that both the contempt and investigatory powers of Congress are prone to abuse.

The exercise and acceptance of deliberative powers to conduct investigations and punish for contempt complete our picture of the federal legislative power foundations laid during the formative constitutional era. The early historical and judicial precedents for the deliberative powers confirm the establishment of Congress as a true legislative body with plenary legislative power over enumerated subjects. Indeed, the recognition of this inherent authority derived from the institutional necessities of Congress as a legislative body goes beyond even *McCulloch's* broad interpretation of the power to enact necessary and proper laws, because it does not require either bicameralism and presentment or the delegation of executive and judicial authority to the other branches of government.

THE ANTEBELLUM ERA

Even as the Supreme Court upheld the assertion of broad federal legislative power and accorded Congress the inherent powers of legislative bodies, the political influence of the Federalists was waning. Although the Republicans (or anti-Federalists) had come to power opposing the Federalists' bold assertions of national power, following the War of 1812, they began to assert relatively broad federal authority as a means of promoting internal economic development and westward expansion. This period of Republican mercantilism came to a close in 1828 with the election of Andrew Jackson, who campaigned as a states' rights candidate. Jackson's election signaled a withdrawal from federal involvement in many areas of commercial activity and a corresponding growth in state legislative and regulatory activity. Although the Court lost a powerful voice for federal power when Chief Justice Marshall (who died in 1835) was replaced by Chief Justice Roger Taney, the Court during the antebellum period did not retreat substantially from the Marshall Court's precedents. Overall, the period leading up to the Civil War was one of relatively few significant developments for the federal legislative power, the most important of which were the rise of the dual sovereignty theory of federalism, the recognition of some inherent federal legislative powers, and renewed debate in Congress over its deliberative powers.

Dual Sovereignty Theory and Mutual Exclusivity

Dual sovereignty theory postulated that the national and state governments occupied two mutually exclusive spheres of sovereign authority. Thus, while it accepted the supremacy of federal legislative action within the sphere of the enumerated powers, dual sovereignty recognized a countervailing and equivalent sovereign authority of the states within the reserved sphere of state powers. Like many other issues of the time, dual sovereignty theory was interwoven with growing tensions over slavery, as it figured prominently in the defense of that "peculiar institution." While the emergence of dual sovereignty theory was of considerable importance because it laid the foundations for resistance to broad assertions of federal legislative authority later in the nineteenth century, in the antebellum period its development was related to limitations on state power.

In support of states' rights, President Jackson articulated a vision of dual sovereignty under which state and national governments stood as equals with mutually exclusive spheres of governmental sovereignty. While Jackson advocated a more restrictive view of federal power than the Federalists, dual sovereignty theory did not deny sovereignty or plenary legislative power to the federal government within its constitutionally specified sphere of authority. In this respect, it differed from the compact theory of federal power rejected by the Supreme Court in *McCulloch* and Martin v. Hunter's Lessee (1816), under which federal authority was granted by states and subordinate to state sovereignty. Thus, Jackson vigorously defended federal prerogatives when states defied federal action he regarded as legitimate, as in the case of the nullification crisis of 1832–33, when South Carolina asserted the power of the states to nullify federal tariff legislation. Nonetheless, insofar as dual sovereignty emphasized the reserved sovereignty of the states, it supported a Madisonian reading of the Necessary and Proper Clause. Dual sovereignty was later used by the Supreme Court toward the end of the nineteenth century to sharply limit federal legislative authority.

The implications of dual sovereignty for the Necessary and Proper Clause are well illustrated by Jackson's challenge to the constitutionality of the Bank of the United States, although that had apparently been settled by *McCulloch*. Supporters of the second bank, perhaps taking a lesson from the fate of the first, sought to renew the bank's charter well in advance of its expiration. Although the bank remained unpopular and was under attack as corrupt and antidemocratic, a bill renewing the charter was passed by Congress in 1832. Jackson was a vocal critic of the bank and vetoed the bill. Not content to rely on policy arguments against the bank, Jackson's veto message argued that some features of the bank were not necessary and proper and that Congress had a duty to regard them as unconstitutional notwithstanding *McCulloch*:

A bank is constitutional, but it is the province of the Legislature to determine whether this or that particular power, privilege, or exemption is "necessary and proper" to enable the bank to discharge its duties to the Government, and from their decision there is no appeal to the courts of justice. Under the decision of the Supreme Court, therefore, it is the exclusive province of Congress and the President to decide whether the particular features of this act are *necessary* and *proper* in order to enable the bank to perform conveniently and efficiently the public duties assigned to it as a fiscal agent, and therefore constitutional, or *unnecessary* and *improper*, and therefore unconstitutional.[38]

Jackson then proceeded to argue that various particular provisions of the bill were unconstitutional because they were not "necessary," even in the broader sense of the term adopted by *McCulloch*.

Ironically, dual sovereignty theory found its way into judicial doctrine during the antebellum era as a way of limiting state power to regulate matters touching on interstate commerce. Decisions of the Marshall Court, particularly Gibbons v. Ogden (1824), suggested that the vesting in Congress of power to regulate interstate commerce implicitly deprived the states of any power to do so, because the power to regulate interstate commerce by its nature could be possessed by only one sovereign authority. At the same time, however, the states retained the general police power to legislate for the well-being of their citizens—see, for example, Willson v. Black-Bird Creek Marsh Co. (1829).

Although these decisions may have generally favored strong federal authority, their view of federal and state authority as mutually exclusive also paved the way for the use of reserved state powers to limit the scope of federal legislative authority. If a matter is within the scope of federal power (e.g., the commerce power), it is by definition beyond the scope of the police power. Conversely, if the matter is within the scope of the police power, it is by definition beyond the scope of federal authority. Thus, decisions addressing the scope of state power, such as Mayor, Aldermen and Commonalty of the City of New York v. Miln (1837), the *License Cases* (1847), the *Passenger Cases* (1849), and Cooley v. Board of Wardens of the Port of Philadelphia (1851), also defined the scope of federal power. To the extent that the Court read the state police power broadly in these cases, they implicitly narrowed the scope of federal legislative power. The full implications of this theory for the meaning of the federal legislative power would not become apparent, however, until the latter part of the nineteenth century.

These cases also illustrated an inherent difficulty with the mutual exclusivity premise of dual sovereignty theory—it does not correspond to the real-world exercise of governmental authority. In practice, the enumerated powers of the federal government and the reserved police powers of the state inevitably overlap. The same type of regulation of the same people engaged in the same activity can fall within the scope of either federal or state power. This is especially true if, as Hamilton postulated, each government possesses plenary legislative power with respect to matters within its authority. In situations in which the powers overlap, the scope of either government's powers depends on where the analysis begins. If we begin by asking whether a matter is necessary and proper to a legitimate purpose within the authority of the federal government, the answer is yes and, under dual sovereignty, the power is denied to the states. If we ask whether the same matter is within the scope of the state police power, the answer is yes, and it follows that the power is denied to the federal government. At a practical level, this could also mean that the failure of Congress to adopt necessary regulations could create a significant gap that the states would be powerless to fill.

These difficulties are reflected in the facts of *Cooley*. Regulation of shipping in and around major port cities (such as Philadelphia), specifically the licensing of ships' pilots, could legitimately fall within the scope of either the commerce power or the police power. The regulation of pilots in and around ports is surely necessary and proper to the regulation of interstate or international commerce. At the same time, regulation of pilots is also necessary and proper to ensure the health and safety of those in and around the port, and therefore within the scope of the police power. Thus, if the analysis begins by asking whether the regulation of pilots in harbors is necessary and proper to the regulation of commerce among the states and with foreign countries, the answer will be yes, and mutual exclusivity would preclude the states from acting. If, as in *Cooley*, Congress does not act to regulate pilots in ports, the lack of state or local authority would expose local shipping to significant risks. Conversely, if the analysis begins by asking whether the regulation of pilots is necessary and proper to the protection of health and safety, the answer likewise would be yes. Under mutual exclusivity, however, this conclusion would preclude Congress from regulating in this area, even to prevent or override protectionist actions by the states that are contrary to the underlying purposes of the Commerce Clause.

It was apparently this conundrum that led the Court in *Cooley* to seek a way out of the mutual exclusivity trap set by dual sovereignty theory. By adopting a doctrine commonly known as "selective exclusivity," the Court held that the state and federal governments had concurrent power over matters that were within the scope of the commerce power but nonetheless "local" in character. This doctrine, which eventually evolved into modern "dormant Commerce Clause" jurisprudence, is inconsistent with the mutual exclusivity premise of dual sovereignty. Indeed, mutual exclusivity is so unworkable that it was never applied in absolute terms, even if the Court later would frequently invoke reserved state powers as a limit on the scope of federal legislative power.

Inherent Legislative Powers

Although the period leading up to the Civil War was one of relatively modest federal legislative activity, there were a few precedents involving the exercise of federal legislative power. Several cases upheld the exercise of the commerce power, including United States v. Coombs (1838), United States v. Marigold (1850), Pennsylvania v. Wheeling & Belmont Bridge Co. (1856), and Foster v. Davenport (1859). The Court also upheld federal legislation authorizing bankruptcy trustees to pass clear title in Houston v. City Bank (1848). While these cases tended to confirm *McCulloch's* relatively broad reading of the Necessary and Proper Clause, they broke little new ground. The most significant and controversial cases during the antebellum era concerned implied power to enforce the Fugitive Slave and Extradition Clauses and inherent federal legislative power over acquired territories, but their subtext was the critical issue of the time—slavery.

In Prigg v. Pennsylvania (1842) and Kentucky v. Dennison (1860), the Court concluded that Congress had implied power to implement the Fugitive Slave Clause (Art. VI, § 2, cl. 3) and the Extradition Clause (Art. IV, § 2, cl. 2). *Prigg* invalidated a state law requiring a hearing before the removal of fugitive slaves by their owners and prohibiting the kidnapping of alleged fugitive slaves, relying in part on the preemptive effect of federal legislation on the subject. *Dennison*, which arose when Ohio refused to return to Kentucky a person whose crime was helping slaves to escape, held that while Congress had power to implement the Extradition Clause, it could not impose a duty on a state officer:

> [W]e think it clear, that the Federal Government, under the Constitution, has no power to impose on a State officer, as such, any duty whatever, and compel him to perform it; for if it possessed this power, it might overload the officer with duties which would fill up all his time, and disable him from performing his obligations to the State, and might impose on him duties of a character incompatible with the rank and dignity to which he was elevated by the State.

This reasoning appears to be an early example of the "no-commandeering" rule that emerged in the 1990s. In both cases, the assertion of federal legislative power does not fall easily within the text of the Necessary and Proper Clause, because neither provision is phrased as granting a power to Congress or the federal government by the Constitution; the federal laws in question are not "carrying into execution" such a power. Moreover, other provisions of the same Article, such as the Full Faith and Credit Clause, contain express grants of federal legislative power.

Ironically, the infamous *Dred Scott* decision (1856) provided the occasion for the Court's affirmation of federal legislative authority respecting newly acquired territory,[39] even though the Court invalidated the federal law in question on due process grounds. After concluding that the federal courts lacked jurisdiction because Scott was not a citizen of any state for purposes of establishing diversity jurisdiction, the Court nonetheless addressed the merits of his claim that his transport through federal territories in which slavery was prohibited had effected his freedom. Before invalidating the law as a violation of due process, the Court indicated that the federal legislative power included the inherent power to regulate newly acquired territories that were not yet states.

This conclusion is particularly significant in light of the fact that there was no textual basis for such a power. Article IV, section 3, clause 2 authorizes Congress to "make all needful rules and regulations respecting the Territory or other Property belonging to the United States," but the Court construed this provision as applicable only to lands ceded by states under the Articles of Confederation to satisfy war debts, relying on other language in the Clause preserving state claims.[40] The Court nonetheless confirmed congressional authority to legislate for newly acquired territories notwithstanding the lack of any explicit constitutional authorization. The power to regulate the territories was inherent in the right to acquire them, a right which itself is not expressed anywhere in the constitutional text. Thus, even as it invalidated federal legislation as interfering with the slave owner's due process rights, *Dred Scott* confirmed that Congress had implicit powers, inherent in its status as a legislative body vested with sovereign authority by its people.

Constraints on the Deliberative Powers

There were no significant Supreme Court decisions concerning the deliberative powers of Congress during this period, but there was renewed debate in Congress over the scope and limitations of these powers. Although investigations, subpoenas, and contempt citations continued to be common practices throughout the period, prominent advocates emerged for a narrow conception of the deliberative powers of Congress.

Several incidents related to investigatory powers. Toward the end of 1827, for example, the constitutionality of equipping a House committee considering tariff legislation with the power to send for people and papers was unsuccessfully resisted on the ground that this power was limited to cases of impeachment and contested elections; however, the resolution authorizing the committee to exercise these powers was passed by a narrow 102–88 margin.[41] From his position in the House of Representatives during the Jackson Administration, John Quincy Adams became a vocal opponent of broad investigatory powers, particularly in connection with investigations into the activities of the Bank of the United States. He successfully moved to narrow the subpoena powers of a committee investigating the bank in 1832 and opposed contempt sanctions against bank officials for refusing to permit an examination of its books, introducing a resolution suggesting that an attempt to punish the officials through contempt sanctions would be unconstitutional.[42] A congressional committee investigating patronage in the Jackson Administration accepted Jackson's claim that its inquiry into his use of the removal power invaded the rights of the executive branch, reporting to the House that it lacked authority to conduct the investigation because it was not in relation to either impeachment or legislation.[43]

Another fascinating incident arose in 1832, when the House reprimanded Samuel Houston, the then-former governor of Tennessee and later to be president of the Republic of Texas, for an assault on Representative William Stanbury of Ohio.[44] Stanbury had, in a speech before the House, criticized President Jackson's secretary of war. Houston, who was a close friend of the President, was apparently provoked to the point of physical violence as Stanbury claimed that he was "knocked down by a bludgeon, and severely bruised and wounded." Notwithstanding the highly partisan character of the matter, Jackson's political strength at the time, and Stanbury's status as a member of the minority party, the House eventually found Houston guilty of contempt and directed that he be brought before the House to be reprimanded by the speaker. The Houston incident confirms that, although there may have been somewhat greater opposition to the assertion of broad investigatory and contempt powers by Congress during the antebellum period, this power continued to be exercised and its existence was not seriously doubted, even if some members construed it narrowly.

As the Civil War approached, the pace of congressional investigations increased and included some notable incidents. In 1857, one instance of refusal to testify before a House investigative committee prompted the passage of a statute making contempt of Congress a criminal offense that could be prosecuted and adjudicated in the ordinary manner.[45] The difficulty was that, as had been held in Anderson v. Dunn and accepted by the committee in question, the power of the House to punish for contempt did not extend beyond the legislative session, the close of which was fast approaching. The statute thus permitted the imposition of punishment for contempt in some cases in which direct congressional action would be impossible or severely limited. At the same time, however, it raises the question why Congress was not always required to exercise its inherent power to punish for contempt through the enactment of necessary and proper laws. In any event, over time statutory prosecutions replaced direct congressional action as the principal means of punishing contempt of Congress.

Several Senate investigatory committees were operating in 1860, including one investigating the Harper's Ferry raid.[46] The refusal of witnesses to testify before that committee led to spirited debate over the constitutionality of contempt sanctions by the Senate, with some senators arguing that the Senate lacked the power to bring a citizen out of state and others arguing that it involved the improper exercise of the judicial power. Nonetheless, proponents of the contempt power easily carried the day, based on the argument that such a power was necessary to preserve the proper functioning of the Senate and on the many precedents in the House of Representatives. Of course, this debate and the ultimate vote was heavily influenced by the battle over slavery. The use of investigatory committees with subpoena power backed by contempt sanctions continued through the Civil War and, by then, had become an accepted practice whose constitutionality was not in doubt.

Conclusion

Although assertions of legislative power remained modest and faced new challenges during the antebellum period, many of the principles recognized during the founding period were reconfirmed, even by those who were relatively more supportive of states' rights. Congress asserted and the Supreme Court confirmed inherent federal authority to legislate for newly acquired territories. Congressional investigations and contempt sanctions continued unabated, even over somewhat more vocal opposition. At the same time, however, state sovereignty began to emerge as a potential limit on federal legislative authority, even if its primary immediate effect was a somewhat narrower congressional view of its own powers, particularly in regard to investigations and contempt. In the final analysis, these developments paled in significance to the constitutional transformation wrought by the Civil War.

THE CIVIL WAR AND RECONSTRUCTION

It is unnecessary to recount here in detail the events leading up to the Civil War, the course of the War, or the political and social upheavals that characterized its aftermath. Among the many constitutional changes resulting from the war, the most important for purposes of this study were the consolidation of the union and the addition of a new field of federal legislative power: individual rights protection. The secession of southern states was the most significant challenge to the existence of the union since its founding, and the victory of the union resolved doubts about its character and continued viability. In the wake of the war, the ultimate authority of the national government could no longer be doubted. The Reconstruction Amendments added new federally protected rights to the Constitution and expressly authorized Congress to adopt "appropriate" legislation to implement their substantive provisions. The consolidation and expansion of federal power after the Civil War, however, did not end the debate over the scope of federal legislative authority or the dual sovereignty doctrine. Indeed, political and judicial enthusiasm for reconstruction soon dissipated and dual sovereignty doctrine reemerged as a limit on federal legislative power.

Secession and the Sovereignty of States

The southern states' claim of a right to secede was based on the compact theory of the Constitution. If the Constitution is merely a compact (i.e., international agreement) among independent states, these states could reassert their sovereignty at any time by withdrawing from the agreement. As noted previously, the Supreme Court rejected the compact theory in McCulloch v. Maryland and other early Supreme Court decisions, but the theory retained political currency in the period before the war, particularly in the South. Insofar as the right to secede is an inescapable component of state sovereignty under the compact theory, the Union's Civil War victory also vanquished the compact theory as a viable characterization of the Constitution. Primary sovereignty in practice rested with the national government; the sovereignty retained by the states was significant, but nonetheless subordinate to the reality of national power.

One critical postwar question in this regard was the constitutional status of the defeated secessionist states and the scope of federal legislative authority to deal with them. At one extreme, some argued that these states were conquered enemies with no constitutional status. Others argued in response that, because these states had failed in their attempts to secede, they remained full states with equal constitutional status. Ultimately a compromise prevailed under which the southern states remained members of the union, but were subject to federal control under the Guaranty Clause (Art. IV, § 4) on the theory that through secession they had been deprived of a "republican form of government." This basis for federal legislative authority was supplemented by the war power, on which proponents relied to support federal action dictating features of the postwar constitutions and laws of secessionist states. Whatever the ultimate justification for federal authority after the war, Presidents Lincoln and Johnson took the initiative during reconstruction, with Congress settling into a more reactive role. Many reconstruction era laws and other measures raised serious constitutional questions on a variety of fronts, but the Supreme Court appeared to go out of its way to avoid confronting military rule in the South.[47]

Reconstruction and Federal Power

One cornerstone of reconstruction policy that had important implications for the federal legislative power was securing the rights of the newly freed slaves.

The first order of business was the adoption of the Thirteenth Amendment in 1866 (with the coerced approval of newly reconstituted southern state legislatures), prohibiting slavery and authorizing legislative action to enforce the prohibition. Congress also quickly extended the Freedmen's Bureau created during the war and adopted the Civil Rights Act of 1866, which provided that all people born or naturalized in the United States—including former slaves and the descendants of slaves—were citizens and that every citizen would have the same rights "to make and enforce contracts, to sue, be parties, and give evidence, to inherit, purchase, lease, sell, hold, and convey real property," and to equal protection of "all laws and procedures for the security of person and property."

The source of congressional authority to adopt the Civil Rights Act was unclear. While there was some basis for arguing that it was "appropriate" to the enforcement of the Thirteenth Amendment or even necessary and proper legislation under the war power, the issue was sufficiently unclear that an important purpose of the Fourteenth Amendment, ratified in 1868, was to resolve doubts about this authority. The Amendment provided for national and state citizenship (overruling *Dred Scott*) and prohibited states from denying (1) the privileges and immunities of U.S. citizenship, (2) due process of law, or (3) the equal protection of the laws. In addition, it contained provisions reducing the representation of states who had denied the right to vote to male persons over the age of 21 (i.e., slave states), disqualifying people who fought for the South from holding public office, and prohibiting the repayment of debts incurred in aid of the South during the war. Finally, section 5 of the Amendment authorized Congress to enforce its provisions "by appropriate legislation."

Notwithstanding these constitutional and statutory actions to secure the rights of the former slaves, reconstruction proved controversial. Immediately following the war, the mood in Congress favored aggressive measures against southern states, such as the three Military Reconstruction Acts of 1867, which gave federal military authorities increasingly broad power to control the reconstitution of state governments. President Johnson, who looked toward reconciliation and reintegration, vetoed these Acts, but his vetoes were overridden. When Johnson declined to enforce the Acts aggressively, Congress sought to force his hand by limiting his power to remove officers whose views did not coincide with his own. It was Johnson's refusal to comply with these attempted limits on his removal power that provided the grounds for his impeachment. Johnson was acquitted by the narrowest of margins and most of the southern states were readmitted to the union shortly thereafter.

The final phases of reconstruction came during the administration of Ulysses S. Grant, which saw the adoption of both the Fifteenth Amendment (in 1870) and new civil rights legislation. The Fifteenth Amendment, which prohibits the denial or abridgement of the right to vote on account of race, color, or previous condition of servitude, was intended to ensure that readmitted southern states could not alter their constitutions to disenfranchise blacks. Additional civil rights legislation was needed to stem the growing problem of violence against the freed slaves, which was perpetrated by private organizations who used intimidation to prevent voting and oust the governments that had been installed by the federal government immediately after the war. The most important of these statutes was the Ku Klux Klan Act of 1871. While the federal government used these statutes to prosecute a number of cases successfully, over time, public enthusiasm for protecting the rights of the freed slaves began to subside. This culminated in the narrow and controversial election of Rutherford B. Hayes in 1876, which marked an end to Republican control of the national government.

Throughout most of the reconstruction era, the Court refrained from addressing the constitutionality of legislation providing for the governance and eventual restoration of the southern states to coequal status. A few cases invalidated some components of the reconstruction agenda, such as *Ex parte* Milligan (1866), which required the use of civil courts as opposed to military tribunals where the civil courts were operational, and *Ex parte* Garland (1867), which invalidated the Federal Test Act of 1865 as a bill of attainder and ex post facto law. Nonetheless, the Court managed to avoid the most serious challenges to reconstruction in cases such as Mississipi v. Garland (1867), Georgia v. Stanton (1868), Texas v. White (1869), and *Ex parte* McCardle (1869). To the extent that the cases challenged congressional authority to enact reconstruction legislation, the Court generally relied on the political question doctrine to conclude that the issues were nonjusticiable. In Texas v. White, for example, the Court relied on Luther v. Borden (1849) to hold that enforcement of the Guaranty Clause was a nonjusticiable political question, in the process implicitly endorsing the Guaranty Clause theory of federal power to enact reconstruction legislation.

Dual Sovereignty and the Scope of the Reconstruction Amendments

By the mid-1870s, political and judicial enthusiasm for federal enforcement of civil rights on behalf of southern blacks had dissipated. With the decline of federal enforcement, whites reasserted power in the South, and such practices as peonage laws, intimidation and disenfranchisement of black voters, and racial segregation flourished and were tolerated by the national government and the Supreme Court. For purposes of this study, the key feature of these developments was the Court's narrow construction of federal legislative power under the Reconstruction Amendments, particularly the Fourteenth Amendment. Ironically, while the Civil War established the primacy of national sovereignty and produced three constitutional amendments explicitly authorizing congressional enforcement, the Supreme Court nonetheless relied on dual sovereignty theory and the preservation of reserved state powers to reject a broad construction of these new federal legislative powers.

First, the Court construed the scope of substantive rights protected by the Fourteenth Amendment narrowly in the *Slaughterhouse Cases* (1873), holding that the amendment did not prevent the state from granting to a particular slaughterhouse the exclusive right to slaughter livestock within the City of New Orleans. In the course of its reasoning, the Court distinguished state citizenship from national citizenship and concluded that the Privileges and Immunities Clause of the Fourteenth Amendment protects only the rights pertaining to national citizenship. Because the right to pursue a calling was one of the privileges and immunities of state citizenship, it was not one of the privileges and immunities of national citizenship. This reasoning extended the concept of mutually exclusive spheres of sovereignty beyond the issue of substantive legislative authority to encompass both citizenship and rights. Dual sovereignty and the preservation of reserved state powers also figured prominently in the Court's justification for this construction:

> Was it the purpose of the fourteenth amendment, by the simple declaration that no State should make or enforce any law which shall abridge the privileges and immunities of *citizens of the United States*, to transfer the security and protection of all the civil rights . . . from the States to the Federal government? And where it is declared that Congress shall have the power to enforce that article, was it intended to bring within the power of Congress the entire domain of civil rights heretofore belonging exclusively to the States?
>
> All this and more must follow, if the proposition [that the pursuit of a calling is within the Privileges and Immunities Clause] be sound.

Given the historical context of the Fourteenth Amendment, it is not so unreasonable to suppose that Congress meant to transfer the protection of individual rights to the national government at the expense of states—there were certainly some in Congress who intended to do so, even if the precise intent of the Fourteenth Amendment's Framers is difficult to ascertain.[48] Critically, however, the Court in the *Slaughterhouse Cases* embraced dual sovereignty theory as a powerful tool to limit the scope of the Fourteenth Amendment.[49]

Second, the Court also employed dual sovereignty theory to support the imposition of a "state action" requirement to limit the scope of federal legislative authority under section 5. In United States v. Cruikshank (1876), United States v. Harris (1883), and the *Civil Rights Cases* (1883), the Court reasoned that the Fourteenth Amendment protected individual rights only against action by the states and that congressional authority under section 5 of the Amendment could not reach private conduct, at least in the absence of some showing that the state had failed to provide equal protection of the laws. To support this requirement, the Court relied on both the text of the Fourteenth Amendment's substantive provisions and concern that a contrary reading would encroach upon reserved state powers. As the Court put it in the *Civil Rights Cases*,

> Such legislation [under the Fourteenth Amendment] cannot properly cover the whole domain of rights appertaining to life, liberty and property, defining them and providing for their vindication. That would be to establish a code of municipal law regulative of all private rights between man and man in society. It would be to make Congress take the place of State legislatures and supersede them.

Again, the Court's reliance on the preservation of state prerogatives is a particularly striking justification for limiting congressional authority to punish private conduct under the Fourteenth Amendment, especially in light of the clear intention of Congress to provide constitutional authority for the Civil Rights Act of 1866, which expressly protected rights between private persons. Indeed, even if the substantive rights provisions of the Fourteenth Amendment are textually limited to prohibiting state action, it is hard to see why Congress could not determine that state remedies were inadequate in light of the southern states' persistent failure to provide blacks with legal protection. Alternative federal remedies against private persons would certainly be an "appropriate" legislative response to such a determination. Nonetheless, the Supreme Court has recently reaffirmed the holding of the *Civil Rights Cases* in United States v. Morrison (2000).

Thus, fifty years after Andrew Jackson embraced the dual sovereignty theory, the Court had returned to it notwithstanding the intervention of a Civil War and three constitutional amendments confirming and expanding federal power. While this theory has important implications for the scope of federal legislative powers, it does not seek to define or interpret those powers directly; the theory is more concerned with defining the reserved sphere of state powers. In this sense, it represents the reemergence of the Madisonian and Jeffersonian justification for the narrow construction of federal legislative power and the decline of the Hamiltonian conception, notwithstanding the continued force of McCulloch v. Maryland. The dual sovereignty conception of federal legislative authority would dominate the Court's constitutional jurisprudence though the New Deal constitutional crisis of the 1930s.

LAISSEZ FAIRE CONSTITUTIONALISM AND FEDERAL LEGISLATIVE POWER

In the final decades of the nineteenth century, the progressive era was characterized by increasing federal and state regulation of economic activity to protect the health and safety of workers, to control the concentration of corporate wealth and power, and to otherwise ameliorate the social and economic effects of industrialization. As might be expected, business interests burdened by these regulations challenged the constitutionality of regulatory legislation on a variety of grounds. These challenges eventually found a receptive audience in the Supreme Court. Invoking both structural and individual rights doctrines, the Supreme Court developed a jurisprudence of laissez faire constitutionalism that stood as an obstacle to both federal and state regulation of economic activity from the close of the nineteenth century until the mid-1930s, when a series of high-profile decisions invalidating important components of President Franklin D. Roosevelt's New Deal Program provoked a constitutional crisis. Laissez faire constitutionalism incorporated a constrained view of federal legislative power, the most important manifestation of which was the Supreme Court's use of the dual sovereignty theory to narrowly construe federal legislative authority. Laissez faire constitutionalism also affected the Court's analysis of legislative delegations and of congressional investigatory and contempt powers. Nonetheless, the impact of laissez faire constitutionalism should not be overstated, as the Court upheld much of the regulatory legislation to come before it.

Restricting the Scope of Legislative Power

Under the dual sovereignty theory, the Court relied on the reserved powers of the states to limit the scope of federal legislative authority, particularly under the Commerce Clause. This analysis began with the proposition that the Tenth Amendment reserved to the states all governmental authority not delegated to the federal government by the Constitution, including the general "police power" to protect the health, safety, property, and morals of the populace. Because dual sovereignty postulated that federal and state powers were mutually exclusive, it followed that federal legislative authority could not extend to activities that were subject to the state police power. Thus, when federal legislation was challenged as beyond the scope of the enumerated powers, the Court was often more concerned with determining whether the regulated activity fell within the scope of the state police power than with defining the scope of federal legislative power. Moreover, because the police powers operated as a limit on each of the enumerated powers, the scope of each of these powers tended to converge.

The seminal case for dual sovereignty limits on federal legislative power was United States v. E.C. Knight Co. (1895), which held that the Sherman Antitrust Act could not be applied to a monopoly in the refinement of sugar. As is typical of dual sovereignty analysis, the Court began its inquiry with the reserved police powers of the state:

> It cannot be denied that the power of a state to protect the lives, health, and property of its citizens, and to preserve good order and the public morals, "the power to govern men and things within the limits of its dominion," is a power originally and always belonging to the states, not surrendered by them to the general government, nor directly restrained by the constitution of the United States, and essentially exclusive. The relief of the citizens of each state from the burden of monopoly and the evils resulting from the restraint of trade among such citizens was left with the states to deal with, and this court has recognized their possession of that power. . . .

While Congress had the exclusive power to regulate interstate commerce, that power did not include sugar refining, because "[c]ommerce succeeds to manufacture, and is not a part of it." The Court acknowledged that "the power to control the manufacture of a given thing involves, in a certain sense, the control of its disposition, but . . . although the exercise of that power may result in bringing the operation of commerce into play, it does not control it, and affects it only incidentally and indirectly." Thus, the Court reasoned, the conclusion "that the power of dealing with a monopoly directly may be exercised by the general government whenever interstate or international commerce may be ultimately affected" would have "far-reaching" implications and overwhelm the states' police power.

Although the Court followed the reasoning of *E.C. Knight* to invalidate or narrow federal economic regulation in a number of other cases during the early twentieth century, it also upheld expansive federal regulation under the commerce power in many cases. At times, the Court invoked a "stream of commerce" metaphor to uphold regulation, as in Swift & Co. v. United States (1905), which distinguished *E.C. Knight* and upheld the application of the Sherman Act to a price-fixing agreement between meat dealers bidding at stockyards. Under this approach, Congress could regulate activity at any point along the stream of commerce, even if the activity was purely intrastate, because an obstruction of the stream of commerce would have a direct effect on interstate commerce. In another leading case, the *Shreveport Rate Case* (1914), the Court upheld the Interstate Commerce Commission's authority to regulate *intrastate* shipping rates because these rates had a direct effect on interstate commerce.

Another important line of cases reflecting similar difficulties dealt with federal legislation banning the shipment of particular goods in interstate commerce. In several cases, the Court upheld federal legislation of this type, including *The Lottery Case* (1903), which upheld a ban on interstate shipment of lottery tickets; Hipolite Egg Co. v. United States (1911), which upheld a ban on interstate shipment of dyed margarine; and Hoke v. United States (1913), which upheld the Mann Act's ban on interstate transportation of women for immoral purposes. In each of these cases, the Court reasoned that Congress was acting within the scope of its powers because it was directly regulating interstate commerce. These cases therefore contrasted with cases like *E.C. Knight*, in which Congress had attempted to regulate an activity that was not interstate commerce but that allegedly affected it. Notwithstanding *The Lottery Case*, *Hipolite Egg*, and *Hoke*, however, in *The Child Labor Case* (1918) the Court invalidated a similar ban on the interstate shipment of goods manufactured with child labor. Although the law was similar in form to those upheld in the earlier cases, the Court concluded that the law encroached on the state police powers and therefore was beyond the scope of the commerce power. The Court distinguished the earlier cases on the ground that the prohibited items in those cases had been "evil" in and of themselves so that their prohibition had protected the stream of commerce.[50] In contrast, there was nothing inherently evil about the *goods* manufactured with child labor, merely a congressional purpose of prohibiting such child labor. Because the regulation of child labor was within the police powers of the state, however, this was an impermissible purpose and the law was invalid.

If the police power is "exclusive" and operates to limit federal legislative power, it follows that those limits are not confined to the Commerce Clause. Thus, dual sovereignty principles also limited the exercise of the taxing and spending powers to prevent encroachment on the police power. In *The Child Labor Tax Case* (1922), for example, the Court invalidated a tax on goods manufactured with child labor and shipped in interstate commerce. The obvious intent of the federal law was to evade the holding in the *Child Labor Case* by using the taxing power to penalize child labor, and the Court would have none of it. Instead, the Court concluded that the tax was not really a revenue measure, but rather an attempt to regulate manufacture that ran afoul of the state police power. The Court had previously upheld tariffs on imported goods even though the tariffs had a regulatory purpose, but in the *Child Labor Tax Case* it distinguished those cases on the ground that the regulatory purposes of those tariffs had been within the scope of federal power, whereas the purpose in the *Child Labor Tax Case* was within the state police power. Similar reasoning was used to constrain the spending power in United States v. Butler (1936).

One interesting exception to the premise that the federal government could not regulate activities within the scope of the state police power is Missouri v. Holland (1920), which upheld a federal statute adopted to implement a treaty with Canada providing for the protection of migratory birds. The state argued that the statute impermissibly impinged on its reserved powers to manage the birds, which under then-current doctrine were regarded as the property of the state. In an opinion by Justice Holmes, the Court concluded that the treaty power was not limited by the Tenth Amendment or the reserved powers of the state. This conclusion followed from the text of the Supremacy Clause, which makes federal legislation supreme law of the land if adopted "in pursuance" of the Constitution, but which provides that treaties made "under the authority of the United States" are supreme. According to Justice Holmes, the difference in wording meant that treaties did not have to comply with constitutional requirements.[51]

Two aspects of Missouri v. Holland are worth noting here. First, although the result would appear to be inconsistent with the mutual exclusivity premise of dual sovereignty because the Court acknowledged federal power to legislate regarding matters within the reserved authority of the states, the Court did not disavow that premise. Instead, the Court carved out a narrow exception to it under the treaty power. Second, the case reflects a particular solicitude for national prerogatives in the realm of foreign affairs that has been evident in the design of federalism since the time of the Articles. Thus, the Court's willingness to countenance such an encroachment on the reserved sphere of state authority did not signal any broader willingness to tolerate expansive assertions of federal legislative power.[52]

Overall, the Court's cases concerning the scope of federal power during this period were plagued by inconsistencies. Although the Court struck down a number of laws as beyond the scope of federal legislative authority, it upheld many others, often on facts that seem indistinguishable. One problem that may have contributed to these difficulties was the Court's failure to develop a coherent account of the federal legislative authority as such. Indeed, one thing that is conspicuously absent from the Court's analysis in cases invalidating statutes as beyond the scope of federal legislative authority was any discussion of the Necessary and Proper Clause. The Court addressed federal power questions as questions about the scope of particular enumerated powers and did not apply the ends-means test of *McCulloch*. Thus, for example, in *E.C. Knight*, the *McCulloch* inquiry would be whether the prohibition of a monopoly in sugar refining was an appropriate means to an end within the scope of the commerce power. The facilitation of interstate trade in sugar is an end within the scope of the commerce power and preventing a monopoly in sugar refining would seem to be a logical means of promoting that end. The contrary result reached by the Court might be justified by reference to the third component of the *McCulloch* test—that Congress cannot use means that are prohibited by or contrary to the letter and spirit of the Constitution. Under this view, laws that impinge upon the reserved sphere of state authority would be invalid even if they are otherwise appropriate means to legitimate ends.

The inconsistency of the Court's federal legislative power decisions illustrates the fundamental problem with dual sovereignty's assumption that federal and state power are mutually exclusive. As discussed previously, state and federal power necessarily overlap in the sense that the same regulation of the same activity may fall within the scope of either power, because the same means might be used to accomplish different legislative ends. As a result, the Court's starting point often determined its destination. In cases like *E.C. Knight*, the Court began with the premise that manufacture of sugar was within the police powers of the states and consequently concluded that it was beyond the scope of the federal commerce power. But when the Court began with the premise that a law was necessary and proper to an enumerated power, as in the *Shreveport Rate Cases*, the Court upheld the law even though it regulated an activity that was within the states' reserved authority.

In light of the overall context of the decisions, it is difficult to say whether they were animated by concerns about federalism as opposed to disagreement with the regulatory policies of particular statutes. For example, while the Court refused to apply the antitrust laws to a monopoly over sugar manufacture in *E.C. Knight*, it had no difficulty applying the same law to bar a labor strike in the mining industry in United Mine Workers v. Coronado Coal Co. (1922), although mining, like manufacture, was within the state police powers. Indeed, the Court's opposition to organized labor was palpable throughout this period.[53] Moreover, moving beyond the federal power cases to consider the Court's treatment of state police power measures in other contexts, the cases exhibit little solicitude for state sovereign authority. At the same time that the Court held that regulation of the terms and conditions of employment in agriculture, mining, and manufacturing were beyond the federal *legislative* power, it did not hesitate to exercise the federal *judicial* power to dictate a laissez faire regulatory regime for the states by invalidating regulations that interfered with property rights or freedom of contract.[54]

In the notorious decision in Lochner v. State of New York (1905), the Court relied on the doctrine of substantive economic due process to invalidate a state law prescribing the maximum number of hours for bakery workers as an improper interference with liberty of contract. The Court reasoned that the state's purported health justification was implausible because there was nothing unhealthy about working in a bakery and that the law was a regulation of the terms and conditions of employment, which was not a legitimate police power purpose. As a result of *Lochner* and many cases following its reasoning to invalidate state regulation of economic activity in the name of freedom of contract or protection of property rights, the Court asserted the very power it had denied to Congress—the power to prescribe the regulatory regime for employment in the areas of agriculture, mining, and manufacture.

Lochner and its progeny are interesting for another reason—their incorporation of the ends-means approach from *McCulloch* to determine whether state legislation was within the police powers. In effect, *Lochner* reasoned that the means chosen by the state (regulation of the hours of bakery workers) was not sufficiently related to the asserted end (protection of health). Given the failure of this ends-means connection, the Court concluded that the real legislative end was to regulate employment relations, an end that was not within the scope of the police powers because it violated freedom of contract. Thus, the *Lochner* approach, like the *E.C. Knight* approach to the commerce power, placed certain areas outside the scope of legislative authority, and required a tight ends-means fit to protect those fields from legislative encroachment. Both lines of cases, then, accord less deference to legislative powers than suggested in *McCulloch*, which implies a great deal of deference to the legislature's choice of means.

Legislative Delegations

One common feature of federal regulatory legislation, even in the early days of the progressive era, was the delegation of significant discretionary authority to administrative agencies such as the Interstate Commerce Commission and the Federal Trade Commission (FTC). This sort of delegation is a matter of practical necessity for regulatory legislation because Congress lacks the expertise and the resources to enact comprehensive statutes specifying all the details of complex regulatory schemes. Thus, it is not surprising that adversely affected parties often invoked the nondelegation doctrine to challenge regulatory statutes as unconstitutional. Although the Court rejected these challenges throughout most of the pre–New Deal period, it continued to acknowledge the doctrine, used the doctrine to construe statutes narrowly, and developed the "intelligible principle" test for permissible delegations. Ultimately, the nondelegation doctrine figured prominently in some of the cases precipitating a showdown between the Court and President Roosevelt that spelled the demise of laissez faire constitutionalism.

The initial decision during this period was Marshall Field & Co. v. Clark (1891), in which the Court upheld statutory provisions authorizing the President to suspend duty free importation of some commodities upon a finding that their country of origin had imposed reciprocally unequal tariffs on goods from the United States. The Court relied on the decision in the *Brig Aurora* case, discussed above, which also upheld legislation authorizing the President to determine whether international trade restrictions should apply by finding that other countries were engaged in unfavorable action toward the interests of U.S. citizens. The Court also reviewed the longstanding legislative practice and state court precedents, concluding that there is no improper delegation of legislative authority when Congress determines the legislative policy that will become effective upon a specified factual contingency and enlists the aid of other officials in determining when and if the contingency arises.

Although *Marshall Field* involved the paradigm of contingent legislation, in a number of cases the Court also upheld delegations authorizing agencies to fill in the details of statutes by issuing binding regulations or decisions. Buttfield v. Stranahan (1904), for example, upheld the delegation of authority to exclude teas of inferior quality by setting standards for the importation of teas. Similarly, in Union Bridge

Co. v. United States (1907), the Court upheld a statute authorizing the secretary of war to determine whether particular bridges constituted unreasonable obstructions of the navigable waters of the United States. Likewise, in United States v. Grimaud (1911), the Court upheld delegation of authority to make regulations for the protection and preservation of the public lands of the United States, stating flatly that "the delegation of authority to make administrative rules is not a delegation of legislative power, nor are such rules raised from an administrative to a legislative character because the violation thereof is punished as a public offense." In each of these cases, the Court acknowledged that an excessive delegation would be improper, but it found that the particular delegation was not excessive. The cases, however, did not articulate a clear standard for excessive delegations.

This line of cases culminated in J. W. Hampton, Jr. & Co. v. United States (1928), which upheld the delegation to the President of authority to equalize tariffs. The Court's discussion of the issue acknowledged that the legislative power itself cannot be delegated, but emphasized the practical necessity of delegating some authority and the impossibility of legislatively specifying all contingencies and all details. Thus, as various federal and state precedents had recognized, Congress could delegate substantial discretion and authority to implement a statute without violating the nondelegation doctrine. The Court then stated the rule that "[i]f Congress shall lay down by legislative act an intelligible principle to which the person or body authorized . . . is directed to conform, such legislative action is not a forbidden delegation of legislative power." The "intelligible principle" test articulated by the Court, which continues to be the controlling test for legislative delegations, is generally understood to require statutory standards that bind and control administrative discretion.

This approach to delegations reflected a shift in the focus of the analysis from the considerations that animated early discussions of the limits of permissible delegation. In Wayman v. Southard, for example, Chief Justice Marshall had suggested that some legislative powers were too important to delegate, which implies that the line between permissible and impermissible delegations depends on the subject of the legislation or type of power being exercised.[55] *Hampton*, however, focuses the analysis on the type of policy decision delegated. Major policy decisions must be made by Congress as manifested in the incorporation of statutory standards reflecting that policy. Congress may then delegate subsidiary policy choices regarding implementation of the policy reflected in the statutory standards. The critical question is how specific these standards must be.

One corollary of the requirement that Congress must incorporate standards is that these standards in turn limit the scope of authority delegated. Thus, the agency cannot adopt policies or regulations that are not fairly implicated by the statute because that would be a legislative act. The Court applied this principle in Morrill v. Jones (1883), for example, to invalidate an agency rule requiring that imported animals be of "superior quality" to obtain the benefit of a statutory provision permitting duty free importation. The statutory language providing for duty free import referred to "all" livestock and therefore reflected no congressional policy of preferring only animals of superior quality. The agency was not implementing statutory policy, but rather formulating its own. In a similar vein, the Court in United States v. Eaton (1892) held that violations of administrative regulations were not punishable as criminal offenses in the absence of legislation specifying that criminal penalties apply. *Eaton* construed statutory penalty provisions applicable to violations of statutory requirements for manufacture and sale as inapplicable to violations of administrative regulations concerning recordkeeping. Critically, the penalty provision applied to violation of "any of the things required by law" in the manufacture and sale of oleomargarine, and the Court considered the regulations not to be "laws" within the meaning of this provision.

Although not as dramatic as the cases soon to come, the Court's decisions concerning the nondelegation doctrine in the pre–New Deal period contained some indications of a more aggressive posture toward broad legislative delegations. The adoption of the intelligible principle test clarified the doctrine and laid the foundations for its enforcement. By narrowly construing statutes to constrain agency action, moreover, the Court acknowledged the preeminence of federal legislative authority while at the same time making administrative implementation of legislative policies more difficult.

Deliberative Powers and Laissez Faire Constitutionalism

Laissez faire constitutionalism's constrained view of federal legislative power had important implications for the power of Congress to conduct investigations and its associated powers to subpoena witnesses, compel production of documents, and punish for contempt. Although the Court accepted such actions as necessary and proper to the exercise of the federal legislative power, the Court adopted a requirement that such investigations must be incident to a valid legislative function and used this requirement to hold that some investigations were beyond the scope of federal legislative power. In addition, while the Court upheld the contempt statute adopted shortly before the Civil War, it interpreted the statute to incorporate a similar requirement that the contempt prosecution must be in aid of a valid legislative function.

The seminal case for limiting congressional investigatory powers was Kilbourn v. Thompson (1880), which involved a House investigation into a bankrupt real estate partnership that was in debt to the United States. Kilbourn, a member of the partnership, was imprisoned for contempt when he refused to answer questions and declined to produce documents sought by the investigating committee. Upon a determination that Kilbourn was in contempt, the speaker of the house issued a warrant for his arrest, which Thompson, the house sergeant-at-arms, enforced. When Kilbourn filed suit, Thompson relied in defense on the warrant, invoking Anderson v. Dunn. Although *Anderson* had suggested that such a warrant was an absolute defense, the Court in *Kilbourn* held that the warrant was void because the investigation was beyond the legitimate scope of congressional authority.

Initially, the Court expressed doubt about whether either House had any power to punish directly for contempt, as opposed to enacting a statutory contempt provision.

This discussion echoed concerns that had been expressed in Congress many years earlier and never really answered,[56] but it called into question historical practices that had prevailed since the founding and endured for nearly one hundred years. Ultimately, the Court found it unnecessary to decide the issue, because it concluded that Congress had exceeded the scope of any power that might exist. Although *Kilbourn* cast doubt on the power of Congress to impose contempt sanctions directly, that aspect of the opinion had no lasting impact and was later disavowed. In contrast, the Court's treatment of the scope of the investigatory power has become an integral part of the doctrine.

The Court reasoned that if the contempt power was justified as necessary to preserve the legislative function, then its use could only be justified in connection with the exercise of that function. In the case of Kilbourn, the investigation was not incident to proposed legislation or any other constitutional duty of Congress, but rather was an attempt to investigate a bankrupt business of which the United States was a creditor. Thus,

the resolution of the House of Representatives authorizing the investigation was in excess of the power conferred on that body by the Constitution; the committee, therefore had no lawful authority to require Kilbourn to testify as a witness, . . . the orders and resolutions of the House, and the warrant of the speaker, under which Kilbourn was imprisoned, are . . . void for want of jurisdiction, and . . . his imprisonment was without any lawful authority.

The Court distinguished Anderson v. Dunn on the ground that the plea in that case did not reveal either the basis of the contempt or the absence of congressional authority.

The *Kilbourn* principle remains an important limitation on congressional investigatory authority and was applied in several other cases during this period. One of the most important of these cases was Marshall v. Gordon (1917), which overturned a contempt citation that arose out of a battle between a member of the House of Representatives and the U.S. attorney for the southern district of New York. The U.S. attorney was conducting a grand jury investigation of alleged criminal antitrust violations in the labor movement that implicated the member, who was eventually indicted. The member responded by accusing the attorney of misconduct and introducing a resolution calling for the House Judiciary Committee to investigate the charges against the attorney. A subcommittee of the Judiciary Committee traveled to New York to take the attorney's testimony, but he resisted. Meanwhile a newspaper article appeared alleging that the House investigation was an effort to thwart the grand jury investigation. The subcommittee demanded that the reporter reveal his sources, threatening contempt sanctions against him when he refused. At this point, the attorney wrote a letter to the committee admitting that he was the reporter's source and repeating the charges in language that, in the Court's words, "was certainly unparliamentary and manifestly ill-tempered, and which was well calculated to arouse the indignation not only of the members of the subcommittee, but of those of the House generally." This letter was the basis for the contempt proceeding.

The Court concluded that the implied power of either house of Congress to punish directly for contempt was strictly limited and "rests only upon the right of self preservation; that is, the right to prevent acts which, in and of themselves, inherently obstruct or prevent the discharge of legislative duty or the refusal to do that which there is an inherent legislative power to compel in order that legislative functions be performed." Reviewing historical legislative practices, the Court concluded that nearly all past exercises of the contempt power involved physical obstruction of legislative duties, physical assaults for legislative actions taken by members, obstruction of congressional officers in the performance of official duties, prevention of attendance by members, or the refusal to give testimony or produce documents that there was a right to compel. The letter giving rise to the contempt citation in Marshall v. Gordon did not fall into these categories and its only impact might be "on the public mind." The contempt citation therefore crossed "the broad boundary line which separates the limited implied power to deal with classes of acts as contempts for self-preservation and the comprehensive legislative power to punish for wrongful acts." This latter statement suggests that the legislative power to enact necessary and proper laws punishing for contempt might be broader than either house's power to cite for contempt directly. In particular, it raises the possibility that Congress might make statutory provisions providing for punishments of contempts that do not arise from particular legislative action within the scope of congressional authority or that do not directly obstruct legislative action.

Notwithstanding cases like *Kilbourn* and Marshall v. Gordon, the Court upheld several contempt citations in the 1920s and 1930s.[57] In McGrain v. Daugherty (1927), for example, the Court upheld a warrant authorizing the sergeant-at-arms of the Senate to take a former attorney general into custody and bring him before a committee investigating charges of misconduct in the Department of Justice during his tenure. After reviewing historical and judicial precedents, the Court concluded that "the power of inquiry—with process to enforce it—is an essential and appropriate auxiliary to the legislative function." The only question, then, was whether the testimony was sought in aid of the legislative function. The Court concluded that it was because the purpose of the investigation was to gather information that could be the basis for future action within the power of Congress, relying on statements in the preamble to the resolution authorizing the investigation. Thus, the Court rejected the lower court's finding that the committee had put the former attorney general "on trial" and usurped the judicial function.

Another case, Jurney v. MacCracken (1935), rejected the argument that Congress had no power to punish for contempt for the destruction of papers sought in a valid committee investigation. The petitioner sought a writ of habeas corpus, arguing that his detention as punishment for destroying papers sought by a committee (whose jurisdiction he did not contest) was improper because it could no longer cause him to produce the papers in question. He contended that the contempt power "may be used by the legislative body merely as a means of removing an existing obstruction to the performance of its duties; that the power to punish ceases as soon as the obstruction has been removed, or its removal has become impossible. . . ." The Court rejected this argument, however, relying on both historical precedent and the necessity of this punishment to vindicate the admitted powers of the Congress.

In addition to addressing direct contempt sanctions issued by Congress in aid of its investigatory powers, the Court during the pre–New Deal period also decided a number of cases arising under the 1857 contempt statute. First, *In re* Chapman (1897) upheld the statute, rejecting separation of powers and double jeopardy arguments against it. The witness, who sought a writ of habeas corpus directing his release, argued that the statute either improperly divested the Senate of its inherent power to punish contempt directly or, if the Senate retained the power to punish directly, violated the prohibition on double jeopardy by authorizing both a direct citation for contempt and a criminal prosecution. The Court, however, concluded that the statute was necessary and proper to the legislative function, that Congress retained the power to punish contempt directly, and that there was no violation of the prohibition on double jeopardy. In the course of its opinion, the Court distinguished *Kilbourn* on the ground that the investigation in *Chapman* concerned alleged misconduct by a senator and therefore was clearly within the jurisdiction of the Senate, which is expressly authorized to punish or expel members.

Likewise in Sinclair v. United States (1929), the Court found that there was sufficient proof of a legislative purpose attached to a committee investigation to sustain a criminal conviction under the contempt statute. Although *Sinclair* upheld the contempt prosecution on the facts, it is significant that the Court applied *Kilbourn's* requirement that the contempt prosecution be in aid of a legitimate legislative function to a statutory prosecution. It is unclear whether this limitation is a constitutional requirement or a matter of statutory interpretation, but *Sinclair* seemed to reject the suggestion in Marshall v. Gordon that the requirement might not apply under statutory provisions punishing contempt of Congress. In any event, after *Sinclair*, both direct contempt citations and statutory prosecutions for contempt were subject to similar requirements that reflect the Court's understanding of the federal legislative authority.

Overall, the Court's decisions during this period concerning the investigatory powers of Congress are, like its decisions on the scope of federal legislative authority, something of a mixed bag. *Kilbourn* and Marshall v. Gordon stand as important decisions restricting that power. *Kilbourn* was the first Supreme Court case to invalidate a contempt sanction imposed by either chamber of Congress, and the principle it announced was applied aggressively in *Marshall*. The constrained view of federal legislative power in these cases is consistent with laissez faire constitutionalism and dual sovereignty, insofar as it links the investigatory power to the exercise of enumerated legislative powers and conceives of those powers relatively narrowly. At the same time, however, the Court reconfirmed that the powers to investigate, to compel testimony and the production of documents, and to issue contempt sanctions are necessary and proper to the federal legislative power and can be exercised directly by either chamber or through the enactment of legislation making contempt of Congress a criminal offense. It also upheld the specific use of contempt sanctions in several cases, including *Daugherty*, in which it accepted a vague reference to possible legislation of an unspecified nature as a sufficient link to the exercise of a valid legislative function.

THE NEW DEAL CRISIS AND THE DEMISE OF LAISSEZ FAIRE CONSTITUTIONALISM

The tension between laissez faire constitutionalism and the modern regulatory state came to a head in the New Deal crisis of the mid-1930s.[58] The federal legislative power was the focal point of this crisis, because a series of controversial Supreme Court decisions invalidated important New Deal statutes on the ground that they exceeded the scope of federal legislative power or improperly delegated that power to administrative agencies. These cases prompted a strong reaction from President Roosevelt, who proposed the so-called "court packing plan" as a means of reconstituting the Court to make it more receptive to federal regulatory legislation. The controversial plan became moot after a critical change of heart by Justice Roberts, typically and cynically referred to as the "switch in time that saved nine," shifted the balance of power on the Court. The result was a series of decisions broadly construing federal legislative authority and accepting very broad legislative delegations (as well as repudiating the substantive economic due process of *Lochner*). These decisions ushered in an era of virtually unlimited federal legislative power.

Reserved Powers, Nondelegation, and the New Deal

Franklin Delano Roosevelt was elected in 1932 with a mandate to combat the Great Depression and he proposed a number of bold legislative initiatives known as the "New Deal." A series of Supreme Court decisions in 1935 and 1936, however, invalidated some of the key components of this legislative program. These decisions included Panama Refining Co. v. Ryan (1935), which invalidated the "hot oil" provision of the National Industrial Recovery Act (NIRA); Railroad Retirement Board v. Alton R. Co. (1935), which invalidated the Railroad Retirement Act; A.L.A. Schechter Poultry Co. v. United States (1935), which invalidated the rest of the NIRA; United States v. Butler (1936), which invalidated the Agricultural Adjustment Act; and Carter v. Carter Coal (1936), which invalidated the Bituminous Coal Conservation Act. These decisions generally relied on either a narrow construction of federal power, the nondelegation doctrine, or both.

The Court's narrow construction of federal power in these cases employed dual sovereignty theory to conclude that the laws in question exceeded federal authority by regulating matters within the scope of the state's police powers. Thus, for example, regulation of labor in coal production was beyond the scope of the commerce power in *Carter v. Carter Coal* and payments to farmers for reducing production exceeded the scope of the spending power in *Butler*, because mining and agriculture, respectively, were within the reserved sphere of the state police powers. Railroad Retirement Board v. Alton R. Co. represents a particularly striking application of the reserved powers doctrine. The Act in question regulated employee pension systems for railroad workers. Because the railroads were instrumentalities of interstate commerce, the Court had previously upheld regulation of the working conditions of railroad employees as within the scope of the federal commerce power. The Court in *Alton*, however, distinguished the earlier decisions on the ground that those statutes related to the safety or efficiency of rail transport, whereas the regulation of pensions related to the "social welfare" of railroad workers. Any connection between the moral and financial security of railroad workers and commerce was too indirect to justify such an encroachment on the state police powers.

There was nothing new in the use of dual sovereignty theory and reserved powers reasoning in these cases. As discussed previously, this framework had been employed since *E.C. Knight* to strike down federal legislation, albeit inconsistently. But the scope and importance of the New Deal programs, the concatenation of decisions in rapid succession, and their broad language and reasoning had profound implications. It appeared that the Court was prepared to block federal legislation aimed at ameliorating the problems of the Great Depression.

The Court's reliance on the nondelegation doctrine in *Panama Refining* and *Schechter Poultry* was also a dramatic step, insofar as no Supreme Court decision before or since has invalidated a federal statute on nondelegation grounds (although *Carter Coal* also has some suggestions of a nondelegation rationale). The earlier of the two decisions, *Panama Refining*, dealt with a relatively minor provision in the NIRA authorizing the President to prohibit the transportation in interstate and foreign commerce of oil produced in excess of any limits established by state law. The Court was careful to recognize that delegation was permissible if the statute contains an intelligible principle, but it concluded the hot oil provision contained none. The provision left the decision whether to prohibit transportation of oil produced in violation of state limits entirely to the President's discretion. The Court rejected the suggestion that the Act's broad statement of purposes provided the necessary standard because it was "simply an introduction of the act, leaving the legislative policy as to particular subjects to be declared and defined, if at all, by the subsequent sections." Although *Panama Refining* dealt with a relatively minor provision, it was a harbinger of things to come.

Only a few months later the Court invalidated the NIRA as a whole in *Schechter Poultry*, concluding that the Act was beyond the scope of the commerce power and improperly delegated legislative authority. The key provisions of the Act provided for the development of industry codes of fair competition that, upon approval by the President, would become binding and subject to criminal enforcement actions. The defendant poultry company had allegedly permitted customers to select their chickens for purchase in violation of a provision in the code applicable to the industry that required sales to follow the "run of the coop" (i.e., the first chickens to come out). (For this reason, *Schechter Poultry* is sometimes known as the "sick chicken" case.) The Court unanimously agreed that the law effected an improper delegation of legislative authority because there were insufficient standards for the codes and presidential approval of them.

In reaching this conclusion, the Court considered and rejected a number of possible standards. The concept of fair competition was, in and of itself, insufficient because it was too open ended. On this point, the Court distinguished the concept of "unfair competition," as used in the FTC Act, because the common law concept of unfair competition gave that term a defined content. "Fair competition," on the other hand, had no generally understood meaning and did not constrain the content of the codes. Although there were statutory conditions for presidential approval, these conditions did not provide standards for the content of the codes themselves. They required the President to approve the codes if the process for making them was representative and they did not oppress any segment of the industry. Finally, while many cases before and after *Schechter Poultry* relied on statutory purposes as a source of an intelligible principle, the purposes of the Act were so varied and pointed in so many different directions that any code could be justified in terms of one or more of these purposes. In addition to the absence of meaningful standards, the Court also pointed to other problematic features of the delegation: government authority was delegated to private parties, there were no procedures governing the adoption of the codes, and violation of the codes would be subject to criminal prosecution.

Two other cases from this period involving nondelegation issues warrant some discussion. In Carter v. Carter Coal Co., which invalidated federal regulation of labor relations in the mining industry as beyond the scope of the federal legislative power, the Court also indicated that the law in question impermissibly delegated authority to set prevailing wage rates for a region to a private body from the industry, reinforcing this factor in *Schechter Poultry*.[59] Another case, United States v. Curtiss-Wright (1936), upheld a delegation of power to the President to determine whether a ban on arms exports to a certain region, enforced by criminal sanctions, should take effect. The Court was willing to assume that the statute would have been unconstitutional under *Schechter Poultry* in the domestic arena, but it reasoned that broader delegations are permissible in the realm of foreign affairs because the President has significant independent constitutional authority to conduct foreign affairs. This decision parallels Missouri v. Holland in its application of a different set of rules for the federal legislative power in its international dimensions.

The Switch in Time That Saved Nine

President Roosevelt responded to the Supreme Court decisions invalidating New Deal programs by proposing legislation that would authorize the appointment of one new federal judge or Supreme Court Justice (up to a maximum of six new Justices) for every judge or Justice over the age of 70. In support of the plan, Roosevelt claimed that the courts were overburdened and that many judges were too old to handle the workload, but his obvious goal was to reshape the ideology of the courts, particularly the Supreme Court, and thereby procure more favorable decisions. The denomination of the proposal as the "court packing plan" reflected broad public recognition of its true purpose. Although Roosevelt's New Deal legislative agenda was very popular, the plan was perceived as an attack on judicial independence and proved controversial for that reason.

The court packing plan became moot, however, as a result of a series of decisions in which the Court repudiated laissez faire constitutionalism, upheld broad assertions of federal legislative authority, and accepted open-ended legislative delegations. The key figure in this transformation was Justice Roberts, who had been part of the laissez faire majority on the Court, but changed his position and, in 1937, began to vote in favor of upholding federal and state regulatory legislation. There is considerable debate concerning the reasons for Justice Roberts' transformation or even whether he really changed his position at all. Some scholars have suggested that Roberts was cowed by the court packing plan and the threat of political reprisals against the Court. Certainly the timing of the change, which came on the heels of Roosevelt's landslide reelection in 1936, fuels speculation that the switch was politically motivated. Others, however, including Justice Frankfurter, have defended Roberts' change of position as a principled one.[60]

Whatever the reason for the switch, it produced a series of decisions that departed from and ultimately rejected the Court's pre–New Deal jurisprudence of the federal legislative power.[61] The Court upheld broad assertions of federal authority notwithstanding apparent encroachment on the states' police powers. Similarly, the Court upheld broad delegations of authority to administrative agencies, distinguishing *Panama Refining* and *Schechter Poultry* on various grounds. Ultimately, these decisions rejected dual sovereignty theory, the mutual exclusivity of federal and state power, and the very notion that reserved state police powers limited the scope of federal legislative power. Instead, these decisions embraced the plenary power principle and in practical effect removed any judicially enforceable federalism-based limits on the scope of federal legislative power.

Federal Legislative Power as Plenary

The expansion of federal legislative power began with NLRB v. Jones & Laughlin Steel Corp. (1937), which upheld the National Labor Relations Act even though it set the terms and conditions for labor-management relations in manufacturing and other activities within the state police power and, therefore, would appear to be in conflict with a number of earlier decisions. *Jones & Laughlin Steel* did not expressly repudiate those earlier decisions, but its reasoning essentially ignored the reserved powers of the states. Instead, the Court emphasized that the Act was concerned with the effect of labor-management relations on interstate commerce and reasoned that this effect was sufficient to justify federal legislation as necessary and proper to the exercise of the commerce power, even if the effect was not direct.

In the same year, the Court upheld key components of the Social Security Act in a pair of companion cases, Steward Machine Co. v. Davis (1937) and

Helvering v. Davis (1937). These cases, which upheld the use of the taxing and spending powers to create a national system of unemployment insurance and old age pensions, refused to link the scope of the taxing and spending powers to the scope of the commerce power or to apply the reserved state police powers as a restriction on the uses of the taxing and spending powers. Although *Steward Machine Co.* and *Helvering* are important decisions, the commerce power was the most important single source of federal authority, and two decisions from the early 1940s appeared to remove any and all limits on that power.

In United States v. Darby (1941), the Court unanimously upheld the Fair Labor Standards Act (FLSA), which prohibited the interstate shipment of goods manufactured in violation of the Act's minimum wage and maximum hour standards. To "enforce" this ban on interstate shipment, the FLSA directly required compliance with the standards and imposed recordkeeping and other requirements. The Court upheld the FLSA in its entirety, starting with the ban on interstate shipment. The Court reasoned that the ban was plainly within the scope of the commerce power, regardless of its purpose, overruling Hammer v. Dagenhart (*The Child Labor Case*) (1918) in the process. The Court then upheld the direct imposition of wage and hour standards and recordkeeping requirements as necessary and proper to the enforcement of the ban on interstate shipment. *Darby* took the Court several steps farther down the road toward plenary power. First, using the "bootstrap" approach approved in *Darby*, Congress could regulate virtually any activity by prohibiting interstate shipment first and then directly regulating the activity to facilitate enforcement of the prohibition. Second, *Darby* also expressly rejected the notion that the reserved state police powers operated as a limit on federal legislative authority, stating that the Tenth Amendment was merely a "truism" and not an independent limit on federal power. Thus, *Darby* expressly repudiated dual sovereignty theory: if federal legislation was necessary and proper to the exercise of an enumerated power, it was irrelevant whether the activity regulated was also subject to the state police power.

Wickard v. Filburn (1942), which upheld a federal quota on the production of wheat as applied to a farmer who grew a small amount of wheat and fed it to his own livestock, was the final straw. If any activity would appear to be beyond the reach of the commerce power, the production of food for on-site consumption would appear to be it. Nonetheless, the Court upheld the quota, accepting the government's argument that the law was sufficiently related to interstate commerce. The purpose of the law was to support the price of wheat shipped in interstate commerce, a legitimate end within the scope of the commerce power. The quota's application to production for on-site consumption was appropriate to the end, because such production reduced demand for wheat sold in interstate commerce, causing prices to sink. Although the impact of this farmer's violation may have been trivial, the cumulative or aggregate effects of similar activity was substantial. After *Wickard*, it appeared that the commerce power was sufficiently broad to justify any federal regulation of any activity, because the cumulate or aggregate effect of almost any activity on interstate commerce could be characterized as substantial. Indeed, the Court did not strike down a law as beyond the scope of the commerce power for another fifty years after *Wickard*.

The Court also accepted broad legislative delegations of authority in the aftermath of the New Deal crisis, although it preferred to distinguish *Panama Refining* and *Schechter Poultry* rather than overrule them. A series of decisions in the 1940s made clear that broad delegations pursuant to general standards were permissible. National Broadcasting Co. v. United States (1943) upheld the Federal Communications Commission's power to allocate broadcast licenses under a "public interest" standard. Yakus v. United States (1944) approved the delegation of authority to set wartime prices at levels that were "generally fair and equitable and [would] effectuate the purposes" of the statute. American Power & Light Co. v. Securities and Exchange Commission (1946) upheld agency authority to structure holding companies to ensure that they were not "unduly or unnecessarily complicate[d]" and did not "unfairly or inequitably distribute voting power among security holders." In some cases, such as Fahey v. Mallonee (1947) and Lichter v. United States (1948), the Court had to be fairly creative to find statutory standards. Indeed, *Fahey* acknowledged that "explicit standards . . . would have been a desirable assurance of responsible administration," but nonetheless found no improper delegation.

In the wake of such decisions upholding broad assertions of federal legislative authority and broad delegations to administrative agencies pursuant to very general standards, there appeared to be few judicially enforceable boundaries to congressional exercise of the federal legislative power. This development was part of a broader jurisprudential shift in which the Court accepted the modern regulatory state. Thus, in such cases as West Coast Hotel v. Parrish (1937) and United States v. Carolene Products (1938), the Court also repudiated the *Lochner* decision and its broad economic rights jurisprudence. Indeed, the jurisprudence of *Lochner* came to be regarded as the epitome of judicial activism. At the same time, the post–New Deal Court began to accord greater protection for certain individual rights, including equal protection, criminal procedure rights, freedom of speech, and right of privacy.[62]

Structural Limits in the Era of Plenary Federal Legislative Power

From the 1940s to the 1970s, limits on federal legislative authority stemmed almost exclusively from individual rights safeguards, as opposed to structural considerations related to the Court's understanding of the legislative power itself. Nonetheless, several developments in this period are of particular relevance to the federal legislative power. These developments include decisions construing the scope of congressional power to enforce the reconstruction amendments, the Court's abortive effort to limit congressional regulation of states as states, and controversial congressional investigations.

First, during the 1960s and 1970s, there was some further development of the power to enforce the Reconstruction Amendments, although this issue was largely rendered moot by the broad scope of the commerce power. In the seminal decision in Katzenbach v. Morgan (1966), the Court held that the language of section 5 of the Fourteenth Amendment, authorizing Congress to enforce the Amendment by "appropriate" legislation, was intended to incorporate the *McCulloch* test for necessary and proper laws. Applying a variation of that test, *Morgan* upheld a federal law banning literacy tests for voting, although the Court had only recently held in Lassiter v. Northampton County Bd. of Elections (1959) that such tests were consistent with the Equal Protection Clause in the absence of discriminatory intent. The Court in *Morgan* reasoned that the ban was necessary and proper to the enforcement of equal protection, because Congress might conclude that such tests were motivated by discriminatory intent or might seek to prevent future equal protection violations likely to arise if non-English speaking groups were systematically excluded from voting. Some language in the opinion might even be read to support congressional power to legislatively expand the rights protected by the Fourteenth Amendment, although the Court never applied such a rationale and later expressly repudiated it in City of Boerne v. Flores (1997).

Other cases followed the lead of *Morgan* and generally upheld civil rights laws enacted pursuant to the Reconstruction Amendments, but congressional authority to enforce the amendments appeared to be less plenary than other powers, such as the commerce power. Most dramatically, in Heart of Atlanta Motel v. United States (1964) and Katzenbach v. McClung (1964), the Court relied on the commerce power to sustain civil rights legislation to avoid revisiting the state action requirement. Both cases dealt with provisions of the Civil Rights Act of 1963 prohibiting private acts of discrimination in public accommodations such as hotels and restaurants. These provisions were essentially identical to provisions that had been invalidated on state action grounds in the *Civil Rights Cases* (1883) and defenders of the statute urged the Court to abolish the state action requirement. Instead, the Court avoided the state action issue by sustaining the statutes under the commerce power. The legislative record indicated that one purpose of Congress in enacting the law was to facilitate interstate travel by blacks. This purpose, which falls within the commerce power, was supported by ample evidence before Congress indicating that discrimination in public accommodations discouraged such travel.

The Court's reliance on the commerce power in *McClung* and *Heart of Atlanta Motel* is another example of that power's virtually unlimited scope, but it also demonstrates the Court's reluctance to read the Fourteenth Amendment enforcement power broadly.[63] There were other indications of this reluctance, as the Court construed various civil rights statutes narrowly to avoid constitutional difficulties. In contrast to the commerce power, moreover, the Court in Oregon v. Mitchell (1970) invalidated at least one provision of a federal statute as beyond the scope of the power to enforce the Fifteenth Amendment. Although the Court's relatively narrow treatment of federal legislative authority to enforce the Reconstruction Amendments imposed few constitutional constraints on the overall scope of federal legislative power so long as other federal powers were virtually limitless, it has taken on added significance with the recent emergence of new doctrines limiting the scope of the federal commerce power.

A second interesting development in relation to the scope of federal legislative power was the abortive holding in National League of Cities v. Usery (1976) that state sovereignty principles, implicit in the Tenth Amendment, limited federal legislative authority to regulate the states "as states." A slim five to four majority of the Court concluded that the extension of the FLSA to cover state employees interfered with state sovereignty in a manner that violated the Tenth Amendment. A series of subsequent cases, however, distinguished *Usery* on increasingly thin grounds, and the Court overruled it less than ten years later in Garcia v. San Antonio Metropolitan Transit Authority (1985). The rejection of *Usery* appeared to be the result of a change of heart by Justice Blackmun, who had been in the *Usery* majority but wrote a separate concurrence and was the critical fifth vote in the new *Garcia* majority. As the author of the *Garcia* opinion, Justice Blackmun explained that the principle of *Usery* was unworkable because it was impossible and improper for federal courts to distinguish between those activities that were sufficiently connected to state sovereignty to warrant protection and those that were not. In addition to overruling *Usery*, *Garcia* contained broad language that came very close to suggesting that the only limits on federal legislative authority were political. Notwithstanding *Garcia*, however, *Usery* laid the groundwork for later development of the no-commandeering rule, as part of a renewed effort to protect state sovereignty that emerged in the 1990s.

A final important development during this period related to the investigatory and contempt powers of Congress, which became an issue with the rise of the House Committee on Un-American Activities. The Committee's investigations into the influence of the Communist Party in the United States presented a variety of constitutional questions and, although the Court's willingness to curb abuses was by no means consistent, it did reverse a number of statutory contempt convictions of recalcitrant witnesses on statutory or constitutional grounds. In keeping with its general view of plenary federal legislative power during this period, however, the Court did not question Congress's general authority to conduct investigations related to valid legislative action, to subpoena witnesses and documents, and to punish individuals for contempt. Nor did the Court question whether investigations into the activities of the Communist Party were sufficiently related to legislative action to satisfy *Kilbourn*, but rather consistently upheld congressional authority to investigate the influence of the Communist Party in cases such as Barenblatt v. United States (1959).

When the Court did reverse contempt convictions, it typically did so on individual rights grounds, particularly due process or the privilege against self-incrimination. The leading example of this tactic is the Court's opinion in Watkins v. United States (1957), which reasoned that a statutory prosecution for contempt required the prosecution to prove that the witness had refused to answer questions that were pertinent to a valid investigation. Because the resolution authorizing the committee's investigation was excessively vague as to the subject matter of the inquiry, it was impossible for the witness to know whether the questions he was compelled to answer were pertinent to the investigation. *Watkins* also contained broad language to the effect that congressional investigations must relate to legislative action and that those solely for the purpose of exposure were improper, that witnesses retained their privilege against self-incrimination, and that congressional investigations were subject to First Amendment restrictions. Although *Watkins* is couched in terms of due process, its reasoning emphasizes the *Kilbourn* requirement that investigations must be related to a valid legislative action, and effectively requires this connection for any question posed to a witness.

Other cases invalidating contempt convictions resulting from the House Committee on Un-American Activities relied on similar reasoning. In Quinn v. United States (1955), the Court held that the defendant had invoked his privilege against self-incrimination and could not be convicted for contempt because the assertion of the privilege had not been overruled by the committee. In Russell v. United States (1962), several convictions were overturned on the ground that the indictment did not specify the subject matter of the inquiry and the defendants therefore lacked adequate notice that would enable them to contest the pertinence of the questions at issue. After a retrial of one of the *Russell* defendants under a proper indictment, the Court in Gojack v. United States (1966) again reversed the conviction, this time because the grant of authority to the committee was insufficiently specific to constitute a proper authorization for the investigation. Another case arising out of a different investigatory committee was Dombrowski v. Eastland (1967), which allowed a suit against a staff member of the committee to go forward on the theory that the staff member had conspired with state officials to conduct an illegal search and seizure of the plaintiff organization.

Conclusion

Overall, then, by the 1960s and 1970s it appeared that the plenary power principle had emerged victorious and that the enumerated powers principle was dead. Limits derived from reserved state powers and dual sovereignty had been rejected and the scope of federal legislative power was determined by a generous construction of both the enumerated powers and the necessary and proper means to implement those powers. Likewise, Congress was free to delegate broad discretion to administrative agencies without fear of violating the nondelegation doctrine. These developments fueled the rise of the modern administrative state. The activist legislature naturally engaged in a wide array of activity related to the exercise of legislative power, including a wealth of committee investigations, and the rule of *Kilbourn* posed few restraints because virtually any area might be the subject for a proper congressional investigation attached to potential legislative acts. Nonetheless, the McCarthy-era precedents do require that the connection between specific questions and avenues of inquiry be formally established and clearly articulated.

THE "NEW" FEDERALISM AND THE FUTURE
OF FEDERAL LEGISLATIVE POWER

For several decades after the New Deal it appeared that there were few, if any, structural constraints on the federal legislative power, but, by the end of the twentieth century, the enumerated powers principle and dual sovereignty emerged once again as potentially significant restrictions on that power. In the 1980s and 1990s, Presidents Ronald Reagan and George H. W. Bush effected a significant shift in the composition of the Court, which brought jurisprudential changes of some significance for the scope of the federal legislative power. In a series of high-profile decisions, the Court demonstrated renewed interest in limiting the scope of federal authority in order to preserve the traditional powers of the states. As part of this development, the Court engaged in a particularly aggressive effort to protect the sovereignty of the states against legislative and judicial encroachment. While these developments reflected the use of enumerated powers and dual sovereignty principles to limit the plenary federal legislative power, they do not appear to signal a return to the pre–New Deal jurisprudence of the federal legislative power.

The New Federalism and Federal Legislative Power

The "new federalism" incorporates three lines of cases in which the Court has invalidated federal statutes to preserve the sovereign status and authority of the states. Although not as explicit as the pre–New Deal decisions, these cases appear to resurrect a modified form of dual sovereignty. One line of cases in particular emphasizes reserved state police powers as a reason to limit the scope of the commerce power and the power to enforce the Fourteenth Amendment. In the second line of cases, the Court fashioned a no-commandeering rule that prevents Congress, when acting pursuant to the commerce power, from compelling the legislature or executive officials of a state to implement a federal mandate. The third line of cases constitutionalizes the sovereign immunity of the states in both state and federal courts and prevents Congress from abrogating that immunity pursuant to the commerce power. These three lines of cases interact in important ways and leave open critical questions that remain to be resolved.

The most dramatic of the new federalism decisions, if only because it was the least expected, was United States v. Lopez (1995), which held that the Federal Gun Free School Zones Act was beyond the scope of the commerce power. *Lopez* incorporated a comprehensive restatement of the federal commerce power under which Congress may regulate three categories of activity: (1) it may regulate the use of the instrumentalities of interstate commerce; (2) it may regulate and protect persons and things in commerce; and (3) it may regulate activities having a "substantial" effect on interstate commerce. The latter category has been the source of the most expansive readings of the commerce power, and the Court in *Lopez* went to great lengths to narrow it, emphasizing that the effect on interstate commerce must be "substantial" and limiting the consideration of aggregate effects under *Wickard* to cases in which the regulated activity is commercial or economic. The Court followed the *Lopez* analysis in United States v. Morrison (2000), which invalidated the Federal Violence Against Women Act.

Two features of the *Lopez-Morrison* analysis are worth noting in this historical discussion. First, the new categories of federal commerce power authority, which will be discussed more fully in Part II, are an apparent departure from the ends-means test of *McCulloch*. Instead of determining whether the ends of the law are within the scope of the commerce power and whether the means are appropriate or plainly adapted to the ends, the Court attempted to categorize the permissible uses of that power. Second, in both cases, the Court emphasized that the underlying activities in question—crime and education in *Lopez* and crime and domestic violence in *Morrison*—were within the traditional police powers of the state. Thus, the government's arguments in favor of federal power in those cases proved too much because, if accepted, they would justify general federal authority over police power matters pursuant to the commerce power. This reasoning incorporates components of the dual sovereignty theory that prevailed before the New Deal shift.

While the results in *Lopez* and *Morrison* are striking, they apparently do not signal a broad-based restriction of the scope of federal power based on dual sovereignty reasoning. In its most recent commerce power cases, the Court has upheld the assertion of federal authority, distinguishing *Lopez* and *Morrison*. In Pierce County, Washington v. Guillen (2003), the Court upheld a federal law specifying that federally required reports on road conditions could not be used in litigation against the state or local governments. Because Congress was regulating the use of the channels of interstate commerce (roads) and regulating and protecting persons and things in commerce (being transported on the roads), the first two of the three *Lopez* categories sustained the statute and the remainder of the *Lopez* discussion did not apply. Similarly, in Citizens Bank v. Alafabco (2003), the Court upheld the application of the Federal Arbitration Act to intrastate banking transactions, indicating that under *Lopez* the cumulative or aggregate effects of a commercial or economic activity may be considered in determining whether there is a substantial effect on interstate commerce.

Pierce County and *Alafabco* were relatively easy cases and received little attention, but the Court's most recent commerce power decision, Gonzales v. Raich (2005), involved the Justices in a high-profile debate over federal authority to prohibit "medicinal marijuana" that is grown for personal consumption. The facts of the case are quite analogous to *Wickard*, and the majority of Justices upheld the federal statute under the cumulative effects doctrine, rejecting the argument that medical use of marijuana is not a commercial or economic activity. Aside from Justice Thomas, even the dissenting Justices accepted the validity of *Wickard*, although they would require a more convincing showing that the cumulative effect of medical marijuana use on interstate commerce is significant. Thus, *Raich* clearly suggests that the Court is unlikely to go much further in narrowing the scope of the federal commerce power. In addition to its treatment of *Wickard*, *Raich* is also significant for Justice Scalia's separate concurring opinion, which expressly invoked the Necessary and Proper Clause and explained its relation to the *Lopez* test.[64]

The Court has also significantly restricted the scope of congressional authority to enforce the Fourteenth Amendment. The seminal decision for this development is City of Boerne v. Flores (1997), which invalidated the Religious Freedom Restoration Act's requirement that state and local laws burdening religious practices must be necessary to further a compelling interest. The Act was passed after Employment Division, Oregon Department of Human Resources v. Smith (1990) held that "strict scrutiny" does not apply to neutral measures that burden religious exercises. *Boerne* began with the premise that Congress did not have the power to define the substantive content of the rights protected by the Fourteenth Amendment and could only act to remedy or prevent violations as defined by the Court. This remedial or preventive power, moreover, only extended to measures that are "congruent and proportional" to the underlying violation. The congruence and proportionality test appears to derive from the *McCulloch* variation adopted by the Court in Katzenbach v. Morgan, but it requires a much closer "fit" between the means and ends than traditionally has been applied under that test. Applying this test in United States v. Morrison, for example, the Court concluded that the Federal Violence Against Women Act could not be sustained as an exercise of the Fourteenth Amendment power.

The narrowing of the Fourteenth Amendment power has particular practical significance as a result of the state sovereign immunity line of cases, because Congress may (as will be discussed below) abrogate state sovereign immunity when enforcing the Fourteenth Amendment. Thus, in a series of recent decisions, the Court has applied the congruence and proportionality test to determine whether statutory remedies against states could be upheld as within the scope of the Fourteenth Amendment power. In Florida Prepaid Postsecondary Education Expense Board v. College Savings Bank (1999), the Court held that a cause of action against states was not congruent and proportional to any violation of the due process rights of patent holders in the absence of any evidence that states violated such rights. In Kimel v. Florida Board of Regents (2000), the Court held that the Age Discrimination in Employment Act's (ADEA's) remedy against states for age discrimination was not congruent and proportional to any equal protection violation because age was not a suspect classification and states could rationally consider it in making employment decisions. Employing nearly identical reasoning, the Court held in Board of Trustees of the University of Alabama v. Garrett (2001) that the Americans with Disabilities Act's (ADA's) remedy against states was not congruent and proportional to any equal protection violation.

More recently, however, the Court has found some statutory remedies to be within the scope of the Fourteenth Amendment. In Nevada Department of Human Resources v. Hibbs (2003), the Court upheld remedies against states under the Family Leave Act (FLA) as a congruent and proportional response to historical discrimination against women based on the stereotype that caring for family members is a woman's job. The critical distinction in *Hibbs* appears to be that, under equal protection doctrine, the classification in question, gender, is a "quasi-suspect" one subject to intermediate scrutiny, as opposed to the rational basis test. And in Tennessee v. Lane (2004), the Court upheld remedies under the ADA against states for claims based on the denial of access to courthouses, distinguishing *Garrett* on the ground that access to court is a fundamental right for due process purposes. Like the most recent commerce power cases, these decisions are not inconsistent with the *Boerne* line of cases, but they may signal that the Court is unwilling to go much further in restricting the scope of federal legislative power.

While the Court has construed the commerce and Fourteenth Amendment powers somewhat more narrowly, it has to this point continued to read other federal powers broadly. Most significant, the use of the spending power to influence conduct is still governed by the generous test of South Dakota v. Dole (1987), under which conditions attached to receipt of federal funds are valid if (1) the purpose of the federal spending program is for the "general welfare," (2) the conditions are expressed "unambiguously," (3) the conditions are "not unrelated" to the purposes of the program, and (4) the conditions do not violate independent constitutional limits. In addition, *Dole* suggested that conditional spending might be improper if it is "coercive." The first and third components of the *Dole* test carry forward the ends-means analysis of *McCulloch*, but they are much more generous than the *Boerne* test for two reasons. First, Congress may pursue any ends related to the general welfare by means of the spending power and these ends are not restricted to the fields encompassed in the other enumerated powers. Second, the means (i.e., the conditions on spending) are permissible if they are "not unrelated" to the spending program, as opposed to "congruent and proportional" to it.

The potential breadth of the spending power may undermine the Court's effort to preserve the reserved state powers and protect state sovereignty, because Congress can regulate nearly as effectively through conditional spending as through direct regulation.[65] Moreover, as will be discussed more fully below, because acceptance of federal funding is considered to be voluntary (unless the penalty is in some way coercive), the spending power can be used to induce states to do things that Congress may not directly compel them to do without infringing on state sovereignty, such as waive sovereign immunity. During the pre–New Deal era of laissez faire constitutionalism, the Court moved to prevent the spending power from being used to circumvent limits on the commerce power, and it may do so again in the wake of decisions like *Lopez* and *Morrison*.[66] On the other hand, because the spending power is less coercive than direct regulation, the Court may regard conditional spending as less threatening to the states. A recent example of a continued broad reading of the spending power is Sabri v. United States (2004), which upheld a federal statute prohibiting bribery in programs receiving federal funds as necessary and proper to the exercise of the spending power, even as applied to bribes not directed toward the expenditure of federal funds.

The Court has also recently upheld legislation pursuant to other enumerated powers. In Eldred v. Ashcroft (2003), the Court upheld the 1998 Copyright Term Extension Act as within the scope of the Patent and Copyright Clause, Article I, section 8, clause 8. While much of the Court's analysis focused on the construction of the Clause itself, particularly the requirement that copyrights be for "limited [t]imes," the Court also rejected the argument that the *Boerne* congruence and proportionality test should apply, explaining that the test derives from the language of section 5 of the Fourteenth Amendment, which confers only the power to *enforce* the substantive provisions of the Fourteenth Amendment. And in Jinks v. Richland County, S.C. (2003), the Court held that a federal statute requiring states to toll their statutes of limitations while litigation is pending in federal court was a necessary and proper law, pursuant to Congress's Article I, section 8, clause 9 power to constitute inferior tribunals and pursuant to Article III's provisions concerning federal courts and their jurisdiction.

One overarching feature of the recent decisions construing the scope of federal legislative power is that they do not consistently invoke or discuss the Necessary and Proper Clause. At times, the Court has treated the power to enact necessary and proper laws as a component of each enumerated power, most explicitly in Katzenbach v. Morgan and more generally through the use of ends-means scrutiny derived from the *McCulloch* test. But *Lopez* seems to replace ends-means scrutiny for purposes of Commerce Clause analysis, and it is not clear why the level of scrutiny should vary as widely as it does between the spending power and the power to enforce the Fourteenth Amendment. In a few cases, the Court or individual Justices have treated the Necessary and Proper Clause as a separate issue for purposes of constitutional analysis.

The No-Commandeering Rule

In addition to limiting the substantive scope of the commerce and section 5 powers so as to preserve the reserved powers of the states, in a second line of cases from the 1990s, the Court created a new limitation on necessary and proper laws—they may not "commandeer" state legislatures or executive officials by compelling them to implement federal law. Although the Court employed this sort of reasoning as early as Kentucky v. Dennison (1860), this rule has its modern roots in the *Usery-Garcia* line of cases. Like the *Usery-Garcia* line, the no-commandeering rule reflects concern for the regulation of states as states, but the no-commandeering rule concerns a subclass of such regulation in which Congress seeks to compel the states to implement federal law as it applies to their citizens. The Supreme Court has invalidated this kind of statute on the ground that it interferes with state sovereignty by treating states as a subordinate enforcement apparatus of the federal government.

The seminal modern decision for the no-commandeering rule is New York v. United States (1992), which invalidated the "take title" provisions of the Federal Low Level Radioactive Waste Policy Amendments Act. Under the Act, states were required to meet certain federal deadlines for developing low-level radioactive waste disposal sites or face increasingly stiff sanctions—first the loss of funds, then higher charges for disposal in other states, and finally the obligation to "take title" to radioactive waste generated in their state and thus be responsible for its disposal. Although *Garcia* had suggested that the use of state sovereignty to limit the exercise and scope of federal legislative power was a thing of the past, the Court in *New York* distinguished *Garcia* on the ground that it involved legislation that applied to both states and private parties but did not explain why this distinction was material. More fundamentally, the Court resurrected the use of the Tenth Amendment as a limit on federal legislative power. The Court acknowledged that the enumerated powers and reserved Tenth Amendment powers were merely "flip sides" of the same coin, but it found that state sovereignty imposed implicit limitations on the enumerated powers. In other words, the power to enact necessary and proper laws for the regulation of interstate commerce did not include the power to interfere with state sovereignty. The Court then proceeded to advance precedential, historical, and policy arguments as to why commandeering was an impermissible interference with state sovereignty.[67]

New York dealt with a federal mandate that effectively required state legislatures to enact legislation and the Court distinguished the compulsory application of federal laws in state courts, which is clearly contemplated by the Supremacy Clause. This reasoning left open the question whether Congress could compel state executive officials to implement federal law. That question was resolved in Printz v. United States (1997), which extended the no-commandeering rule to state executive officials and invalidated provisions of the Brady Handgun Violence Prevention Act requiring state and local law enforcement personnel to conduct background checks on prospective gun purchasers. The Court restated and expanded on *New York's* rationales, which it considered to be equally relevant in the context of compelled executive action by states, but in *Printz* it added a separation of powers rationale, reasoning that delegation of executive authority to state officials interfered with the President's duty to take care that the laws be faithfully executed.

New York and *Printz* left open several issues surrounding the scope of the no-commandeering rule. One questions is the extent to which the rule applies to federal powers other than the commerce power. Another is what exactly constitutes commandeering. In Reno v. Condon (2000), for example, the Court distinguished *New York* and *Printz*, concluding that a statute prohibiting state motor vehicle departments from disclosing personal information regarding licensed drivers did not commandeer the states because it did not "require the states in their sovereign capacity to regulate their own citizens." A related question is what constitutes compulsion. These and other questions concerning the application of the no-commandeering rule will be discussed in greater detail in Part II.

State Sovereign Immunity

One longstanding attribute of sovereignty is immunity from suit, both in the sovereign's own courts and in the courts of other sovereign nations. Although not absolute and frequently waived, sovereign immunity is generally regarded as essential to the dignity and status of a state as sovereign. The extent to which the states retained sovereign immunity under the Constitution is a recurring issue of federalism, which has taken on renewed importance in the wake of recent Supreme Court decisions expanding and strengthening that immunity. These decisions also have important implications for the federal legislative power.

The sovereign immunity of states first became a controversial issue in Chisholm v. Georgia (1793), in which the Supreme Court held that the diversity jurisdiction of federal courts extended to suits against a state by citizens of another state. The Eleventh Amendment was quickly adopted to reverse that result and by its terms provides only that "[t]he Judicial power of the United States shall not be construed to extend to any suit . . . commenced or prosecuted against one of the United States by Citizens of another State or by Citizens or Subjects of any Foreign State." Nonetheless, in Hans v. Lousiana (1890), the Supreme Court held that states are also immune in federal court from suits brought by their own citizens arising under federal law. The Court has long held, however, that the sovereign immunity of states does not preclude suits for injunctive relief against state officers—see *Ex parte* Young (1908)—and that Congress may require states to waive sovereign immunity as a condition of receiving federal funds (provided that condition is germane to the funding program and clearly stated).

For purposes of this study, the critical question is whether Congress, in the exercise of its legislative powers, may abrogate state sovereign immunity. In Fitzpatrick v. Bitzer (1976), the Court held that Congress could abrogate state sovereign immunity when acting pursuant to its power to enforce the Fourteenth Amendment. The Court reasoned that because the Fourteenth Amendment came after the Eleventh Amendment and by its terms authorizes Congress to enforce substantive rights against state action, the Fourteenth Amendment implicitly authorizes the abrogation of immunity. This conclusion seems inescapable, especially in light of the state action doctrine that prevents Congress from creating remedies against private persons, for otherwise Congress's enforcement power is a dead letter. While *Fitzpatrick* is thus unsurprising, in Pennsylvania v. Union Gas Co. (1989), the Court held that Congress could abrogate state sovereign immunity under the commerce power as well.

Union Gas cannot be sustained by the same reasoning as *Fitzpatrick*, because the Commerce Clause does not expressly contemplate remedies against states and was not enacted after the Eleventh Amendment. A plurality of the Court reasoned, however, that the Eleventh Amendment was directed at the courts rather than Congress, because its language specified how the "judicial power" was to be construed. This analysis, of course, is untenable, because if the federal judicial power cannot be construed to extend to a particular type of case, then Congress cannot give the courts jurisdiction over it. Thus, *Union Gas* was an easy target for proponents of states' rights and the Court overruled it in Seminole Tribe of Florida v. Florida (1996). *Seminole Tribe*, however, continued to recognize the doctrine of *Ex parte* Young and the validity of conditional spending requirements to induce waivers.

Not long after *Seminole Tribe*, the Court held in a trilogy of cases that Congress could not abrogate state sovereign immunity in state courts, which are otherwise constitutionally required to hear federal causes of action within their jurisdiction. See Alden v. Maine (1999), Florida Prepaid Postsecondary Education Expense Board v. College Savings Bank (1999), and College Savings Bank v. Florida Prepaid Postsecondary Education Expense Board (1999). Although the language of the Eleventh Amendment speaks only of the *federal* judicial power, the Court reasoned that the Amendment reflected and confirmed a broader principle that states retained their sovereign immunity as part of the constitutional structure of federalism. Thus, although the Eleventh Amendment says nothing about state courts and although state courts are generally bound to adjudicate suits arising under federal law if Congress so provides, they could not be made to accept federal suits in violation of their sovereign immunity. *Alden* dealt with an enactment under the commerce power and the *Florida Prepaid* cases dealt with enactments under the Patent and Copyright Clause.

The *Alden* trilogy nonetheless confirmed that Congress could abrogate immunity pursuant to the Fourteenth Amendment, that conditional federal spending provisions may require waiver, and that suits under the doctrine of *Ex parte* Young remain available. In light of *Seminole Tribe* and the *Alden* trilogy, many federal statutes abrogating immunity and creating remedies against states were called into question, including the ADA, the ADEA, and the FLA. The sovereign immunity cases increased the importance of the scope of the power to enforce the Reconstruction Amendments, because the remedy provisions of these statutes could no longer be sustained under the commerce power. When defenders of the statutes relied on section 5 of the Fourteenth Amendment, however, their efforts met with limited success. As discussed above, the ADEA and ADA failed to satisfy the congruence and proportionality test for exercise of the power to enforce the Fourteenth Amendment, and the Court invalidated their remedies against states in *Kimel* and *Garrett*, respectively. On the other hand, the Court upheld the remedies provisions of the FLA in *Hibbs* and a narrow remedy for denial of access to court under the ADA in *Tennessee v. Lane*.

More recently, in Central Virginia Community College v. Katz (2006), the Court has upheld the abrogation of state sovereign immunity under the Bankruptcy Clause, an issue that it had previously left open in Tennessee Student Assistance Corp. v. Hood (2004). Although the Bankruptcy Clause is part of the original Constitution and the rationale of *Fitzpatrick v. Bitzer* does not apply, the Court relied on historical evidence to conclude that it was understood at the founding that sovereign immunity would not apply in bankruptcy. *Central Virginia Community College* applies only to the bankruptcy power, but it nonetheless leaves open the possibility that similar reasoning might apply to other enumerated powers, provided the historical evidence supports it.

The sovereign immunity line of cases, like restrictions on the scope of federal power and the no-commandeering rule, also raises questions about the Court's continued adherence to the *Dole* test for the federal spending power. Insofar as conditional spending provisions can be used to induce a waiver of sovereign immunity, reading the spending power broadly may undermine the Court's recent efforts to protect state sovereign immunity, whether in federal or state courts. Nonetheless, there is currently little indication of a move to restrict the use of spending conditions as a means of inducing states to waive immunity.

Legislative Delegations and the Rehnquist Court

While the new federalism decisions reflect a renewed commitment to limiting federal authority so as to preserve state prerogatives, there is little indication that the Court will constrain the regulatory state by limiting legislative delegations. There were some signs in the early 1980s that the Court might reinvigorate the nondelegation and other separation of powers constraints, but subsequent decisions consistently rejected nondelegation arguments. Nonetheless, and notwithstanding some Justices' recent suggestion that the Court abandon the doctrine entirely, the Court continues to acknowledge the rule against delegating legislative power and has used that rule to invalidate the Line Item Veto Act, but only after distinguishing it from the more usual case of delegation.

The nondelegation doctrine received some new life in Industrial Union Dept., AFL-CIO v. American Petroleum Institute (*Benzene*) (1980), in which the Court invalidated an agency regulation setting maximum workplace exposure levels for the carcinogenic chemical, Benzene. Both a plurality opinion authored by Justice Stevens (joined by Chief Justice Burger and Justices Powell and Stewart) and a separate concurrence by (then) Justice Rehnquist invoked the nondelegation doctrine to support this conclusion, but did so in different ways. The plurality used the doctrine to support a narrow reading of the agency's statutory mandate under which the agency was required to demonstrate that a chemical posed a "significant risk" at a given exposure level before the agency could prohibit exposures at that level. Among other reasons for such an interpretation, the plurality emphasized that a contrary reading "would give [the agency] power to impose enormous costs that might produce little, if any, discernible benefit" and that "such a 'sweeping delegation of legislative power' . . . might be unconstitutional under the Court's reasoning in [*Schechter Poultry*] and [*Panama Refining*]."[68]

Justice Rehnquist's concurring opinion went a step further to argue that the statute authorizing the agency regulation should be invalidated as a violation of the nondelegation doctrine. In Justice Rehnquist's view, there was no intelligible principle in the statute and Congress had not resolved the fundamental policy question whether regulation of toxic chemicals should be pursuant to a feasibility or cost-benefit standard. This question, which effectively determined whether human lives would be balanced against the cost of saving them, was too important to be delegated to an agency and had to be resolved by the legislature. Justice Rehnquist's restatement and explanation of the nondelegation doctrine has been particularly influential and is frequently quoted. In a subsequent decision, American Textile Manufacturers Institute, Inc., v. Donovan (1981), the Court held that, once the threshold of significant risk was met, a feasibility standard applied to the regulation of toxic chemicals in the workplace. So construed, the majority found no nondelegation problems with the statute, but Justice Rehnquist's dissent, which repeated his nondelegation objections, was joined by Chief Justice Burger.

The possibility that *Benzene* might presage a more significant reinvigoration of the nondelegation doctrine was given an added boost by INS v. Chadha (1983), which (as discussed in the introduction to this book) held that the legislative veto violated the bicameralism and presentment requirements. Although the Court was careful to distinguish the legislative veto from traditional statutory delegations to executive agencies, which (unlike the legislative veto) are subject to statutory standards and judicial review for compliance with those standards, the Court's formalistic analysis suggested a broader willingness to aggressively enforce separation of powers principles. Although they addressed different issues, other decisions in the 1980s also suggested a renewed vigor in enforcing separation of powers. Thus, in Northern Pipeline Construction Co. v. Marathon Pipe Line Co. (1982), the Court held that Congress had improperly vested judicial power in the bankruptcy courts, whose judges did not enjoy the life tenure and salary protections required by Article III. Similarly, in Bowsher v. Synar (1986), the Court held that Congress could not vest executive functions in the comptroller general, who was subject to removal by Congress rather than the President.

Whatever the possible implications of these cases, however, the Court soon indicated that it was not prepared to enforce the nondelegation doctrine aggressively. In United States v. Mistretta (1989), the Court upheld the Federal Sentencing Guidelines Commission against a nondelegation challenge. Although the statutory standards in *Mistretta* were clearly adequate under the intelligible principle test, *Mistretta* presented the distinctive problem of delegating rulemaking authority to the judiciary, which troubled only Justice Scalia, who vigorously dissented. That same year, in Skinner v. Mid-America Pipeline Co. (1989), the Court rejected another nondelegation challenge, this one involving a statute authorizing the secretary of transportation to impose user fees to pay for federal pipeline safety programs. Although the standards in this case again easily met the intelligible principle test, the Court rejected the argument that a more specific statutory standard was necessary because Congress had delegated the taxing power. This argument draws on the suggestion in some early cases that some powers are too important to be delegated, but the Court found "no support" for the contention that the delegation of authority under the taxing power required "the application of a different and stricter nondelegation doctrine."

The Court's most recent nondelegation decision, Whitman v. American Trucking Associations (2001), also rejected a nondelegation claim, concluding that the discretion granted was "well within the outer limits of our nondelegation precedents." First, the Court rejected the premise, embraced by some lower court decisions, that an otherwise unconstitutional delegation might be saved if an agency promulgated regulations confining its own discretion. Second, the Court indicated that "the degree of agency discretion that is acceptable varies according to the scope of the power congressionally conferred." In other words, the broader the scope of agency regulatory authority, the more specific the standards must be; the narrower the scope of that authority, the more open ended those standards may be. It is also worth noting that Justice Stevens, joined by Justice Souter, urged the Court to frankly admit that the power to promulgate binding regulations is legislative power and to hold that the delegation of legislative power is permissible provided that it is constrained by standards. This approach appears to be primarily a semantic difference, insofar as the basic requirement of statutory standards would remain the same. Nonetheless, it would indicate a significant change in the logic of the federal legislative power that could, in the long run, have an impact on the overall substantive analysis.

A final recent precedent of importance for the issue of legislative delegations is Clinton v. City of New York (1998), in which the Court invalidated the Federal Line Item Veto Act. The Act authorized the President to "cancel" certain budgetary items if he or she determined that cancellation would reduce the federal deficit without impairing essential government functions or harming the national interest. Although it might appear that the nondelegation doctrine should apply to this delegation of authority and that the question would be whether the Act contained an intelligible principle or standard to guide and control its exercise, a majority of Justices did not view the case in those terms. For the majority, the critical feature of the Act was that it permitted the President to "cancel" items of spending that had been enacted into law, which the majority viewed as the functional equivalent of amending or repealing a statute. Because it takes a statute to amend or repeal a statute, the Act necessarily delegated legislative authority, regardless of the standards it imposed.[69]

The case was in some respects similar to *Chadha*. First, in both cases the Court rejected what it perceived as statutory provisions authorizing a deviation from the constitutional requirements of bicameralism and presentment. Second, in both cases the Court concluded that legislative power had been improperly delegated—to either chamber of Congress in *Chadha* and to the President in *Clinton*. Finally, in both cases the Court distinguished the usual cases involving the application of the intelligible principle test under the nondelegation doctrine. As a result, they are not necessarily inconsistent with the Court's apparent willingness to tolerate broad legislative delegations.[70]

THE STATE OF FEDERAL LEGISLATIVE POWER

The foregoing historical account of the federal legislative power provides the raw material for the analysis of federal legislative power in Part II. The historical and judicial precedents offer some general answers to recurring questions concerning the federal legislative power. First, the federal legislative power is the plenary authority to enact necessary and proper laws with respect to the enumerated powers. Congress may enact laws to implement legislative ends within the scope of the enumerated powers and may use appropriate means to do so, which includes the delegation of enforcement authority to executive officials pursuant to statutory standards that executive officials and courts are bound to observe. Congress also possesses broad authority in relation to the legislative process itself, which is not limited to governance of its own internal affairs, but includes the power to command private parties to provide information and to impose sanctions on private parties who interfere with the legislative process.

This concept of federal legislative power, however, remains in tension with the enumerated powers premise of federalism. The power to enact necessary and proper laws as the means for implementing ends within the enumerated powers, if construed broadly, effectively authorizes virtually any conceivable legislative act and threatens to obliterate reserved state powers. Yet there is no intrinsic limit within the legislative power itself that can prevent this outcome without also impeding legitimate congressional efforts to pursue important national policies. Aggressive judicial review of the ends and means of legislative action, moreover, cannot be accomplished without converting the Court to a superlegislature.

Thus, when the Court has attempted to limit federal legislative authority, it has seldom focused on any concept of the federal legislative power itself, but rather relied on dual sovereignty theory to construct external limits on that power. Whether in the form of reserved state police powers or state sovereignty itself, these external limits operate in much the same way as individual rights do to limit the exercise of the federal legislative power based on considerations extrinsic to that power. Even as to this sort of external limit, moreover, the Court has vacillated and inconsistency has been the rule rather than the exception. As of this writing, with the passing of Chief Justice Rehnquist and the resignation of Justice O'Connor, the Court has experienced its first personnel changes since Justice Breyer's appointment in 1994. It remains to be seen how the appointments of Chief Justice Roberts and Justice Alito will affect the Court's treatment of the federal legislative power.

NOTES

1. Edward S. Corwin, "The Progress of Constitutional Theory Between the Declaration of Independence and the Meeting of the Philadelphia Convention," 30 *Am. Hist. Rev.* 511, 527 (1925), reprinted in *American Constitutional History: Essays By Edward S. Corwin* 1, 16 (Mason & Garvey eds., 1964).

2. I. Charles Ticknor Curtis, *Constitutional History of the United States from their Declaration of Independence to the Close of their Civil War* 99 (1889).

3. Carl Brent Swisher, *American Constitutional Development* 23 (2d ed., 1954).

4. By resolution of July 23, 1787, proposed by Elbridge Gerry of Massachusetts. For a detailed account of the drafting history of the Necessary and Proper Clause, see Joseph M. Lynch, *Negotiating the Constitution: The Earliest Debates Over Original Intent* 4–26 (1999); Robert G. Natelson, "The Agency Law Origins of the Necessary and Proper Clause," 55 *Case W. Res. L. Rev.* 243 (2004).

5. Max Farrand, 2 *The Records of the Federal Convention* 18 (Yale University Press rev. ed., 1937). Other resolutions were similarly worded. *Id.*

6. See, e.g., Randy E. Barnett, "The Original Meaning of the Necessary and Proper Clause," 6 *U. Pa. J. Const'l L.* 183, 185 (2003) (observing that the Clause was added "by

the Committee on Detail without any previous discussion" by the convention and that it was not "the subject of any debate" before the Constitution's approval by the convention).

7. Robert G. Natelson, "The Agency Law Origins of the Necessary and Proper Clause," 55 *Case W. Res. L. Rev.* 243 (2004).

8. See, e.g., Brutus, in 2 *The Complete Antifederalist* at 367–68 (Herbert J. Storing ed., 1981).

9. The Federalist Papers are available in a variety of editions from a number of publishers and I will omit citations to any particular editions or pages. A searchable online version is available through the Yale Law School's Avalon Project at http://www.yale.edu/lawweb/avalon/federal/fed.htm.

10. For comprehensive analysis of the activities of the early Congresses, see David P. Currie, *The Constitution in Congress: The Federalist Period, 1789–1801* (1997) (hereinafter Currie, *Federalist Period*) and David P. Currie, *The Constitution in Congress: The Jeffersonians, 1801–1829* (2001) (hereinafter Currie, *The Jeffersonians*).

11. Currie, *Federalist Period*, at 296.

12. *McCulloch* was not the first Supreme Court decision to construe the Necessary and Proper Clause, however. In United States v. Fisher, 6 U.S. (2 Cranch.) 358 (1805), the Court upheld a bankruptcy statute giving the United States priority as a debtor. In *Fisher*, Chief Justice Marshall reasoned that:

In construing this clause it would be incorrect and would produce endless difficulties, if the opinion should be maintained that no law was authorized which was not indispensably necessary to give effect to a specified power.

Where various systems might be adopted for that purpose, it might be said with respect to each, that it was not necessary because the end might be obtained by other means. Congress must possess the choice of means, and must be empowered to use any means which are in fact conducive to the exercise of a power granted by the constitution.

This language foreshadows, in abbreviated form, some of the reasoning in *McCulloch*, but it is *McCulloch's* more extended analysis and the resulting ends-means test for necessary and proper legislation that have stood the test of time.

13. See Alexander Hamilton, Report to the House of Representatives (Dec. 13, 1790), reprinted in *Legislative and Documentary History of the Bank of the United States* 15–35 (M. St. Clair Clarke & D.A. Hall eds., 1832). Hamilton's use of his position to propose legislation to Congress set an important early precedent for executive officials' actively promoting a legislative agenda in Congress.

14. See 2 *Annals of Cong.* 1894 (1791).

15. See Opinion of Thomas Jefferson, Secretary of State of the United States (Feb. 15, 1791), reprinted in Legislative and Documentary History of the Bank of the United States, at 91–94; Opinion of Edmund Randolph, Attorney General of the United States (Feb 12, 1791), reprinted in Legislative and Documentary History of the Bank of the United States, at 86–91.

16. See Opinion of Alexander Hamilton on the Constitutionality of the Bank of the United States (Feb 23, 1791), reprinted in Legislative and Documentary History of the Bank of the United States, at 95–112.

17. Madison's Speech, 2 *Annals of Cong.* at 1947.

18. See Jefferson's Opinion, *supra* note 15.

19. Madison's Speech, 2 *Annals of Cong.* at 1948–949; *accord* Jefferson's Opinion ("If such a latitude of construction be allowed to this phrase as to give any non-enumerated

power, it will go to everyone, for there is not one which some ingenuity may not torture into a *convenience* in some instance *or other*, to *some one* of so long a list of enumerated powers . . . .").

20. Hamilton's Opinion, *supra* note 16. I shall not encumber the discussion that follows with repetitive notes citing Hamilton's opinion.

21. See Dumas Malone, *The Sage of Monticello* 352 (1977) (Hamilton's opinion on the constitutionality of the bank "had come into Marshall's hands in the papers of Washington and was directly drawn upon in his own opinion in the case of McCulloch vs. Maryland, sometimes almost word for word").

22. Later in the opinion, Marshall also advanced textual arguments based on the phrasing of the Clause, which purports to enlarge congressional power, and its placement among the other grants of legislative authority, rather than among the limitations on federal legislative power.

23. This test is arguably more cautious and restrictive than the "in fact conducive" language Marshall had used in United States v. Fisher, 6 U.S. (2 Cranch.) 358 (1805). See David P. Currie, *The Constitution in the Supreme Court: The First Hundred Years 1789–1888*, 163–64 (1985).

24. Having upheld the bank as a valid exercise of federal legislative authority, the Court also held that the State of Maryland's effort to tax the bank violated the Supremacy Clause.

25. See generally Currie, *Federalist Period* at 90–93.

26. 1 Stat. 109, 110 § 1 (April 10, 1790).

27. See generally Richard E. Levy, "Of Two Minds: Charitable and Social Insurance Models in the Veterans Benefits System," 13 *Kan. J. L. & Pub. Pol'y* 303, 307–10 (2004) (discussing early history of veterans benefits system).

28. See Currie, *Federalist Period* at 146–49.

29. The latter point is significant because the President has independent authority in the field of foreign relations and the Court would later suggest on analogous facts in United States v. Curtiss-Wright Export Co., 299 U.S. 304 (1936), that the scope of permissible delegations to the President may be broader in the foreign relations field.

30. See Skinner v. Mid-America Pipeline Co., 490 U.S. 212 (1989).

31. See generally Hans Linde, "Due Process of Lawmaking," 55 *Neb. L. Rev.* 197 (1976).

32. For a brief overview of early exercises of the investigatory and contempt powers, see Telford Taylor, *Grand Inquest: The Story of Congressional Investigations* 32–35 (1955).

33. For a discussion of these historical precedents, see James M. Landis, "Constitutional Limitations on the Congressional Power of Investigation," 40 *Harv. L. Rev.* 153, 170–94 (1926).

34. The Supreme Court would later reject this broad view of the investigatory authority of Congress and confine that authority to investigations related to some valid legislative action. See Kilbourn v. Thompson, 103 U.S. 168 (1880).

35. See C.S. Potts, "Power of Legislative Bodies to Punish for Contempt (Part I)," 74 *U. Pa. L. Rev.* 691, 719–20 (1926).

36. *Id.* at 720.

37. Thomas Jefferson, *A Manual of Parliamentary Practice: For the Use of the Senate* (U.S. Government Printing Office, 1993) (1801). Jefferson updated the manual in 1812.

38. President Jackson's Veto Message is available online through the Yale Law School's Avalon Project at http://www.yale.edu/lawweb/avalon/presiden/veto/ajveto01.htm.

39. For detailed discussion of the historical origins of inherent power over newly acquired territory, see Sarah H. Cleveland, "Powers Inherent in Sovereignty: Indians,

Aliens, Territories and the Nineteenth Century Origins of Plenary Power Over Foreign Affairs," 81 *Tex. L. Rev.* 1 (2002).

40. U.S. Const. Art. IV, § 3, cl. 2 ("Nothing in this Constitution shall be so construed as to Prejudice any Claims of the United States, or of any particular State.")

41. See Landis, *supra* note 31, at 177–78.

42. *Id.* at 179–81.

43. *Id.* at 181–82.

44. This incident is summarized in Potts, *supra* note 33, at 723–24.

45. See generally Landis, *supra* note 31, at 185–86.

46. *Id.* at 186–88.

47. See Mississipi v. Garland, 71 U.S. (4 Wall.) 333 (1867); Georgia v. Stanton, 73 U.S. (6 Wall.) 50 (1868); *Ex parte* McArdle, 74 U.S. (7 Wall.) 506 (1869); Texas v. White, 74 U.S. (7 Wall.) 700 (1869).

48. See Jacobus tenBroek, *The Antislavery Origins of the Fourteenth Amendment* 185, 204 (1951).

49. The Court in the *Slaughterhouse Cases* also read the Due Process and Equal Protection Clauses narrowly, but its principal focus was on the Privileges and Immunities Clause, which is also the most significant for purposes of this discussion.

50. It is unclear whether the Court thought women in general, or only immoral women, to be evil in themselves.

51. This reasoning makes no sense, of course, insofar as the Constitution contains specific requirements for making treaties that would be irrelevant if Holmes was correct. The more plausible and currently accepted reading of the Clause is that the difference in language was intended to preserve the validity of treaties made under the Articles of Confederation. At any rate, it is currently clear that treaties are subject to constitutional limitations. See Reid v. Covert, 454 U.S. 1, 16 (1957).

52. In a similar vein, the Court exhibited special solicitude for legislative delegations to the President with respect to foreign relations in United States v. Curtiss-Wright Export Co., 299 U.S. 304 (1936). See also Marshall Field & Co. v. Clark 143 U.S. 649 (1892).

53. See generally William E. Forbath, "The Shaping of the American Labor Movement," 102 *Harv. L. Rev.* 1109 (1989).

54. See Stephen Gardbaum, "New Deal Constitutionalism and the Unshackling of the States," 64 *U. Chi. L. Rev.* 483 (1997).

55. Likewise, the early congressional debate over the delegation of authority to designate post roads was over whether a power expressly enumerated could be delegated. See *supra* note 26 and following text.

56. See *supra* note 35 and following text.

57. These cases clearly put to rest any suggestion in *Kilbourn* that the House and Senate could not impose contempt sanctions directly.

58. For a general treatment of this period, see G. Edward White, *The Constitution and the New Deal* (2000).

59. Although the significance of delegation to a private body appears to have faded under the federal nondelegation doctrine, perhaps because few federal statutes do so, the issue continues to be an important one under many state constitutions. See Gumbhir v. Kansas State Bd. of Pharmacy, 228 Kan. 579, 618 P.2d 837 (1980).

60. One scholar has even suggested that Frankfurter fabricated a memorandum from Justice Roberts as a means of vindicating Roberts and, more important, the Supreme Court, from charges of unprincipled, political decisionmaking. See Michael Ariens, "A

Thrice-Told Tale, or Felix the Cat," 107 *Harv. L. Rev.* 620 (1994). For a vehement response, see Richard D. Friedman, "A Reaffirmation: The Authenticity of the Roberts Memorandum, or Felix the Non-Forger," 142 *U. Pa. L. Rev.* 1985 (1994).

61. Not all scholars agree with this characterization, and there are some pre–New Deal cases that suggest the change of direction had begun before the crisis. See, e.g., Richard D. Friedman, "Switching Time and Other Thought Experiments: The Hughes Court and Constitutional Transformation," 142 *U. Pa. L. Rev.* 1891 (1994).

62. See generally Richard E. Levy, "Escaping *Lochner's* Shadow: Toward A Coherent Jurisprudence of Economic Rights," 73 *N.C. L. Rev.* 329 (1995).

63. Richard E. Levy, "An Unwelcome Stranger: Congressional Individual Rights Power and Federalism," 44 *U. Kan. L. Rev.* 61 (1995).

64. This opinion will be discussed further in Part II.

65. See generally Richard E. Levy, "Federalism: The Next Generation," 33 *Loy. L.A. L. Rev.* 1629 (2000).

66. Indeed, proponents of the limited federal power have urged the Court to do so. See, e.g., Ilya Somin, "Closing Pandora's Box of Federalism: The Case for Judicial Restriction of Federal Subsidies to State Governments," 90 *Geo. L.J.* 461, 484 (2002).

67. I have previously argued that these rationales, at least as presented by the Court, are unpersuasive at best and, in some instances, disingenuous in their mischaracterization of precedent. See Richard E. Levy, "New York v. United States: An Essay on the Uses and Misuses of Precedent, History, and Policy in Determining the Scope of Federal Power," 41 *Kan. L. Rev.* 493 (1993).

68. As will be discussed further in Part II, it is not entirely clear why the power to impose costs without concomitant benefits is relevant to the nondelegation analysis.

69. In light of this analysis, a statute that authorized the President to impound funds or decline to spend them without canceling the item would present a different case.

70. Clinton v. New York also points up the potential significance of Justice Stevens' approach in *American Trucking*. Because he would accept the delegation of legislative authority as consistent with separation of powers, provided there are sufficient standards, the Court's analysis in Clinton v. New York would not resolve the issue. Even if the cancellation of budgetary items is an exercise of legislative authority, under Justice Stevens' analysis it would be permissible if the Act's standards are sufficient.

Part II

Analysis of the Federal Legislative Power

This part of the book undertakes a doctrinal and theoretical analysis of the federal legislative power, including (1) the power to make "necessary and proper" laws; (2) the legislative delegation of power; and (3) the deliberative powers to investigate, compel testimony and production of documents, and punish for contempt. The doctrinal dimension focuses on describing, explaining, and synthesizing the decisions in each area, with the ultimate aim of clarifying the constitutional framework and identifying critical unresolved questions. The theoretical dimension attempts to distill from the doctrine a deeper understanding of the federal legislative power. Both components of the analysis draw on and are informed by collective action theory, which uses economic principles to examine the dynamics of group behavior.[1] This part therefore begins with a general description of collective action theory and its implications for the federal legislative power.

COLLECTIVE ACTION AND THE FEDERAL LEGISLATIVE POWER

The term "collective action" refers to cooperation among individual members of a group in an effort to obtain a common benefit. Collective action takes a variety of forms in our society, including families, business enterprises, religious groups, and many other collective endeavors. Government, too, is a form of collective action, through which society as a whole seeks to attain societal benefits, such as common defense and security, a functional legal system, a market economy, and a social safety net. Notwithstanding its prevalence, the dynamics of collective action raise a variety of barriers to effective cooperation among individuals. Thus, the structure and operation of many institutions, including government, represent pragmatic responses to the dynamics of collective action. This perspective on the constitutional structure of government has important implications for understanding legislative power both generally and in the particular context of a federal system.

The Dynamics of Collective Action

Even when collective action would produce a clear net benefit for the collective as a whole, there are inherent barriers that the collective must overcome to achieve this benefit. As Mancur Olson famously argued in his seminal work, *The Logic of Collective Action*, the incentives of individual members tend to undermine collective action. The benefit of collective action is often a "public good," in the sense that once it is produced, all members of the collective will share in it regardless of their contribution to its production. As a result, individuals have the incentive to "free ride" on the efforts of others, producing what is referred to in game theory as a "prisoner's dilemma." Just as the incentive for individual prisoners to seek a deal may lead them to confess, even when it would be in their common interest for each to remain silent, collective benefits that are public goods will not be produced, or will be underproduced, if individuals act independently to maximize their own interests. To achieve the benefits of collective action, individual members of the collective must agree on a course of action and perform that agreement. Given the incentives of individual members, there are significant costs associated with both reaching and enforcing any agreement on collective action. These costs can be grouped under the general term "transaction costs."

According to the "Coase theorem," in the absence of transaction costs, if collective action produces a net collective benefit, members of the collective should be able to reach agreement.[2] This is true even if the incidence of expected benefits is uneven and even if some members would be net losers, because the collective could agree on a redistribution of benefits so that each member is better off.[3] In practice, however, there are significant transaction costs associated with reaching agreement. Members of a collective must gather information on the costs and benefits of various courses of action, identify and communicate with other members, and negotiate and compromise to obtain consent. Reaching agreement is complicated by strategic behavior, such as holding out, through which members attempt to secure the best possible deal for themselves. For small, clearly defined groups, the costs of reaching agreement are often relatively easy to overcome, but as the collective becomes larger and more diffuse, the costs increase exponentially until they become insurmountable.[4]

Even after agreement has been reached, enforcing it also creates transaction costs because individual members have incentives to "cheat" on the collective. Most generally, to the extent that the benefit is a form of public good, the incentives to act as free riders remain notwithstanding the existence of an agreement. In the prisoners' dilemma, even if the prisoners had agreed in advance to remain silent if caught, once they are caught and placed in separate rooms for interrogation, they still have individual incentives to confess and make a deal. In many instances, moreover, members may have particular incentives to cheat, such as when the costs of the agreement fall particularly heavily on them. Thus, the collective incurs "agency costs," because the incentives of the principal (the collective) and agent (members implementing collective action) diverge.[5] Agency costs include both the net loss from noncompliance and the cost of monitoring and enforcing compliance. As in the context of reaching agreement, these costs increase with the size of the collective.

Government as Collective Action

Governments are structural mechanisms that reduce the costs of making and enforcing societal agreements to act collectively. From this perspective, the core component of "sovereign authority" is the power of the state to make and enforce collective decisions. In a polity of any size, it is not possible to obtain individual consent for every collective action decision, that is, to govern by consensus. Although delegating authority to a government results in some actions that make us worse off when viewed in isolation (e.g., the imposition of taxes), most of us recognize that, in comparison to a Hobbesian state of nature, the overall benefits of government greatly outweigh its costs.[6] At the same time, the benefits of collective action must be balanced against the fundamental right of individual autonomy and the risk that the power of the collective will be abused by those in authority.

Taking the example of a common defense, which is widely regarded as a public good, collective action to protect against external invasion produces a significant benefit for a society. Yet, except in extreme cases, it would be nearly impossible to negotiate participation in that defense by individual agreement and consensus, because of the free-rider problem, and equally impossible to rely entirely on voluntary contributions and participation to constitute that defense.[7] These barriers are overcome through the institution of government, which is accorded the power to provide for that defense, including the power to conscript soldiers and collect taxes to finance its operations. In the United States and other constitutional republics, the antecedent collective agreement creating the government and empowering it to act is the Constitution. The Constitution, moreover, establishes the basic mechanism for collective action by the government: the rule of law. Government decisions on behalf of the collective are embodied in laws that bind members and are enforced through a legal system that deters, identifies, and punishes violations of the law.

The Legislative Power in Collective Action Perspective

If our government is a form of collective action that operates by means of laws, the role of the legislative power comes into sharper focus; it is the power to make decisions on behalf of the collective by enacting laws that bind its members. Vesting this power in a representative body, such as Congress, facilitates its exercise by greatly reducing the costs of reaching agreement. First, because each legislator represents many members of the collective, the number of people whose agreement is needed is greatly reduced; 538 members of Congress make decisions on behalf of hundreds of millions of citizens. Second, the legislature does not require unanimous agreement to act, but rather makes decisions through some variation of majority rule.

The inherent risk of government, however, is that governmental power will be abused, particularly because the ability to act without individual consent will typically eliminate the need to compensate individual members who experience a net loss as a result of the collective action. Thus, just as there are agency costs from the perspective of the collective, individual members must be concerned about agency costs because the government's interest may not coincide with their own. The social contract for collective action is possible because people recognize that, viewed as a whole, these costs are more than offset by the benefits of government. Nonetheless, the structure of government under the Constitution reflects concern that the majority might abuse the power to make collective decisions at the expense of the minority and incorporates various safeguards against such abuse.

The Constitution vests authority to make laws in Congress, which is designed to be both representative and deliberative in character. The representative structure of Congress reflects the premise that the government is the agent of the members of the collective—the "people." Political accountability is the essential means of monitoring and enforcing that relationship. The deliberative character of Congress is reinforced through the requirements of bicameralism and presentment, which require the concurrence of representative bodies with somewhat different constituencies. This structure is a self-conscious effort to increase transaction costs by requiring negotiation and compromise among the House, Senate, and president to enact legislation. The representative and deliberative structure of Congress helps to constrain the ability of groups within the collective to gain control of its processes and use governmental authority in ways that are contrary to the interests of the broader collective.

Congress makes collective decisions by enacting laws that operate within a rule of law framework, which both enhances the effectiveness of collective decisions and constrains them. Under the rule of law, government action must be grounded in legal authority to act, government actors are bound by the law, and the legality of government action is subject to independent review. The rule of law enhances the effectiveness of collective action by reducing agency costs. One essential characteristic of a society based on the rule of law is the widely shared acceptance of the law as binding. People obey the law not only out of fear of direct enforcement (i.e., that they will be caught and punished), but also because they have internalized a sense of obligation to comply with the law. This sense of obligation is the glue that makes government work. Notwithstanding Olson's insights, social science research suggests that people will engage in collective action when they believe that other members of the collective will reciprocate, but not when they believe others will free ride or cheat.[8] Universal acceptance of the rule of law fosters reciprocal trust among members of society and thus greatly reduces enforcement costs by promoting voluntary compliance. It also provides a structure for enforcement when there are violations.

At the same time, the rule of law, coupled with the separation of powers, helps to protect members of the collective from the abuse of power. The representative and deliberative character of Congress is at best an imperfect means of guarding against such abuse. First, the fact that Congress acts by means of generally applicable laws reinforces political accountability for those laws, reflected in the premise that laws targeting minorities may be the result of a failure of the political process.[9] Second, while Congress makes decisions by enacting laws, under separation of powers, it must rely on independent executive and judicial institutions to secure compliance. This arrangement further diffuses governmental power and imposes additional transaction and agency costs on collective action. Overall, then, the constitutional structure of the legislative power reflects a delicate balance between facilitating and constraining collective action.

Collective Action Among States

Within the system of nation states, each state is a collective with its own distinctive organizational structure to facilitate collective action. Collective action also helps to illuminate the behavior of states at the level of international relations, with each state understood as an individual actor with its own interests (i.e., the collective interest of its citizens).[10] Just as individuals within a society have reasons to act collectively, states too may benefit from various forms of cooperation, such as collective security, free trade, or environmental protection agreements.[11] In this sense, each state is both the embodiment of a collective and an individual member of a collective of states. When states act collectively, their behavior is subject to the same kinds of collective action problems described above; that is, states experience transaction costs associated with reaching and enforcing international agreements. Like individuals, moreover, states may seek to create structures that facilitate collective action.

Thus, federalism can be understood as a form of interstate collective action and analyzed in those terms.[12] It creates a structure that reduces the costs of making and enforcing agreements among the member states. Just as government in general reflects a compromise between the delegation to government of authority to make collective decisions and the incorporation of institutional safeguards to protect the interests of individual members, federalism represents a compromise between the collective and individual interests of member states.

From this perspective, the problems that arose under the Articles of Confederation can be understood as the result of their failure to respond adequately to collective action problems arising at the level of interstate relations.[13] Collective decisions under the Articles were difficult to reach because the Articles only departed from decision by consensus in a few narrow areas and even then only to a limited degree.[14] More fundamentally, because the Articles relied entirely on the states to implement collective decisions internally, enforcement of collective decisions was very difficult if states resisted. Thus, the difficulties typically identified as creating the need for a constitutional convention—protectionism in interstate trade, failure of states to honor their debts, and a general inability to enforce congressional decisions—are precisely the kinds of problems one would expect as a result of barriers to collective action.

By the same token, the Constitution responds to these collective action problems through improved structures for making and enforcing collective decisions among the states. The Constitution facilitates collective decisionmaking by vesting in Congress authority to act by majority vote (subject to bicameralism and presentment) with respect to an expanded array of federal powers, including such critical new powers as the power to tax and spend and the power to regulate commerce among the states, with the native tribes, and with foreign nations. Equally important, enforcement costs were reduced by authorizing the national government to act through directly binding laws and by creating national executive and judicial institutions to enforce those laws. These changes reduced enforcement costs by removing the states as intermediaries between the national government and its citizens and permitting the national government to act by means of laws.

Federalism and the Dual Collective

The central feature of federalism is the division of power to make decisions on behalf of the collective between two levels of government. Some collective decisions are allocated to a central or national government, while others are retained by smaller, more local units of government. This is what is meant by divided sovereignty. The division of authority reflects commonsense judgments about whether national or localized collectives will best further collective interests. From the perspective of individual citizens, smaller and more localized collectives have advantages in terms of what Albert Hirschman described as "voice" and "exit."[15] In smaller units, members are more likely to have shared interests and they have an enhanced voice in the form of greater control over elected representatives. In addition, it is easier for members to leave smaller collectives, and state or local governments are therefore subject to interjurisdictional competition. Enhanced voice and exit reduce the agency costs experienced by citizens vis-à-vis their government, which would tend to favor delegating decisional and enforcement authority to smaller, as opposed to larger, regional units. At the same time, however, the individual interests of states may lead them to act in ways that are contrary to the interests of the collective as a whole, and the citizens of those states may benefit in the long run from action by the larger collective. With respect to those matters, it makes sense for members of the collective to delegate decisional and enforcement authority to a larger collective authority. In essence, the issue is when the interests of the members of the larger collective are best served by regulatory competition and when they are not.[16]

This differentiation is reflected in the constitutional structure of federalism. The Constitution allocates decisional and enforcement authority to the national government in those areas in which collective action among the peoples of all the states is most desirable. The Constitution reserves power for smaller governmental units, the states, in the residual categories of sovereign authority, thereby increasing accountability and reducing agency costs from the perspective of individual citizens. This basic principle animated the drafting of the Constitution and is reflected in its enumeration of federal legislative power in Article I, section 8.[17] For example, it is generally understood that free trade produces net benefits for participating states, even if some industries in each of those states will suffer. From the perspective of states (or of politically powerful groups within states), there are ongoing incentives to act in protectionist ways respecting at least some domestic industries, and the lack of a centralized decisional authority under the Articles of Confederation resulted in the proliferation of trade barriers. The commerce power reflects the Framers' recognition of this reality, and allocated the authority to determine the rules of interstate trade to the national government.[18] Other areas of federal authority likewise encompass matters for which interstate collective action is beneficial.[19]

The critical difficulty with this division of power between the national government and the states is the absence of sharp lines of demarcation between the respective spheres of state and federal decisional authority. Unlike the geographic boundaries separating the territory of individual states, it is not possible to draw clear boundary lines between powers, such as the federal power to regulate interstate commerce and the states' police power to provide for the health and safety of their citizens.[20] Even if these powers are conceptually distinct, they can provide the basis for legislation that acts in identical ways on the same activity. Thus, it is hardly surprising that questions concerning the division of authority between the national and state governments have pervaded the history of the federal legislative power.

Implications for the Federal Legislative Power

As this brief account of government and federalism reveals, collective action theory offers important insights into the structure of government. It has significant implications for each aspect of the federal legislative power discussed in this book and can foster a deeper understanding of the federal legislative power itself.

The power to enact necessary and proper laws lies at the core of the federal legislative power. At its most fundamental level, it expresses the power to reach agreement on behalf of the collective regarding the ends of collective action and the means of achieving them. It prescribes the manner through which these agreements are to be effected: through the enactment of laws, understood as binding rules of general applicability, that are necessary and proper to the implementation of ends within the sphere of authority delegated to the collective by its members. The representative and deliberative character of Congress facilitates decisions that further the collective interest and protect against abuse of power. Because ours is a federal system, legislative power is divided between the national government and the states pursuant to the enumerated powers principle. In this sense, the concept of necessary and proper laws also serves to confine the federal legislative power to the enumerated powers, and its interpretation has profound implications for the allocation of legislative power within the dual collective.

While the legislative power is the power to reach agreement on the ends and means of collective action, it does not include the authority to enforce compliance with those agreements. Under separation of powers, this task falls to the executive and the judiciary, to whom Congress must delegate enforcement authority. This separation of powers protects the members of the collective against abuse of power by requiring the concurrence of all three branches to effectuate collective decisions, which increases the costs of collective action. At the same time, the power to make the antecedent collective agreement, the federal legislative power, is vested in Congress and cannot be delegated. This rule against delegation protects the representative and deliberative processes for reaching collective agreement and the separation of powers generally. The line between making collective decisions and enforcing them is defined by the "nondelegation doctrine," which requires that legislation contain an "intelligible principle" or standard to guide and control the exercise of delegated authority.

Finally, Congress's deliberative powers have the distinctive characteristic that Congress may exercise them through means other than the enactment of necessary and proper laws. In these areas, Congress may take direct action without following the structural requirements for legislation and without requiring the assistance of either the executive or judicial branches. Because these actions operate as exceptions to the usual rules for the exercise of legislative power, they would seem to require special justification. In collective action terms, they may be explained, at least to some extent, as touching in a particularly direct way on the interests of Congress as an independent institution. Because of this particular concern for institutional autonomy, the costs of adhering strictly to bicameralism and presentment or separation of powers may simply be too high.

The analysis that follows will consider in greater detail the power to enact necessary and proper laws, the limits of legislative delegations, and the deliberative powers of Congress. A concluding section considers the implications of that analysis for our understanding of the legislative power itself. While the analysis is primarily doctrinal, it is founded on the collective action principles outlined above.

NECESSARY AND PROPER LAWS

The power to enact necessary and proper laws defines the legislative power itself. In a constitutional democracy, even a unitary state, laws must be necessary and proper to an end within the sphere of governmental power. In the United States, however, the meaning of necessary and proper laws has been approached as a question of federalism. Indeed, there are few questions more central to the operation of federalism than the meaning of the Necessary and Proper Clause. This point was certainly recognized during the debates surrounding ratification of the Constitution and its early implementation, as typified by the controversy surrounding the national bank. These early controversies came to a head in *McCulloch*, which adopted the controlling test for necessary and proper laws: (1) the ends must be legitimate and within the enumerated powers; (2) the means must be appropriate and plainly adapted to the ends; and (3) the means may not be inconsistent with or prohibited by the Constitution.

Ironically, however, since *McCulloch* the Court has neither devoted significant attention to the Necessary and Proper Clause nor offered much guidance concerning the application of the *McCulloch* test. Instead, the Necessary and Proper Clause has receded into the background, and subsequent struggles over the scope of federal power have tended to focus on particular enumerated powers or on whether the reserved powers of states operate as an external limit on federal legislative power. As a consequence, there are a host of unresolved questions concerning the *McCulloch* test. Some of these questions are fundamental and overarching, such as the nature of the relationship between the Necessary and Proper Clause and the enumerated powers or the level of ends-means scrutiny that is required by the test. Other questions arise concerning each of the three components of the test—legitimate ends, appropriate means, and improper means. The difficulty resolving these questions arises from the fundamental tension between the "plenary power" principle that Congress has the full legislative power with respect to enumerated fields and the "reserved power" principle that federal power is limited and states retain general police power authority.

The *McCulloch* Test and the Enumerated Powers

The power to enact necessary and proper laws is inextricably intertwined with the enumerated powers. As discussed in Part I, the Framers understood the Necessary and Proper Clause to express the inherent character of legislative power as the authority to make decisions for the collective through enactment of binding rules to govern the behavior of its members. In this sense, the Necessary and Proper Clause, standing alone and by its own force, does not confer on Congress any authority to act. It has effect only when joined with an enumerated power or other grant of federal authority. Conversely, none of the enumerated legislative powers can be exercised effectively in the absence of the power to enact necessary and proper laws. As a consequence, one cannot analyze the Necessary and Proper Clause except in relation to the particular enumerated powers with which it is conjoined. Indeed, since *McCulloch*, the Court's cases have for the most part focused on enumerated powers and have mentioned the Necessary and Proper Clause, if at all, only in passing. Further insight into the meaning of the power to enact necessary and proper laws and into the application of the *McCulloch* test therefore must be sought in cases considering the scope of particular enumerated powers. The most significant enumerated powers from a practical and historical perspective have been the commerce power, the taxing and spending powers, and the power to enforce the Fourteenth Amendment. The case law regarding these and other powers confirms the close relationship between the enumerated powers and the Necessary and Proper Clause, but it also raises some fundamental questions about that relationship.

The Supreme Court's analysis of federal legislative power has been driven primarily by cases dealing with the commerce power, which figured prominently in the Court's pre–New Deal efforts to constrain federal regulatory authority and which provided the basis for far-reaching post–New Deal legislation.[21] The Court adopted the current test for the scope of the commerce power in United States v. Lopez (1995), which reoriented the doctrinal framework for commerce power analysis with important implications for the Necessary and Proper Clause.

From the post–New Deal period until *Lopez*, the Court applied the rational basis test in commerce power cases. Under this approach, the Court would ask whether there was a rational basis for a congressional determination that a regulated activity (substantially) affected interstate commerce.[22] The rational basis test reflected *McCulloch*-type ends-means scrutiny insofar as the effect on commerce established the link between the means chosen (regulation of the activity) and the ends within the commerce power (preventing an undesirable effect on interstate commerce). This test appears to combine the commerce power and the Necessary and Proper Clause into a single inquiry insofar as the Court only rarely engaged in a separate application of the *McCulloch* test.[23] In *Lopez*, however, which held that the Federal Gun Free School Zones Act exceeded the scope of federal legislative power, the Court engaged in a fundamental restatement of commerce power doctrine.

After an extensive review of the history of the commerce power, the Court in *Lopez* identified three categories of activity that Congress may regulate under the commerce power: Congress may (1) regulate "the use of the channels of commerce"; (2) "regulate and protect persons and things in commerce"; and (3) regulate "activities having a substantial relation to interstate commerce" or that "substantially affect interstate commerce."[24] While these three categories had appeared in previous cases, they did so as a description of the types of regulation that the Court had upheld under the rational basis test.[25] In *Lopez*, by way of contrast, the rational basis test disappeared from the analysis and these categories defined the commerce power itself, an approach that has been confirmed in subsequent cases, notably United States v. Morrison (2000), which applied the test to hold that the Federal Violence Against Women Act exceeded the scope of the commerce power. The relationship between the new "categorical" approach and the *McCulloch* test remains unclear.

Although the *Lopez* test does not track the *McCulloch* test or use explicit ends-means scrutiny, the test appears to define the scope of federal legislative power under the Commerce and Necessary and Proper Clauses combined because, as presented in *Lopez*, the three categories purport to synthesize the various types of legislation that previous cases had upheld using the rational basis test.[26] In addition, the *Lopez* categories include both legislation that might be within the enumerated commerce power itself and legislation that can only be justified as necessary and proper to some commerce power end.[27] More fundamentally, in both *Lopez* and *Morrison*, the Court concluded that the law exceeded the scope of federal power without any separate inquiry into whether it might be sustained under the Necessary and Proper Clause or any citation to McCulloch v. Maryland. If the *Lopez* test defined only the scope of the commerce power, without regard to the Necessary and Proper Clause, the conclusion that a federal statute did not fall within any of the three *Lopez* categories would not resolve the case, because the Court should also consider the Necessary and Proper Clause as a possible source of legislative authority. Thus, notwithstanding the divergence from the *McCulloch* test, the *Lopez* approach is probably best understood as describing the scope of the commerce power and the Necessary and Proper Clause combined.

Lopez and *Morrison* are also significant because the Court's treatment of the third category of commerce power legislation (regulation of an activity that has a substantial effect on interstate commerce) suggested less deference to congressional judgments than had previously been accorded under the rational basis test. In particular, the Court limited the so-called "cumulative effects" doctrine from Wickard v. Filburn (1942), which permits the consideration of the aggregate or cumulative effects of an activity on commerce and thus obviates the need to establish a connection to commerce in each individual case. The Court characterized the cases applying that doctrine as involving regulation of activities that were themselves commercial or economic in character, and refused to consider the cumulative effects of "noncommercial" activities being regulated: gun possession in *Lopez* and violence against women in *Morrison*. Both decisions include language suggesting that the Supreme Court will make an independent evaluation of the factual basis for Congress's conclusion that an activity has a substantial effect on interstate commerce and suggesting that, when federal laws regulate activity traditionally within the state police power, the Court will not accept broad ends-means arguments that would in effect cede plenary authority over these areas to Congress. The implications of these features of *Lopez* for the application of the *McCulloch* test will be discussed further below.

More recent decisions, however, raise some doubts as to the future of the commerce power and its relation to the Necessary and Proper Clause. First, although it is but a casual reference in a footnote, there is language in Pierce County, Washington v. Guillen (2003) suggesting that application of *Lopez* and the Necessary and Proper Clause are distinct inquiries. In *Pierce County*, a unanimous Court upheld a statutory provision prohibiting information compiled or collected in connection with federal highway safety programs from being used as evidence in civil actions because the provision was "aimed at improving safety in the channels of commerce and increasing protection for the instrumentalities of interstate commerce" and thus fell within the first and second categories of activities that Congress may regulate under *Lopez*. This analysis was unexceptional, whether in terms of the *Lopez* categories or the traditional rational basis test, but the Court also observed in a footnote that "[b]ecause we conclude that Congress had authority under the Commerce Clause [to enact the statutory provisions] we need not decide whether they could also be a proper exercise of Congress' authority under the Spending Clause *or the Necessary and Proper Clause*."

Although this casual observation in a footnote is unlikely to signal a change in the Court's analysis, the relationship between the commerce power and the Necessary and Proper Clause was the subject of extended discussion in Justice Scalia's concurring opinion in Gonzales v. Raich (2005). *Raich* upheld provisions of the Controlled Substances Act prohibiting local cultivation and use of marijuana as within the scope of federal power. Applying the *Lopez* analysis, the majority concluded that local cultivation and use of marijuana had a substantial effect on interstate commerce, relying on the cumulative effects of such activities because they were economic or commercial in character. The dissenters, on the other hand, did not consider the activity to be sufficiently commercial and therefore refused to consider its cumulative effects.

Justice Scalia's concurrence, however, offered a different analysis, relying explicitly on the Necessary and Proper Clause to uphold the law. Justice Scalia observed that the third *Lopez* category, regulation of activity with a substantial effect on interstate commerce, is both "misleading" and "incomplete." It is misleading, he argued, because the power to regulate activities affecting commerce derives not from the commerce power itself, but rather from the Necessary and Proper Clause.[28] It is incomplete, he argued, because authority to enact necessary and proper laws to implement the commerce power "is not limited to laws governing intrastate activities that substantially affect interstate commerce," but rather also includes the power to "regulate activities that do not themselves substantially affect interstate commerce," if such regulation is "necessary to make the regulation of interstate commerce more effective. . . . " Justice Scalia pointedly relied on this application of the Necessary and Proper Clause, rather than the third *Lopez* category, as the basis for upholding the Controlled Substances Act.

While the Court has not generally applied the Necessary and Proper Clause as a distinct supplement to the federal commerce power, it has relied on the Clause and the *McCulloch* test in erecting and strengthening state sovereignty–based limits on the commerce power. In New York v. United States (1992) and Printz v. United States (1997), the Court held that the federal government may not commandeer the states by compelling their legislatures or executive officials to implement federal policy. Similarly, the Court has held that state sovereign immunity principles—arising from the text of the Eleventh Amendment, Seminole Tribe v. Florida (1996), and background understandings at the time of the framing implicitly incorporated into the constitutional structure, Alden v. Maine (1999)—prevent Congress from using the commerce power to create causes of action for damages against the states. In both of these contexts, state sovereignty operates as an external limit on the permissible means of implementing policies that are otherwise within the scope of federal power.

Nonetheless, these cases may also be understood as applying the third part of the *McCulloch* test; that is, they hold that commandeering and remedies against states are "improper" means because they are contrary to the letter or spirit of the Constitution. As the Court explained in New York v. United States:

In some cases the Court has inquired whether an Act of Congress is authorized by one of the powers delegated to Congress in Article I of the Constitution. . . . In other cases the Court has sought to determine whether an Act of Congress invades the province of state sovereignty reserved by the Tenth Amendment. . . . In a case like this one, involving the division of authority between federal and state governments, the two inquiries are mirror images of each other. If a power is delegated to Congress in the Constitution, the Tenth Amendment expressly disclaims any reservation of that power to the States; if a power is an attribute of state sovereignty reserved by the Tenth Amendment, it is necessarily a power the Constitution has not conferred on Congress.

Although the Court in *New York* did not specifically refer to the *McCulloch* test, it later did so in *Printz*, which reasoned that "[w]hen a 'La[w] . . . for carrying into Execution' the Commerce Clause violates the principle of state sovereignty . . . , it is not a 'La[w] . . . *proper* for carrying into Execution the Commerce Clause," and is thus, in the words of The Federalist, 'merely [an] ac[t] of usurpation' which 'deserve[s] to be treated as such.'"[29] The Court used this same reasoning with regard to sovereign immunity in *Alden*.

This understanding of state sovereign immunity as an implicit restriction on the means of implementing the commerce power is consistent with a power-specific application of sovereign immunity. In other words, when an enumerated power contemplates remedies against the state, sovereign immunity should not act as a restriction on the means of implementing that power. This point has been clear with respect to the power to enforce the Fourteenth Amendment since the Court's decision in Fitzpatrick v. Bitzer (1976). Because the Fourteenth Amendment came later in time and repealed any inconsistent provisions or understandings of the original Constitution, it was unclear whether powers enumerated under the original Constitution might be interpreted to have a similar effect. This issue was not resolved by spending power cases either, because those cases assumed that the state voluntarily waives sovereign immunity when it accepts funding to which an explicit condition of waiver attaches.

Thus, the Court's recent decision in Central Virginia Community College v. Katz (2006), in which the Court held that state sovereign immunity did not prevent the assertion of jurisdiction over states under the bankruptcy laws, takes on added significance. The Bankruptcy Clause is not later in time, and the Court did not rely on an implied repeal rationale. Instead, the Court examined the historical evidence to conclude that, at the time of the founding, the Framers contemplated that jurisdiction could be asserted over states under the bankruptcy power. *Central Virginia Community College* opens the door to a similar construction of other Article I powers. It remains to be seen, however, whether the text and history of these other powers will support such a construction.

Next to the commerce power, the most important enumerated powers are the taxing and spending powers. To the extent that a government neither taxes nor spends for its own sake, but rather to achieve some other end, the taxing and spending powers present some unique issues. Article I, section 8, clause 1, which contains these powers, specifies that they must be exercised to provide for the "general welfare." The meaning of this requirement is a question that, like the national bank, divided Hamilton and Madison. Madison argued that the term "general welfare" incorporated by reference the other enumerated powers, that is, that Congress could tax and spend only in furtherance of the enumerated powers.

Hamilton, whose position ultimately prevailed, argued that Congress could tax or spend for purposes beyond the enumerated powers so long as those purposes furthered the welfare of the nation as a whole.[30]

Because the exercise of the taxing and spending powers can be used to accomplish regulatory objectives, the Court's broad construction of the "general welfare" requirement creates the possibility that Congress could use these powers to undermine the principle of enumerated federal powers. Thus, a critical historical question for both powers was the extent to which these regulatory objectives might lead the Court to recharacterize a tax or spending statute as a regulatory measure.[31] Although the Court appeared willing to do so in some pre–New Deal cases,[32] it has not generally followed these cases in the post–New Deal era. If the underlying tax or spending program is valid, it is well established that Congress can require reporting and payment of taxes or an accounting of expenditures, create government agencies and institutions to collect taxes and disburse funds, and impose criminal sanctions for tax offenses or misuse of federal funds.[33] These incidental requirements would seem to be justified not by the taxing power itself, but rather as necessary and proper to its exercise.

There is, however, little contemporary case law concerning the scope of the taxing power or its relation to the Necessary and Proper Clause. This may be because the tax statutes always carry with them an "end" within the scope of the taxing power—to raise revenue—and the Court has never suggested that a federal tax must be defended in terms of the uses to which the revenue raised will be put. As long as a tax raises revenue (and does not violate other requirements concerning the incidents of the tax), it appears to be within the taxing power. Although the pre–New Deal decisions of Bailey v. Drexel Furniture Co. (1922) and United States v. Butler (1936) evinced a willingness to look behind the ostensible revenue-raising purposes of a tax to identify improper regulatory objectives, subsequent cases have not.[34] And while the Court has not adopted a definitive test for necessary and proper legislation in connection with a tax, it has used the language of McCulloch in connection with ancillary provisions of tax statutes.[35] To the extent that the exercise of the taxing power presents current constitutional questions, they relate to independent constitutional requirements, such as those contained in the Bill of Rights.[36]

The Court has engaged in more recent discussions of the scope of the spending power. In South Dakota v. Dole (1987), the Court adopted a four-part test for the spending power that appears to incorporate the components of the McCulloch test: (1) "the exercise of the spending power must be in pursuit of 'the general welfare'"; (2) "if Congress desires to condition the States' receipt of federal funds, it must do so unambiguously . . ."; (3) conditions on federal grants may not be "unrelated" to the purpose of the federal spending program; and (4) other constitutional provisions may provide an independent bar.[37] The parallels between this test and the McCulloch test are obvious—the pursuit of the general welfare is the legitimate end within the scope of the enumerated spending power, the relation between conditions on the receipt of funds and the purposes of the program reflects the ends-means connection (although it is arguably more generous than the corresponding language in *McCulloch*), and the independent bar posed by other constitutional provisions correlates to *McCulloch's* requirement that the means not contravene the Constitution.[38]

A more recent case, Sabri v. United States (2004), upheld a federal statute criminalizing bribery of officials in state and local programs that received federal funds on the ground that it was necessary and proper to a federal spending program.[39] The Court rejected the defendant's argument that federalism required a more specific jurisdictional nexus between the bribery and the expenditure or allocation of federal funds, reasoning that because money is fungible, Congress was legitimately concerned with the integrity of the program as a whole.[40] Of particular interest in *Sabri* was the Court's express reliance on the Necessary and Proper Clause as the basis for upholding the statute and its refusal to apply the *Dole* test, which it limited to conditions attached to federal funding for state programs.

Sabri therefore tends to suggest that, perhaps in contrast to the commerce power, when taxing and spending is at issue, the enumerated powers and the Necessary and Proper Clause are distinct. The actual tax or the appropriation and expenditure of funds seem to be regarded as within the respective enumerated powers themselves, without the benefit of the Necessary and Proper Clause. Ancillary provisions providing for collection or disbursement and enforcement of federal mandates are treated separately under the Necessary and Proper Clause. Within this construct, the *Dole* test would appear to be a particularized application of the Necessary and Proper Clause for conditions attached to a spending provision. As the *Dole* test suggests, when the Necessary and Proper Clause is attached to the taxing and spending powers, the Court appears to apply it generously and with considerable deference to Congressional prerogatives.

The power to enforce the Reconstruction Amendments, particularly the Fourteenth Amendment, is a third significant area of federal legislative authority. From a textual and historical perspective, however, this field of federal authority presents certain distinctive features. Most obviously, the power to enforce these amendments is not among the original enumerated powers; it represents a modification of the original allocation of authority between the state and national government and it is appended separately to the Constitution rather than incorporated as part of Article I, section 8. In addition, the phrasing of the power is distinctive. It is the power "to *enforce*, by appropriate legislation, the provisions of this article."[41] Under current doctrine, this power includes the power to address violations of the rights protected in these amendments by providing "congruent and proportional" remedies, a test that explicitly draws on *McCulloch* and reflects the incorporation of the enumerated power and the power to adopt necessary and proper legislation into a single, comprehensive legislative power.

In Katzenbach v. Morgan (1966), the Court concluded that the framers of the Fourteenth Amendment intended the phrase "appropriate legislation" to incorporate the *McCulloch* test for necessary and proper legislation. Thus, *Morgan* articulated a test for the Fourteenth Amendment Power that tracks the *McCulloch* test:

We therefore proceed to the consideration whether [the statute at issue] is "appropriate legislation" to enforce the Equal Protection Clause, that is, under the McCulloch v. Maryland standard, whether [the statute] may be regarded as an enactment to enforce the Equal Protection Clause, whether it is "plainly adapted to that end" and whether it is not prohibited by but is consistent with "the letter and spirit of the constitution."

Morgan applied this test to uphold federal legislation prohibiting states from imposing English literacy requirements as a prerequisite to voting, notwithstanding a then-recent Supreme Court decision rejecting an equal protection challenge to similar literacy requirements in Lassiter v. Northampton County Bd. of Elections (1959). The Court in *Morgan* reasoned that the statutory ban was nonetheless appropriate legislation to enforce the Equal Protection Clause under its *McCulloch*-based test for two reasons. First, employing a "fact-finding" rationale, the Court postulated that Congress might find that such laws were prompted by racially discriminatory motives, which would establish an equal protection violation that had not been proven in *Lassiter*. Second, the Court also employed a "prophylactic" rationale, reasoning that Congress might conclude that literacy requirements would lead to under-representation of minorities, which in turn would lead to discriminatory acts by future government officials.

While *Morgan's* reasoning has broad implications, the scope of the Fourteenth Amendment power was relatively unimportant during the 60s, 70s, and 80s, because at that time the commerce power was, for all practical purposes, unlimited. Thus, Congress seldom needed to rely on its power to enforce the Reconstruction Amendments to support civil rights legislation. In the wake of recent decisions limiting the scope of the commerce power, however, the scope of the Fourteenth Amendment power has become increasingly important. In particular, while Congress may not abrogate state sovereign immunity pursuant to the commerce power (or necessary and proper legislation implementing it), abrogation is permissible under the Fourteenth Amendment, because the Amendment comes later in time than either the structural incorporation of state sovereign immunity in the original Constitution or the Eleventh Amendment, and the Fourteenth Amendment clearly contemplates remedies against states.[42] Thus, with the reinvigoration of state sovereign immunity as a restriction on the scope of the commerce power, the Fourteenth Amendment has become especially important as a basis for federal statutes creating remedies against the states.

The current test for the scope of the Fourteenth Amendment power appears to be a more restrictive variation of *McCulloch*-type ends-means scrutiny. It originated in City of Boerne v. Flores (1997), a case that ironically was less about federalism than about separation of powers. *Boerne* invalidated the federal Religious Freedom Restoration Act (RFRA), which required strict judicial scrutiny of facially neutral laws that burden the free exercise of religion. Relying on its power to enforce the Fourteenth Amendment (through which the Free Exercise Clause of the First Amendment is enforced against the states), Congress adopted RFRA in response to Employment Division, Oregon Department of Human Resources v. Smith (1990). *Smith* had seemingly weakened the protection previously accorded religious practices under the Free Exercise Clause by holding that neutral laws incidentally burdening the free exercise of religion are not subject to strict scrutiny, although prior cases had often been read as applying strict scrutiny to neutral laws.[43] In rejecting this legislative effort to overrule its decision in *Smith*, the Court in *Boerne* tightened both the ends and the means components of *Morgan's McCulloch* variation. As to the ends, the Court rejected any suggestion that Congress can define the substantive content of Fourteenth Amendment rights, holding that the end of Fourteenth Amendment legislation must be to remedy a violation of Fourteenth Amendment rights as defined by the Court.[44] As to the means, because Congress was only given the power to "enforce"—not define—the rights protected by the Fourteenth Amendment, the Court required that the remedy (i.e., the means) must be "congruent and proportional" to the underlying violation of the Amendment as defined by the Court:

While the line between measures that remedy or prevent unconstitutional actions and measures that make a substantive change in the governing law is not easy to discern, and Congress must have wide latitude in determining where it lies, the distinction exists and must be observed. There must be a congruence and proportionality between the injury to be prevented or remedied and the means adopted to that end. Lacking such a connection, legislation may become substantive in operation and effect. History and our case law support drawing the distinction, one apparent from the text of the Amendment.

Applying this test on the facts, RFRA was clearly unconstitutional.

Since *Boerne*, the Court has applied the test in several decisions to hold that federal legislation was beyond the scope of the Fourteenth Amendment power. In United States v. Morrison (2000), the Court held that federal remedies against private actors pursuant to the Violence Against Women Act were beyond the scope of the Fourteenth Amendment power, because the substantive rights in the amendment are guaranteed against adverse *state* action. Although Congress identified an underlying violation by the state—the failure of states to enforce their laws prohibiting violence in cases of gender-related violence—the Court held that remedies against the private perpetrators of this violence were not congruent and proportional to that violation. *Morrison* suggests that the Court will not permit a broad reading of the Fourteenth Amendment power to avoid commerce power limits under *Lopez*.

The more significant application of the congruence and proportionality test, however, has come in the area of federal remedies against states, which (as previously discussed) are impermissible under the commerce power but permissible under the Fourteenth Amendment. In two parallel cases, Kimel v. Florida Board of Regents (2000) and Board of Trustees of the University of Alabama v. Garrett

(2001), the Court held that remedies against states for employment discrimination based on age and disability, respectively, were beyond the scope of the Fourteenth Amendment power, because these classifications are not suspect under the Court's equal protection jurisprudence and the state could therefore rely on these classifications as proxies for other valid employment considerations without violating equal protection. Conversely, in Nevada Department of Human Resources v. Hibbs (2003), the Court upheld the Family and Medical Leave Act's remedies against states, accepting congressional determinations that such remedies were needed to combat gender discrimination and explicitly indicating that the congruence and proportionality test is more generous when Congress creates remedies for discrimination based on suspect or quasi-suspect classifications. Likewise, in Tennessee v. Lane (2004), the Court upheld ADA remedies against states for failure to improve access to public buildings as congruent and proportional to the extent that the fundamental right of "access to courts" is implicated.[45]

Notwithstanding *Hibbs* and *Lane*, the cases suggest that ends-means scrutiny under the congruence and proportionality test is much more stringent than the traditional rational basis variation of the *McCulloch* test as applied in other contexts.[46] Because the Court in *Boerne* appeared to base the test on its interpretation of the term "enforce" in the text of the Fourteenth Amendment, it is unclear precisely how the test relates to the Necessary and Proper Clause.[47] Insofar as the test seems to express the means component of the *McCulloch* test, which *Morgan* had stated was incorporated by the language of section 5 of the Fourteenth Amendment, *Boerne* and its progeny may imply that the scope of the power to enact necessary and proper laws varies with the nature of the substantive power to which it is attached, an issue that will be discussed more fully below.

The commerce power, the taxing and spending powers, and the Fourteenth Amendment power are the most significant areas of federal authority for purposes of this analysis, but some additional areas of federal power warrant further discussion. First, two additional enumerated powers have been the source of some discussion in the Supreme Court of relevance to the meaning of the Necessary and Proper Clause: (1) the war power and related powers to provide for and regulate an army and navy, and to call up the militia (Art. I, § 8, cls. 11–16); and (2) the patent and copyright powers (Art. I, § 8, cl. 8). Second, because the Necessary and Proper Clause authorizes Congress to carry into effect not only the enumerated powers, but also other powers vested in the federal government, at times the power to enact necessary and proper laws has been invoked in connection with the implementation of executive or judicial powers.

In general terms, the Court has construed the war power and related powers, taken together with the Necessary and Proper Clause, broadly. For example, in Woods v. Cloyd W. Miller Co. (1948), the Court upheld the Housing and Rent Act of 1947 as a valid exercise of the war power notwithstanding its adoption *after* the termination of World War II, because it responded to the housing crisis created by the demobilization of the armed forces at the end of the war.[48] In one aspect of these powers, however, the Court has read congressional authority quite narrowly: the power to provide for courts martial. Although this power has long been recognized (and reconciled with Article III), it has at times been construed narrowly out of concern for individual rights.[49] Of particular relevance for the Necessary and Proper Clause is the Court's decision in Toth v. Quarles (1955), which invalidated the court martial of a former member of the military for a nonmilitary crime committed while serving outside the country. The Court reasoned that such a military trial could not be sustained by the power to make rules to govern the armed forces, adopting the premise that this authority was " 'the least possible power adequate to the end proposed.' "[50] This approach is quite contrary to the *McCulloch* test, which imposes no such limitation on Congress's choice of means, and runs counter to the broad construction of the commerce power prevalent at the time.[51] This narrow statement of congressional authority can best be understood as driven by concern over the protection of individual liberties.[52]

As the Court has frequently stated, the Patent and Copyright Clause "is both a grant of power and a limitation,"[53] because the text of the Clause provides that patent and copyright protection must be "for limited Times" and its purpose must be "[t]o promote the Progress of Science and useful Arts." Thus, for example, the Clause has generally been construed to impose a constitutional requirement of originality for patents and copyrights.[54] These limitations, however, have not generally been read as justifying a narrower scope of congressional discretion.[55] In its recent decision upholding the extension of the terms of copyrights for existing works, Eldred v. Ashcroft (2003), the Court applied a deferential rational basis test to uphold the Copyright Term Extension Act, without mentioning the Necessary and Proper Clause or *McCulloch*.[56] In the course of its analysis, the Court rejected the argument that legislation pursuant to the Clause should be subject to "heightened judicial review" because it, like the Fourteenth Amendment power, was substantively limited by the terms of its grant.[57] The Court stated broadly that the congruence and proportionality test "does not hold sway for legislation enacted, as copyright laws are, pursuant to Article I authorization," and went on to explain the congruence and proportionality test as an outgrowth of the language of section 5 of the Fourteenth Amendment, which only authorizes Congress to "enforce" substantive rights granted in the Amendment. In contrast, the copyright power, like other powers in Article I, is the power to "define" the right.

By its terms, the Necessary and Proper Clause attaches not only to the enumerated legislative powers of Article I, but also to "all other Powers vested by this Constitution in the Government of the United States, or any Department or Officer thereof." Thus, the Court has at times assessed whether federal statutes were necessary and proper to other constitutional powers, such as the treaty power[58] or the jurisdiction of federal courts.[59] Recently, in Jinks v. Richland County (2003), the Supreme Court confirmed that *McCulloch* applies to federal statutes grounded on these other constitutional powers as well, upholding 28 United States Code (U.S.C.), section 1367(d), which requires that a state statute of limitations must be tolled during the pendency of a case in federal court. The Court reasoned that:

> § 1367(d) is necessary and proper for carrying into execution Congress's power "[t]o con-
> stitute Tribunals inferior to the supreme Court," U.S. Const., Art. I, § 8, cl. 9, and to assure
> that those tribunals may fairly and efficiently exercise "[t]he judicial Power of the United
> States," Art. III, § 1. As to "necessity": The federal courts can assuredly exist and function
> in the absence of § 1367(d), but we long ago rejected the view that the Necessary and
> Proper Clause demands that an Act of Congress be "'*absolutely* necessary'" to the exer-
> cise of an enumerated power. . . . Rather, it suffices that § 1367(d) is "conducive to the due
> administration of justice" in federal court, and is "plainly adapted" to that end. . . ."

The Court also rejected the contention that the provision interfered with state sovereignty so as to constitute an improper means.

As the foregoing discussion suggests, the Court has not since *McCulloch*
engaged in any focused and sustained analysis of the Necessary and Proper
Clause or its role in the constitutional order. Instead, the Clause has been discussed, if at all, as an incidental factor in cases applying particular enumerated
powers. As a result, while the basic understanding of the Clause as affording
Congress broad discretion over the means to implement any ends within the scope
of the enumerated federal powers has continued to operate as a background principle, a number of significant issues remain unresolved. These issues, which are
discussed below, include both overarching questions about the relationship
between the Clause and the enumerated powers and the degree of deference
afforded under *McCulloch* and more specific doctrinal issues concerning each of
the three components of the *McCulloch* test.

Overarching Questions

McCulloch established certain basic principles concerning the Necessary and
Proper Clause, but it left some fundamental questions unresolved. As an initial
matter, there is a latent ambiguity concerning exactly how the Clause interacts
with the other enumerated powers. Although this ambiguity has received relatively scant attention, it has potentially significant theoretical and doctrinal implications. More attention has been devoted to a second overarching question: the
proper degree of deference that courts must afford Congress in determining
whether a law is necessary and proper to an enumerated power. This question,
which is central to the operation of federalism and to the role of the courts in
enforcing it, has recently reemerged in the wake of the Court's renewed interest
in preserving the role of states by limiting federal power.

While it is clear that the Necessary and Proper Clause must be understood in
relation to the enumerated powers to which it attaches, there is more than one way
to conceive that relationship. One possibility is what I shall call the "additional
power model." Under the additional power model, each of the other enumerated
powers, standing alone, provides significant legislative authority to which the

Necessary and Proper Clause is added. Thus, for example, Congress would have the power to regulate interstate commerce *plus* the power to enact laws that are necessary and proper for the regulation of interstate commerce. A second possibility is what I shall call the "constitutive power model." Under the constitutive power model, the Necessary and Proper Clause defines the content of the legislative power granted with respect to each of the other enumerated powers, which have no content except in conjunction with it. Thus, for example, the power to regulate interstate commerce would be the power to enact necessary and proper laws for the regulation of interstate commerce. Although the additional power model might appear at first glance to be the more generous reading of the federal legislative power, it is not inherently so.

Under the additional power model, the enumerated power and the Necessary and Proper Clause remain distinct sources of authority to be analyzed separately. Legislation may be upheld on the basis of the enumerated power itself without application of the *McCulloch* test, which would be called into play only if a statute is related to, but not within, an enumerated power. This approach resonates with *McCulloch's* notion that the powers encompassed by the Clause are "incidental" to the enumerated powers. It also draws some support from the text of Article I, section 8, which incorporates the Necessary and Proper Clause as the final power in a list of enumerated powers, joined by the conjunctive "and."[60] Moreover, because the Clause also attaches to "other Powers" vested by the Constitution in other branches or officials and some of these other powers can be exercised even without legislative action, a parallel construction would support the notion that the enumerated powers can be distinct bases of authority.[61]

In contrast to the additional power model, under the constitutive power model, the Necessary and Proper Clause merges with each of the other enumerated powers (as well as other federal powers) and determines the scope of legislative authority with respect to that substantive field. As one pair of commentators put it:

There are seventeen substantive powers of Congress specified in the 'foregoing' seventeen clauses of section 8, including powers to regulate commerce and to 'constitute Tribunals inferior to the supreme Court.' Because none of these seventeen powers is self-executing, implementation requires some 'necessary and proper' enactments by Congress.[62]

Under this approach it is not possible to analyze the enumerated power independently of the power to enact necessary and proper laws because that is the authority granted to Congress with respect to each of the enumerated powers. The constitutive power model resonates strongly with Hamilton's defense of the Necessary and Proper Clause in the Federalist No. 33, discussed in Part I, in which he argued that the Necessary and Proper Clause was only "declaratory of a truth" that would arise by unavoidable implication from the enumerated powers themselves, because the legislative power is the power to make necessary and proper laws.[63] It can also draw some support from the language of the Necessary and Proper Clause itself, which authorizes Congress to enact necessary and proper laws "for carrying into execution" the enumerated powers, thus implying that these powers may not be self-executing.

McCulloch reflects elements of both models. For example, Chief Justice Marshall rejected Maryland's argument that the purpose of the Necessary and Proper Clause was to confirm that Congress had the power to enact laws (i.e., to legislate), stating bluntly: "[t]hat a legislature, endowed with legislative powers, can legislate, is a proposition too self-evident to have been questioned." This reasoning reflects the additional power model insofar as it assumes that the Necessary and Proper Clause must add something to the enumerated powers, which have independent content. Indeed, in rejecting the suggestion that the Clause limits the legislative powers of Congress, Marshall specifically states that the Clause "purports to be an additional power, not a restriction on those already granted." On the other hand, some aspects of the *McCulloch* opinion are more consistent with the constitutive power model. For example, Marshall famously relies on first principles to justify implied powers that emanate from the enumerated powers themselves, and only thereafter observes that the Necessary and Proper Clause confirms this construction:

But the constitution of the United States has not left the right of congress to employ the necessary means, for the execution of the powers conferred on the government, to general reasoning. To its enumeration of powers is added, that of making 'all laws which shall be necessary and proper, for carrying into execution the foregoing powers, and all other powers vested by this constitution, in the government of the United States, or in any department thereof.'

In the same passage in which Marshall refers to the Clause as an "additional power," he also describes the Clause in terms consistent with the constitutive power model: "If no other motive for its insertion can be suggested, a sufficient one is found in the desire to remove all doubts respecting the right to legislate on that vast mass of incidental powers which must be involved in the constitution, if that instrument be not a splendid bauble."

As the review of the enumerated powers cases in the preceding section demonstrates, subsequent cases have at times reflected the additional power model and at times the constitutive power model. This inconsistency occurs across the enumerated powers and, at times, within a given enumerated power. A notable example of the additional power model at work is United States v. Darby (1941), which upheld provisions in the FLSA that prohibit the shipment in interstate commerce of goods manufactured in violation of minimum wage and maximum hour requirements, require the production of goods for interstate commerce to comply with minimum wage and maximum hour limits, and impose certain recordkeeping requirements. Addressing the prohibition on shipment first, the Court concluded that it was within the scope of the commerce power, reasoning that the power to regulate commerce includes the power to prohibit it and that the power to prohibit commerce is not limited to goods that are of themselves noxious or harmful to commerce.[64] Critically, the Court did not consider the Necessary and Proper Clause in relation to this part of the statute, apparently finding that the prohibition on commerce was sustainable under the commerce power alone. In contrast, the Court applied the *McCulloch* test to uphold the other two provisions of the statute, reasoning that they were necessary and proper to enforcing the prohibition on interstate shipment.[65]

Although *Darby* is a relatively dated and (in some quarters) controversial case,[66] more recent decisions also reflect the additional power model. As described earlier, Pierce County, Washington v. Guillen (2003) seemed to reflect the additional power model in upholding a federal ban on using information gathered by states under the Federal Highway Safety Act from being used as evidence in a subsequent tort suit against the state as within the scope of federal power.[67] The Court concluded that the ban fell "within Congress' Commerce Clause power" and appended a footnote observing that "[b]ecause we conclude that Congress had authority under the Commerce Clause to enact [the provisions in question], we need not decide whether they could also be a proper exercise of Congress' authority under the Spending Clause *or the Necessary and Proper Clause*."[68] Likewise, Sabri v. United States (2004) also employed the additional power approach, in the context of the spending power, to sustain a conviction under a statute criminalizing bribery in programs receiving federal funds, although the statute did not require a specific link between the bribery and the use of federal funds. The Court reasoned that "Congress has authority under the Spending Clause to appropriate federal monies to promote the general welfare . . . and it has corresponding authority under the Necessary and Proper Clause to see to it that taxpayer dollars appropriated under that power are in fact spent for the general welfare. . . ." Both of these cases seemed to assume the additional power model, but they did not engage in conscious analysis of the matter and the statements in question were not essential to the resolution of either case.

More recently, Justice Scalia's concurring opinion in Gonzales v. Raich (2005), engaged in a more extended discussion of the relationship between the commerce power and the Necessary and Proper Clause that reflected the additional power model. As described earlier, Justice Scalia expressly distinguished congressional power to legislate pursuant to the commerce power itself, which in his view is encompassed by the first two *Lopez* categories, from the power to enact necessary and proper legislation in connection with the commerce power, which provided the basis for the third *Lopez* category (regulating intrastate activities having substantial effects on interstate commerce), as well as legislation necessary to make a regulation of interstate commerce more effective. With respect to the second category of necessary and proper legislation to implement the commerce power, Justice Scalia endorsed the reasoning in *Darby*. None of the other Justices in *Raich* joined Justice Scalia's analysis and it remains to be seen whether it will become the majority view. Nonetheless, it represents a relatively rare discussion of the relationship between the commerce power and the Necessary and Proper Clause that expressly adopts an additional power perspective.

Other cases, however, reflect the constitutive power model. The clearest example is Katzenbach v. Morgan (1966), which as discussed above expressly concluded that congressional authority under section 5 of the Fourteenth Amendment to enact "appropriate" legislation to enforce its substantive provisions incorporated the *McCulloch* test. Thus, the test for the section 5 power is a variation of the *McCulloch* test, and it is impossible to separate the specific legislative authority under section 5 from the power to enact necessary and proper laws. Although recent cases have applied a more stringent variation on the ends-means inquiry demanded by *McCulloch*, the relationship between this test and the section 5 power remains unchanged. Because this power has a distinctive textual and historical context, however, the significance of this approach for the Article I powers is uncertain. Nonetheless there are cases under the Article I powers that also reflect the constitutive power model.

In particular, many of the Court's recent commerce power decisions seem to reflect the constitutive power model. First, as noted above, the *Lopez* test encompasses not only categories of regulatory authority that may be within the commerce power itself, such as the power to regulate the use of the channels of interstate commerce, but also regulatory authority whose justification must derive from the Necessary and Proper Clause, such as the power to regulate activities that have a substantial effect on interstate commerce. Moreover, both *Lopez* and *Morrison*, which applied the *Lopez* test, concluded that the laws in question exceeded the scope of federal legislative authority without inquiry into the Necessary and Proper Clause. The failure to consider the Clause as a separate source of authority is inconsistent with the additional power model. Second, insofar as the Court has explained state sovereignty–based restrictions on commerce power legislation as reflecting inherent restrictions on the proper means of implementing that power, the Court seems to be treating the *McCulloch* test as a restriction on the commerce power itself, not merely as a restriction on the Necessary and Proper Clause.

Ultimately, the Court's approach to the Necessary and Proper Clause remains ambiguous in large measure because the choice of models makes little difference in most cases. Indeed, the choice of approaches is less significant, from a practical perspective, than the scope of the content the Court is willing to accord either component of the equation. Nonetheless, the choice between the additional and constitutive power models has some potentially significant implications, particularly as the Court has begun to find limits on the scope of federal legislative authority. Most clearly, from the doctrinal perspective, under the additional power model the *McCulloch* test should not apply when Congress acts within the scope of an enumerated power without relying on the Necessary and Proper Clause. This result is especially important in connection with the ends component of the *McCulloch* test, which would limit the ends of statutes to purposes within the enumerated powers to which they attach. This may explain *Darby's* conclusion that Congress's purposes or motives for prohibiting the shipment of goods in interstate commerce is irrelevant, a conclusion that would appear to be at odds with the ends component of the *McCulloch* test. For measures that fall directly within an enumerated power, any intrinsic limitation on ends would have to be found in the enumerated power itself, such as the requirement that spending must be "for the common Defence and general Welfare of the United States" or that patents and copyrights can only be granted "to promote the Progress of Science and useful Arts."[69] The inapplicability of the *McCulloch* test is less likely to matter to its requirement of appropriate means or its prohibition on means that contravene the letter and spirit of the Constitution. If it does not rely on the Necessary and Proper Clause, Congress would be limited to means within the enumerated power itself, which would be, a fortiori, "appropriate" for purposes of *McCulloch*.[70] As to *McCulloch's* exclusion of means that contravene the Constitution, such measures would presumably be unconstitutional even without *McCulloch* because the violation of the constitutional norm represents an independent ground for invalidating the legislation.[71]

A more subtle, but nonetheless potentially significant, implication of the choice of models is the extent to which the Necessary and Proper Clause has a consistent meaning regardless of the power to which it attaches. If the Clause is viewed as a separate and additional source of power, its meaning should be the same regardless of the power to which it attaches. Conversely, to the extent that the Clause defines the legislative power, it could have broader or narrower scope, depending on the kind of power being exercised. Thus, for example, Eldred v. Ashcroft (2003) explained the "congruence and proportionality" test for the Fourteenth Amendment power—which clearly employs the constitutive power model—as an outgrowth of the section 5 grant of power to "enforce" the amendment's substantive provisions, thus linking a form of elevated scrutiny of the means-ends connection (the second part of the *McCulloch* test) to the limits of the substantive power granted. At the same time, *Eldred* rejects a similar elevation of scrutiny for the Patent and Copyright Clause, although that Clause also limits the purposes for which patents and copyrights can be granted, reasoning that the Clause means the same thing in relation to all of the Article I powers, which seems to reflect the additional power model. In contrast, Justice Breyer's suggestion in dissent that a more searching rationality review (in comparison to the commerce power) should be applied, because "a particular statute that exceeds proper Copyright Clause bounds may set the Clause and the First Amendment at crosspurposes," would make sense under the constitutive power model.

As this discussion suggests, the choice between the additional and constitutive power models relates to a second fundamental question: how much deference should the courts afford Congress when determining whether legislation is necessary and proper to the execution of an enumerated power? *McCulloch* uses the terms "appropriate" and "plainly adapted" in describing the relationship between the legislative means and ends within the enumerated power.[72] When applying that test, Chief Justice Marshall also employs language of deference to congressional judgments:

Should Congress, in the execution of its powers, adopt measures which are prohibited by the Constitution, or should Congress, under the pretext of executing its powers, pass laws for the accomplishment of objects not intrusted to the Government, it would become the painful duty of this tribunal, should a case requiring such a decision come before it, to say that such an act was not the law of the land. But where the law is not prohibited, and is really calculated to effect any of the objects intrusted to the Government, to undertake here to inquire into the degree of its necessity would be to pass the line which circumscribes the judicial department and to tread on legislative ground. This Court disclaims all pretensions to such a power.

Perhaps in view of such language, ends-means scrutiny under *McCulloch* has, at least since the New Deal period, generally been equated with deferential "rational basis scrutiny" under the Equal Protection and Due Process Clauses. The recent reinvigoration of federalism-based limits on congressional authority has called this conventional understanding into question.

For all practical purposes, the "rational basis" test permits Congress to regulate any activity it may choose, because it is always possible to come up with a rational connection to one of the enumerated powers. Under the ends component of the rational basis test, the courts will accept any plausible legislative purpose, whether or not that purpose was articulated by or actually motivated Congress, and presume that there is a factual basis to support it. Likewise, the courts are relatively unconcerned with a lack of a close "fit" between the means and the ends and defer to any reasonable legislative judgment that a particular means will further the legislative ends. This deferential approach, particularly when coupled with the commerce power in relation to the truly national economy that emerged in the twentieth century, permitted Congress to reach virtually any activity within the scope of powers traditionally reserved to the states.[73] Thus, even if the federal government remained in theory a government of enumerated powers, in practice, the scope of federal legislative power seemed unlimited. But as the Court has begun to reinvigorate limits on the scope of federal legislative authority, the conventional rational basis understanding of the *McCulloch* test has become both uncertain and controversial.

In relation to the commerce power, *Lopez* signals a movement away from the *McCulloch* test without an explicit rejection of the rational basis test.[74] The categorical approach of *Lopez* bears little resemblance to *McCulloch* and appears to supplant ends-means scrutiny. Under the third and potentially most expansive *Lopez* category (power to regulate activities having substantial effects on interstate commerce), the commerce power has a more restricted scope than would likely result under the rational basis test. First, the Court limited the circumstances under which it is permissible to consider the cumulative or aggregate effects on interstate commerce to circumstances under which the regulated activity is commercial or economic in character.[75] Such a restriction could not be justified or explained under the traditional rational basis test, because it is hardly "irrational" to conclude that a noncommercial activity may have a cumulative effect on interstate commerce such that regulating the activity is a reasonable means to effectuate a commerce power purpose. Second, *Lopez* indicated that while it would consider congressional fact-finding, the Court would make an independent judgment about whether a given activity has a substantial effect on interstate commerce.[76] Third, the Court indicated that notwithstanding the plainly rational conclusion—supported by evidence in the legislative record—that crime in schools (in the aggregate) affects interstate commerce, such reasoning could not be accepted because it would permit the federal government broad authority to regulate in traditional areas of state authority.[77] Although the Court in *Lopez* explained the three categories of commerce power authority as a restatement of the kinds of federal laws that are rationally related to the regulation of interstate commerce, by focusing on the categories and developing rules for applying the third category, the Court was able to constrain the commerce powers in a manner that would not be possible under the rational basis test.

The Court has also moved away from the rational basis test in construing the power to enforce the Fourteenth Amendment. The "congruence and proportionality" requirement from *Boerne* is clearly more restrictive than the rational basis test, insofar as it requires a close fit between the ends and the means chosen.[78] Indeed, the parties and the Court in *Eldred* treated the congruence and proportionality test as a form of elevated scrutiny, which the Court refused to apply under the Copyright Clause. Although under *Eldred* this test is apparently confined to the Reconstruction Amendments, it is clear that the power to enforce those amendments is one category of federal legislative power to which the rational basis test simply does not apply. Viewed together with *Lopez*, the development of special tests for particular powers may portend the decline of the rational basis test on a broader scale.

Such a move has been advocated by a number of scholars in recent publications arguing that the rational basis test is inconsistent with the correct interpretation of the Necessary and Proper Clause.[79] At the risk of oversimplifying the arguments advanced in a diverse and nuanced literature, these scholars emphasize that the text requires laws to be "necessary *and proper*," which they interpret as implying a close connection between an enumerated power and the means chosen. This interpretation is bolstered by evidence of the Framers' intent, particularly Madison's and Hamilton's defenses of the Necessary and Proper Clause in the Federalist Papers, as well as the debate surrounding the creation of a national bank, which proponents of a more restrictive view of federal power read as supporting meaningful scrutiny under the Necessary and Proper Clause to preserve the principle of enumerated federal powers. Finally, critics of the rational basis approach argue that it misreads *McCulloch*, which required that necessary and proper laws be "appropriate" and "plainly adapted" to the implementation of ends within the enumerated powers.

This kind of analysis resonates with the Court's recent reinvigoration of limits on federal power, and is apparently gaining some purchase, as recent opinions by Justices Thomas and Scalia suggest. Justice Thomas wrote a separate concurrence in Sabri v. United States (2004) for the primary purpose of questioning the rational basis approach to the *McCulloch* test.[80] The majority in *Sabri* characterized *McCulloch* as "establishing review for means-ends rationality under the Necessary and Proper Clause" and upheld the application of a federal bribery statute to officials in programs receiving federal funds without requiring a connection between the bribery and the federal funds, because it "addresses the problem at the sources of bribes, by rational means, to safeguard the integrity of . . . recipients of federal dollars." Justice Thomas, however, relied on the commerce power to uphold the statute[81] and disputed the Court's characterization of *McCulloch*. Focusing on the language of *McCulloch* itself, Justice Thomas argued that " 'appropriate' and 'plainly adapted' are hardly synonymous with 'means-end rationality.' " In particular, Justice Thomas concluded that "[t]o show that a statute is 'plainly adapted' to a legitimate end, then, one must seemingly show more than that a particular statute is a 'rational means,' . . . to safeguard that end; rather, it would seem necessary to show some obvious, simple, and direct relation between the statute and the enumerated power."

Although less explicit, Justice Scalia's recent opinion for the Court in Jinks v. Richland County (2003) conspicuously omits any reference to the rational basis test and instead focuses on the language of *McCulloch* itself. The Court, per Justice Scalia, upheld a federal law providing that state statutes of limitations are tolled during the pendency of federal actions, reasoning that the law was necessary and proper to Congress's power to establish lower federal courts and provide for the fair and efficient exercise of their Article III powers. In so doing, Justice Scalia did not ask whether the law was rationally related to these powers of Congress, but rather whether the law was " 'conducive to the administration of justice' in federal court" and was " 'plainly adapted' to that end." In addition, Justice Scalia continued, there was no suggestion that the law was a " 'pretext' for 'the accomplishment of objectives not entrusted to the [federal] government' "[82] and the "connection between [the law] and Congress's authority over the federal courts [was not] so attenuated as to undermine the enumeration of powers. . . ."[83] Thus, Justice Scalia's opinion (for a unanimous court) reaches an unexceptional result, but it uses language that is consistent with a more searching inquiry under the Necessary and Proper Clause.[84]

It remains to be seen whether these opinions presage a broader movement away from the rational basis approach to the *McCulloch* test. The Court continues to employ the rational basis formulation in some cases—as the majority did in *Sabri*. Indeed, even Justice Thomas joined an opinion employing the rational basis formulation as recently as Eldred v. Ashcroft (2003). Nonetheless, viewed in combination, the recent scholarship and judicial opinions cast some doubt on the long-term viability of the rational basis test. Ironically, over two centuries after Hamilton and Madison parted company on the scope of the Necessary and Proper Clause, the fundamental problem remains—how to apply the Clause to accommodate both the plenary power principle and the enumerated powers principle. This issue is also reflected in the application of the individual components of the *McCulloch* test.

Ends

The first component of the *McCulloch* test is that the legislative "ends" must be "legitimate" and "within the scope of the constitution." This requirement is generally understood to mean that the purposes of a necessary and proper law must be within one or more of the enumerated powers of Congress.[85] Determining whether this requirement is met entails two distinct inquiries. First, the relevant enumerated power must be defined and given scope. Second, the purposes or ends of the federal statute must be ascertained and characterized. Each of these inquiries presents its own issues and problems.

Defining the enumerated power and determining its scope is a matter of constitutional interpretation. Consistent with their constitutionally assigned role under Marbury v. Madison (1803), this issue falls to the courts. Most recently and explicitly, the Court in *Boerne* rejected any congressional role in defining the content of Fourteenth Amendment rights, requiring legislation to enforce its substantive provisions to be linked to a violation of constitutional rights *as defined by the Court*.[86] Notwithstanding the distinctive nature of the Fourteenth Amendment power, it is also apparent that the Court determines the meaning of the enumerated Article I powers as well. The Court defined the power to regulate commerce among the states in Gibbons v. Ogden (1824). In United States v. Butler (1936), it resolved the question whether the term "general welfare" as used in relation to the taxing and spending powers confines the purposes of federal spending to those within the other enumerated powers. Likewise, the Court has interpreted other textual limitations or qualifications on enumerated powers, such as uniformity requirements[87] and the requirement that patents and copyrights be awarded for limited terms to promote the sciences and useful arts.[88] While a comprehensive catalogue of how the Court has interpreted each of the enumerated powers is neither necessary nor proper here, several general points are worth noting.

First, when the Court has directly confronted such interpretive questions, it has generally construed the enumerated power broadly. Thus, for example, *Gibbons* interpreted the commerce power broadly with respect to the meaning of commerce (to include navigation), the meaning of "among the states" (to include all commerce involving more than one state and the power to regulate intrastate aspects of that commerce), and the power to "regulate" (to include plenary authority to determine the rules under which commerce may be conducted). Likewise, *Butler* construed the power to spend "for the general welfare" broadly, refusing to confine the general welfare to matters within the other enumerated powers.[89] Similarly, under Woods v. Cloyd W. Miller Co. (1948), permissible war power ends appear to encompass not only the conduct of the war itself, but also dealing with the conditions and circumstances caused by the war, even after hostilities have ceased.[90] A possible exception to this pattern is the Fourteenth Amendment power, insofar as Congress apparently cannot seek to remedy discrimination based on classifications that are not suspect or "quasi" suspect even though nonsuspect classifications may in some instances violate equal protection. Like other aspects of the Fourteenth Amendment power, however, the distinctive text and separation of powers considerations involved may explain this result.

Second, the breadth of the ends encompassed by an enumerated power has implications for the effective scope of necessary and proper laws to implement it. The ends reflected in some enumerated powers are relatively narrow, such as the powers to coin money,[91] create post offices and roads,[92] or punish piracy.[93] Because the ends encompassed by these powers are narrow, the range of legislation that might be justified as appropriate to the execution of those ends is correspondingly narrow. Conversely, when the enumerated power contemplates a very broad range of ends, such as the regulation of commerce or spending for the general welfare, legislation addressing virtually any and all activity might be justified as necessary and proper to the execution of some end within the enumerated power. Thus, it comes as no surprise that the battle over the scope of federal legislative power should generally have been waged in cases involving broad powers, particularly the commerce power.

Third, determining the ends encompassed by the enumerated powers is also complicated by the variable phrasing and form of the enumerated powers. Some powers, such as the commerce power, simply refer to a broad or narrow field of authority and contemplate "plenary" authority over that field.[94] For others, the grant of authority over a particular field is qualified by restrictions on means, as in the case of the bankruptcy and naturalization powers, which must be exercised by means of "uniform" laws or rules.[95] Some powers do not refer to a field of authority at all, but rather are phrased as a grant of authority to take a particular type of action coupled with substantive provisions limiting the purposes for which the means can be used, such as the power to spend, which is the power "to provide for the common Defence and general Welfare of the United States."[96] Some powers reflect various combinations of the above forms. Thus, for example, the patent and copyright power is the power to secure exclusive rights for authors and inventors (a particular action not a field of authority), which must be "for limited times" and which can only be exercised "to promote the Progress of Science and the useful Arts."[97]

While interpreting the enumerated powers to determine the permissible ends they encompass can be problematic, the more difficult issue in most cases is the characterization of the ends of a particular statute. This issue is essentially one of historical fact: what purpose did Congress intend when it passed a statute? But this factual determination entails some unique and fundamental problems. To begin with, it is not realistic to seek "the" purpose of legislation adopted by a collective body consisting of hundreds of members, each of whom may have had multiple purposes and mixed motives for approving legislation. Even assuming that there is such a thing as a legislative purpose, what evidence can and should be used to demonstrate it?[98] Any analysis of purpose, moreover, raises questions about the proper deference owed to Congress's own characterization of its purposes.

McCulloch itself did not engage in any extended inquiry into the ends supporting the incorporation of a national bank, but rather seemed to take those ends as a given. At the outset of his discussion of implied powers, Chief Justice Marshall suggested several enumerated powers whose ends the bank apparently served: "Although, among the enumerated powers of government, we do not find the word 'bank' or 'incorporation,' we find the great powers, to lay and collect taxes; to borrow money; to regulate commerce; to declare and conduct a war; and to raise and support armies and navies." Later, in the course of defending the necessity and appropriateness of the bank, he opined there was no longer any controversy that the bank was "a convenient, a useful, and essential instrument in the prosecution of [the federal government's] fiscal operations," which presumably encompasses many of the ends he earlier referenced. Marshall's casual assumption of the ends does not tell us much, however, because it may reflect either deference to Congress on this issue or judicial notice of the ends to be served by the bank, which were well understood at the time. There is language in *McCulloch* that might support an inquiry into the "real" purpose or ends served by a statute, insofar as Marshall suggested that legislation purporting to serve legitimate ends would be invalid if those ends were merely a "pretext" for ends that are beyond the scope of federal power and that deference to Congress's choice of means is appropriate only if legislation is "really calculated to effect any of the objects intrusted to the government."

Since *McCulloch*, the Court has vacillated a good deal in its approach to characterizing legislative ends, at times undertaking to inquire into the real purposes of legislation and at other times apparently accepting without inquiry any plausible statutory purpose. In some famous pre–New Deal cases, the Court invalidated legislation apparently within the scope of an enumerated power because its true purpose was to regulate in areas reserved to the police power of the states. Most prominently, in Hammer v. Dagenhart (*The Child Labor Case*) (1918), the Court concluded that the true purpose of a law prohibiting shipment of goods manufactured with child labor was to regulate employment conditions in manufacture and production, which was not within the commerce power. Likewise, in Bailey v. Drexel Furniture Co. (*The Child Labor Tax Case*) (1922) and United States v. Butler (1936), the Court concluded that legislation in the form of a tax or an expenditure was intended to accomplish an impermissible regulatory purpose within the states' reserved police powers. These cases seemed to imply that even when Congress acts by using means expressly granted to it, the Court would inquire into the ultimate end of the legislation and require that end to be within the enumerated power.[99]

After the New Deal switch, however, the Court disavowed any inquiry into the real purpose or motive behind legislation. In United States v. Darby (1941), for example, the Court stated broadly that "[t]he motive and purpose of a regulation of interstate commerce are matters for the legislative judgment upon the exercise of which the Constitution places no restriction and over which the courts are given no control," overruling *The Child Labor Case* on precisely this point. Likewise, the Court no longer inquires into whether a tax or spending law serves a regulatory purpose, as reflected in the post–New Deal decisions of Helvering v. Davis (1937) and Steward Machine Co. v. Davis (1937), which upheld the Social Security Act notwithstanding the argument that it served an improper purpose. Under current doctrine, it is sufficient that a tax raise revenue or that spending legislation provide for the expenditure of funds, even if there is a regulatory effect that may have been the primary purpose of Congress. Even as to the Fourteenth Amendment power, the Court apparently accepts the characterization of legislative ends if a statute "may be regarded as an enactment to enforce" the amendment's substantive provisions.[100]

Indeed, to the extent that scrutiny of legislation under the *McCulloch* test is equated with the traditional rational basis test, there is virtually no scrutiny of legislative ends.[101] Congress need not state its purposes contemporaneously and the Court will consider any plausible purpose offered in support of legislation, including a post hoc explanation offered for the first time in the context of litigation. Under this approach, moreover, the Court does not generally inquire into whether an asserted purpose is merely a pretext for some other purpose that is not within the enumerated powers.[102] Although Congress is not required to provide a factual record or findings to support its commerce power purposes, it frequently does so and, under the rational basis test, the Court defers.[103] Finally, Congress may rely on various powers and purposes in the alternative, and the statute is within the scope of federal legislative power if it is sufficiently related to any one of them.[104] This approach might be defended on the theory that pretextual ends will more likely fail the means-ends fit component of the rational basis test,[105] but such a defense would require a meaningful scrutiny of fit, which is not typically contemplated by the rational basis test.

Recent cases suggesting potentially more careful scrutiny under the *McCulloch* test reveal some indications of a renewed inquiry into the true purposes of legislation. Most clearly, although City of Boerne v. Flores (1996) did not explicitly alter the prior approach to determining legislative ends, the Court conspicuously rejected Congress's preventive rationale for the RFRA and concluded that its real purpose was to overturn the Court's holding in Employment Division, Oregon Dept. of Social Services v. Smith (1990). The Court in *Boerne* examined the legislative history to conclude that Congress was not concerned with preventing intentional religious discrimination (an end within the Free Exercise Clause as defined by the Court in *Smith*), but rather sought to prevent neutral laws that incidentally burden religious practices (which under *Smith* did not violate the Free Exercise Clause).[106] The Court in *Boerne* also concluded that "RFRA is so out of proportion to a supposed remedial or preventive object that it cannot be understood as responsive to, or designed to prevent, unconstitutional behavior. It appears, instead, to attempt a substantive change in constitutional protections."[107]

Boerne might be viewed as an isolated case reflecting particular separation of powers concerns arising from the distinctive features of the Fourteenth Amendment enforcement power, but there are indications in other cases that the Court may be prepared to examine legislative ends more carefully. Justice Scalia's opinion for the Court in *Jinks* conspicuously quoted *McCulloch's* language in observing that "[t]here is no suggestion by either of the parties that Congress enacted [this law] as a 'pretext' for 'the accomplishment of objects not entrusted to the [federal] government.'"[108] In his concurring opinion in *Sabri*, Justice Thomas referred approvingly to *Jinks'* discussion of *McCulloch*. It is also possible to understand *Lopez* and *Morrison* in these terms, that is, as reflecting the Court's judgment that the real purpose or end of Congress in those cases was to regulate private noncommercial activity within the traditional province of the states on the basis of a pretextual commerce power end. These cases fall short of rejecting the post–New Deal approach of deferring to the congressional characterization of ends, but they may presage a more direct reconsideration of that approach, particularly if the Court follows Justice Thomas's lead in rejecting the rational basis test.

Appropriate Means

The requirement of appropriate means is, in practice, the focus of most cases presenting serious issues about the scope of federal power under the Necessary and Proper Clause.[109] The central question in this regard has been and continues to be just how closely the means must "fit" with the legislative ends, because the answer to this question has critical implications for the scope of federal legislative power. If a loose connection between the ends and the means is acceptable, federal legislative power is relatively broad; if a tight fit is required, the scope of the federal legislative power is relatively narrow. Thus, the fit question figured prominently in the ratification debates and the bank controversy and was not definitively resolved by *McCulloch*, as the subsequent ebb and flow of federal legislative power cases has revealed.

Analysis of the fit issue, however, is further complicated by the fact that ends-means scrutiny may serve a variety of functions. As originally formulated in *McCulloch*, ends-means scrutiny serves a power allocation function, establishing the link between an enumerated power and the means chosen to implement it. But ends-means scrutiny also serves an evidentiary function, because a poor fit between means and ends supports the inference that the asserted ends are not the "real" purpose of legislation. Finally, ends-means scrutiny is also relevant to any balancing of competing interests, because the public purposes of legislation justify the sacrifice of other values only to the extent that these intended benefits are reasonably likely to accrue. All three uses of ends-means scrutiny appear to some extent in the Court's decisions concerning the federal legislative power, with varying implications for the fit inquiry.

The *McCulloch* test was articulated as a power allocation test for determining whether a given law is within the scope of federal authority. If the means are "appropriate" and "plainly adapted" to an enumerated power end, legislation is within the field of authority granted to Congress in Article I. Viewed from this perspective, the *McCulloch* test should be interpreted and applied to reflect the Framers' complementary, but in some respects contradictory, understandings that (1) the legislative power granted Congress with respect to each enumerated power is the full measure of sovereign legislative power traditionally exercised by legislatures as to any given subject within their authority (the plenary power principle), and (2) the legislative power of the federal government is limited by the principle of enumerated powers, with the remaining power reserved to the states (the reserved power principle). The closeness of fit required under the *McCulloch* test is likely to depend on which of these two principles the Court chooses to emphasize.

When the fit inquiry functions as a power allocation principle, its primary focus is the reasonableness of the legislative determination that a particular end within the enumerated powers will in fact be furthered by the chosen means. Thus, *McCulloch* concluded that the bank was appropriate and plainly adapted to enumerated power ends, because there was no longer any "controversy" that the bank was a "convenient, a useful, and essential instrument in the prosecution of its fiscal operations. . . ."[110] Likewise, for example, the inquiry into whether an activity in fact has a substantial effect on interstate commerce serves to establish that the regulation of that activity is necessary and proper to the regulation of interstate commerce. In a number of cases, the Court has referred to the legislative record as supporting Congress's conclusion that a given activity affects interstate commerce, although the Court also emphasized in those cases that Congress is not required to create a factual record or make formal findings to support its legislative judgment.[111] The Court's more recent statements that it must make an independent judgment whether there is a substantial effect on interstate commerce thus reflect a strengthening of the factual predicate requirement that must be met to establish that legislation will further a commerce power end.[112]

In addition to its use as a power allocation principle, the fit inquiry serves an evidentiary function. Under this approach, it is the pursuit of improper ends that places the legislation beyond the scope of federal legislative authority (rather than an insufficient connection to legitimate ends), and a bad fit between the means and the ends tends to show that the ends asserted in support of a statute are merely a pretext. This idea may be foreshadowed by Chief Justice Marshall's statement in *McCulloch* that it would be the Court's "painful duty" to invalidate laws passed by Congress "under the pretext of executing its powers . . . for the accomplishment of objects not intrusted to the government." But the evidentiary approach did not fully emerge until later cases, which, ironically, dealt with the scope of state legislative authority under the doctrine of substantive economic due process. In the notorious decision in Lochner v. State of New York (1905), the Court invalidated a New York statute prescribing the maximum hours for bakery employers. The Court rejected the state's argument that the law was a legitimate police power measure to protect the health and safety of bakery employees,[113] reasoning that the law's tenuous connection to asserted health and safety benefits tended to show that its true purpose was to regulate labor relations, which the Court at the time viewed as an illegitimate end.[114] Although the Court has overruled *Lochner* itself and disavowed many aspects of its reasoning, the use of a poor ends-means fit to infer improper motives has found its way into various areas of constitutional law, most prominently the analysis of classifications under the Equal Protection Clause.[115]

This kind of reasoning also appears in federal legislative power cases, particularly insofar as the Court has undertaken to inquire into the ends of legislation. As noted above, in *Boerne*, the Court concluded that the preventive rationale for RFRA advanced by Congress was a pretext and the true purpose of the law was to effect a substantive change in the scope of the Free Exercise Clause as made applicable to the states by the Fourteenth Amendment.[116] In reaching this conclusion, the Court emphasized that "RFRA is so out of proportion to a supposed remedial or preventive object that it cannot be understood as responsive to, or designed to prevent, unconstitutional behavior. It appears, instead, to attempt a substantive change in constitutional protections." As this language suggests, when poor fit is used to generate an inference as to the real purposes of legislation, the focus of the analysis tends to be on over- and underinclusiveness. In particular, if the law is much too broad, in the sense that most of its applications would not tend to further its stated purpose, the poor fit suggests that some other motive is at work. Conversely, if a law is much too narrow, in the sense that it does not address a lot of activity that would seem to implicate the statutory purpose in the same way as a regulated activity, that too tends to show that some other purpose is at work.

A third function of ends-means analysis is in the weighing of the governmental interest used to justify legislation that burdens constitutionally protected interests. From this perspective, an asserted governmental interest must be weighty enough to justify legislation impeding other constitutional values. An asserted interest, however, is weighty only to the extent that legislation will actually achieve it, and a poor means-ends fit therefore tends to diminish that governmental interest. When the adversely affected constitutional values are particularly important, the level of scrutiny may be raised accordingly. This aspect of means-ends scrutiny is most prominent when the issue is one of individual rights, in which the weighing of competing interests is explicitly incorporated into some tests for constitutionality[117] and in the levels of scrutiny applied.[118] But it has also been used in power allocation cases involving the "dormant" Commerce Clause,[119] in which neutral laws burdening interstate commerce are invalid if the burden is excessive in relation to the purported state interest.[120]

The use of means-ends scrutiny as a part of a broader effort to balance competing interests has not been explicit in the context of federal legislative power, but it may play a role in the recent reassertion of limits on the scope of that power.[121] In particular, *Lopez* and *Morrison* may be understood as effectively raising the level of scrutiny when federal legislation intrudes upon traditional areas of state authority. From this perspective, both cases involved federal legislation addressing private noncommercial activity in areas that are traditionally the province of the state police power (crime and education or crime and domestic relations, respectively), thus burdening a particularly important constitutional value, the reserved powers of the states. Insofar as the Court was unwilling to accept the aggregate effects of noncommercial activity on interstate commerce as a basis for the laws, emphasized the lack of a jurisdictional nexus, and suggested an independent inquiry into the factual basis for the laws in question, the cases seem to apply a higher level of scrutiny than the traditional rational basis test.[122] Indeed, in both cases, the Court suggested that accepting the commerce power arguments advanced in defense of the respective federal statutes would effectively obliterate the principle of enumerated powers and destroy any notion of reserved state power.[123] This reasoning implies that the means-ends fit must be closer when laws burden important federalism values.

The same kind of reasoning may also be reflected in the elevated scrutiny applied to legislation under the Fourteenth Amendment enforcement power, which has from the beginning been viewed by the Court as a potential threat to the principle of enumerated powers and accordingly construed narrowly.[124] In *Morrison*, the scrutiny of fit was particularly rigorous, insofar as the Court indicated that a nationwide remedy against private persons committing violence against women is not a congruent and proportional remedy for some states' failure to provide "equal protection" for women who are victims of violence. The Court accepted that there was a factual basis for Congress's conclusion that states' failure to protect women adequately was the product of improper discrimination, but it reasoned that a remedy against private persons who commit the violence (as opposed to against the states for failure to enforce their laws) is not directed toward the underlying violation. This conclusion seems odd, because it makes perfect sense for a Congress that believes states' failure to enforce laws protecting women is the product of discrimination to offer an alternative remedy for victims in federal court. The refusal to accept (or apparently even consider) such an explanation would seem to be a product of the majority's concern for the impact of a contrary rule on the reserved power of the states.[125]

As the foregoing discussion suggests, scrutiny of the means-ends connection under the Necessary and Proper Clause remains primarily a power allocation inquiry, but elements of the factual inference and balancing approaches appear as well. Under this mixed approach, the Court considers a variety of factors, whether explicitly or implicitly, in assessing whether a given statute is sufficiently related to an end within the enumerated powers of Congress. These factors include the factual record or foundation for the congressional determination that the law will further the end in question, whether the law is especially overbroad in connection with its asserted purposes suggesting an improper motive, and whether the relationship between the law and its stated purposes is too tenuous to justify a particularly significant impingement on state power. More fundamentally, there is considerable uncertainty as to just how aggressive the Court will be when considering these factors. Not only is the level of scrutiny under the *McCulloch* test potentially in play, but under any stated level of scrutiny, the Court's consideration of these factors may be more or less deferential to Congress and more or less favorable to the assertion of federal legislative authority.

Prohibited Means

The third component of the *McCulloch* test is the requirement that the means must not be "prohibited," and must be consistent with "the letter and spirit of the constitution." At a minimum, this component of the *McCulloch* test prevents Congress from using the federal legislative power to violate independent constitutional requirements, such as the explicit prohibitions of Article I, section 9, or the Bill of Rights.[126] In this respect, however, it is also redundant and therefore unnecessary, because a law that violates such a prohibition would be unconstitutional even if it is clearly within the scope of the enumerated powers. While one could say that legislation that violates constitutional rights is beyond the scope of the enumerated powers, the constitutionality of the law would still turn on the meaning of the constitutional prohibition rather than on the scope of federal legislative authority. Thus, individual rights cases involving federal laws do not typically refer to the prohibited means component of the *McCulloch* test, but rather consider directly whether the law violates the individual right asserted. The critical question for purposes of the prohibited means component of the *McCulloch* test is therefore whether it embodies something more—an implicit federalism-based limit on federal legislative power to preserve the sovereignty of states.

This issue, too, is an aspect of the federal legislative power on which the Court has been inconsistent. Under dual sovereignty theory, which (as described in Part I) prevailed during the period before the New Deal, the Court frequently relied on the reserved powers of the states to limit the scope of federal power. At times the Court invoked the Tenth Amendment as an independent bar to the assertion of federal legislative power, reading its reservation of powers not delegated to the national government as creating a sphere of state autonomy that was protected from federal interference. Such reasoning was apparently disavowed after the New Deal in *Darby*, which stated that the Tenth Amendment is but a truism and refused to treat it as an independent bar to commerce power legislation. After a brief resurgence in the mid-1970s, when National League of Cities v. Usery (1976) held that federal laws regulating states as states violated the Tenth Amendment, the Court in Garcia v. San Antonio Area Metropolitan Transit Authority (1985) again apparently disavowed any judicially enforceable Tenth Amendment limitation on federal legislative power.[127]

This history brings into focus the Court's approach in the recent no-commandeering and sovereign immunity cases. In New York v. United States (1992), which first adopted the no-commandeering rule, the Court had to reconcile its reliance on state sovereignty to limit federal legislative power with its statements in *Darby* and *Garcia* that the Tenth Amendment is not an independent limit on federal power. That Court did so by explaining that the scope of federal legislative power under Article I and the limits imposed by the Tenth Amendment were "mirror images" of each other, so that "if a power is an attribute of state sovereignty reserved by the Tenth Amendment, it is necessarily a power the Constitution has not conferred on Congress." As described above, later cases such as Printz v. United States (1997) and Alden v. Maine (1999) expressly linked this kind of reasoning to the concept of "proper" laws under the Necessary and Proper Clause, which in turn finds expression in the third component of the *McCulloch* test.

These developments are closely related to the renewed academic debate on the interpretation of the Necessary and Proper Clause. Scholars who have revisited the historical understanding of the Clause as part of a larger argument for more aggressive enforcement of limits on federal legislative power often place heavy reliance on the term "proper."[128] In this view, the conventional wisdom (including the rational basis formulation of *McCulloch*) relies on a broad interpretation of the term necessary without sufficient attention to the additional requirement that laws must be proper. In particular, the term "proper" arguably imparts more than a redundant requirement that legislation may not violate an independent constitutional bar. Instead, the requirement could impart a concern for limiting federal power so as to preserve the reserved powers of the states or individual liberties, which justifies a more rigorous scrutiny of the basis for federal legislation. This notion is reinforced by the language of *McCulloch* concerning not only the "letter" of the Constitution, but also its "spirit."

It remains to be seen whether the Court will adopt such an interpretation of the Necessary and Proper Clause. To this point, the prohibited means component of the *McCulloch* test has been used narrowly to preclude direct encroachments on state sovereignty through laws that apply to the states themselves, either commandeering them to implement federal policies or creating remedies against them. Nonetheless, to the extent that the Court may wish to engage in more rigorous scrutiny under the Necessary and Proper Clause, the notion of "proper" laws and the spirit of the Constitution may provide a vehicle for so doing. This question, like so many others concerning the *McCulloch* test, remains unresolved.

Necessary and Proper Laws and the Federal Legislative Power

As the foregoing analysis demonstrates, the construction of the Necessary and Proper Clause in relation to the enumerated powers is beset by a variety of uncertainties. To a large extent, these uncertainties reflect the fundamental tension between two core principles of federalism. On the one hand, under the plenary power principle, the Framers intended that Congress would possess the full measure of legislative power with respect to each of the enumerated powers—the same kind of legislative power that state legislatures or Parliament possessed with respect to matters within their spheres of authority. On the other hand, under the reserved power principle, the Framers intended and expected that, by virtue of the enumeration of powers, federal legislative authority would be limited and states would retain a sphere of their own sovereign legislative authority.

These dual principles reflect certain functional considerations arising from the nature of federalism as a pragmatic response to the problems of collective action. The plenary power principle reflects the fundamental goal of the Constitution to "form a more perfect Union," that is, to facilitate more effectively collective action among the states (or among the peoples of the states) in those matters for which collective action would most likely produce a common benefit. True to this goal, *McCulloch* construed the power to enact necessary and proper laws broadly, rejecting any construction that would so limit Congress as to prevent it from acting effectively on behalf of the collective when exercising its enumerated powers. The reserved powers principle reflects, among other things, the recognition that centralized decisionmaking for a large collective poses a potential threat to individual members of the collective, who may be bound by collective decisions that adversely affect them. The preservation of states enhances both the "voice" of individuals in collective decisions and the possibility of "exit" to other states whose policies are more in line with the individual's preferences.

Ultimately, however, these two principles may be impossible to reconcile.[129] The power to make legislative decisions on behalf of the collective—to determine the ends of collective action and the means of achieving them—knows few intrinsic limits. Given the breadth of the enumerated powers—interstate commerce, fiscal and monetary matters (under the taxing and spending powers as well as the power to provide a common currency), foreign relations and military matters, and several others as well—there is simply no activity whose regulation cannot be justified in theory as a means appropriate to some end within the scope of those powers. Thus, if the federal legislative power is the same kind of legislative power possessed by other sovereigns, its limitation to enumerated ends will not effectively reserve any area of collective decisionmaking exclusively to the states. For all practical purposes, that was the state of the doctrine from the New Deal until the emergence of the "new federalism" in the 1990s. The new federalism has begun to impose some limits on federal legislative power, but it leaves both the extent and the source of those limits unclear. If, in light of the recent addition of Chief Justice Roberts and Justice Alito, the Court moves to a more comprehensive restriction of federal legislative authority, giving force to the reserved power principle, it will have to reconcile those restrictions with the plenary power principle.

To this point, however, such a reconciliation has eluded the Court. Instead, the results in the cases tend to depend on which of the two principles the Court emphasizes. When the Court emphasizes the plenary power principle and asks whether the law is necessary and proper to an enumerated power, the law is upheld even if it regulates some activities that would seem to fall within the reserved power of the states. When the Court has invalidated laws as beyond the scope of federal legislative power, it has begun with the postulate that some activity is protected from federal regulation, because it is within the reserved sphere of state sovereignty, and reasoned that the activity is therefore beyond the scope of federal legislative authority notwithstanding powerful arguments about how regulating the activity would further an end within an enumerated power. The cases therefore suggest that limits on the federal legislative power do not derive from any coherent conception of the power to enact necessary and proper laws to implement the enumerated powers, but rather from the treatment of state powers and state sovereignty as external limits on that power, in much the same way that individual rights operate as external restrictions on legislative action that would otherwise be within the scope of legislative powers.

It remains to be seen what direction the new federalism will ultimately take. It could remain a relatively sporadic intervention based on particular laws that strike a majority of Justices as infringing on especially important components of reserved state autonomy. Or the Court might seek to articulate a more comprehensive formulation. One possibility, suggested by Justice Thomas, would be to formally adopt a form of more rigorous ends-means scrutiny under the *McCulloch* test. More rigorous scrutiny would shrink the sphere of legislative authority that attaches to each enumerated power, but to truly preserve state authority, scrutiny might have to be quite rigorous indeed. It would also mean sacrificing the plenary power principle by treating federal legislative power as less plenary than the legislative power of states, insofar as the baseline test for the exercise of state legislative power is generally the rational basis test. The Court might avoid this apparent contradiction by elevating the baseline level of scrutiny for all legislative action, including state legislation under the police powers.[130] Ironically, however, this result would actually reduce rather than enhance state autonomy, to the extent it would interpose the federal courts as a significant constraint on state legislative authority.[131] Notwithstanding the presence of some judicial and scholarly support for elevating scrutiny of ends and means, at the present time the Court does not appear likely to do so.

A related avenue that might be pursued in this regard is the adoption of a "subsidiarity" principle[132] under which federal legislation is primarily justified when there is a reason to believe that the states cannot adequately address an issue.[133] Certainly such a principle appears to be reflected in the Constitution's enumeration of federal powers, which as previously discussed largely fall into those categories for which collective action problems are most likely to prevent desirable national action in the absence of federal power. There is, however, little textual or historical support for the importation of such a principle as a judicially enforceable limit on the application of particular enumerated powers, even if it might be consistent with the general design of federalism or desirable as a matter of legislative policy. Ultimately, like the express adoption of elevated scrutiny, the adoption of a subsidiarity principle to limit federal legislative power seems unlikely to garner the support of a majority of Justices.

A more limited alternative would be to elevate the level of scrutiny for those federal laws that entrench upon traditional areas of state authority. Under this approach, reserved state power would operate as an extrinsic limit on federal legislative authority, but (as under a subsidiarity approach) it would not be an absolute bar. Instead, legislation regulating activity in areas generally reserved to the states would have to be justified by a more substantial linkage to an enumerated federal power. In my view, this approach best captures the actual results of the cases invalidating federal legislation, both during the pre–New Deal period and since the resurgence of federalism-based restrictions on federal power. Nonetheless, the Court has been unwilling to acknowledge elevated scrutiny based on interference with reserved state powers. Were it to do so, the Court would also have to develop some means of determining which areas of traditional state power are of sufficient importance to trigger heightened scrutiny, and it would have to articulate the appropriate level of scrutiny.

In the final analysis, the Court's Necessary and Proper Clause jurisprudence raises more questions than it answers. We know that the legislative power is the power to enact necessary and proper laws and that the power to enact necessary and proper laws includes the power to select ends that are within the scope of the enumerated powers and the appropriate means to achieve them, provided those means are not prohibited. We also know, or at least can predict with some confidence, that the Court will continue to struggle to reconcile two central premises of federalism—the plenary power principle and the reserved power principle. In the end, the scope of federal legislative power will continue to depend on which of these two principles the Court accords priority in any given case.

LEGISLATIVE DELEGATION

Legislative delegation is a second major issue that goes to the core of the federal legislative power. Within the overall structure of separation of powers, the exercise of the legislative power necessarily entails the delegation of authority to executive officials and to courts, because the legislative power to make laws does not include the executive power to implement them or the judicial power to apply them to resolve cases and controversies. At the same time, however, because the federal legislative power is vested in Congress, the legislative power itself cannot be delegated to anyone else. In other words, the problem of legislative delegation requires the Court to define the legislative power in a manner that permits it to distinguish between proper and improper delegations. Thus, like the problem of necessary and proper laws, the problem of legislative delegation draws on an underlying conception of the legislative power. While the analysis of necessary and proper laws has been dominated by issues of federalism, the analysis of legislative delegation addresses the legislative power purely from a separation of powers perspective. Nonetheless, the Court's underlying conception of the federal legislative power in the two areas is remarkably congruent.

Delegation and Separation of Powers

Under the separation of powers, three types of governmental authority are allocated among three distinct branches of government, each designed to reflect the nature of the power it exercises. The legislative power to make laws is vested in Congress, which is representative in character and deliberative in operation and structure. The executive power to implement and enforce the laws is vested in the President, elected by a national constituency, who sits at the apex of a unitary executive branch, which facilitates prompt coordinated action.[134] The judicial power to interpret and apply the laws to resolve disputes is vested in the judiciary, staffed by judges whose independence is ensured by life tenure and salary protections. This basic structure has both political and legal dimensions that bear on the delegation of legislative authority.

The political dimension of separation of powers is the embodiment of Madison's basic idea—articulated in the Federalist No. 10—that the diffusion of governmental authority serves as a check against the problem of faction by making it more difficult for any one group to control the entire government. This diffusion operates "vertically" through the division of power between the federal government and the states and "horizontally" through the separation of powers.[135]

Separation of powers, coupled with certain "checks and balances," creates a kind of dynamic tension in which the natural tendencies of each branch to expand its own authority checks, and in turn is checked by, the corresponding tendencies of the other two branches. In collective action terms, the diffusion of power constrains the ability of any majority within the collective to impose its will on the minority, thus protecting the individual interests of dissenting members of the collective. It therefore acts as a structural counterweight to constitutional provisions facilitating collective action.

The legal dimension of separation of powers is perhaps less well known, but certainly of equal importance. Separation of powers is essential to the operation of the rule of law, by which I mean a constitutional order in which government actors derive their authority from, and are constrained by, law. The separation of legislative and executive power is essential to the rule of law because without it the same government actors can simultaneously make and enforce the law, rendering meaningless the requirements that government action be undertaken pursuant to valid legal authority and constrained by legal standards.[136] By separating legislative from executive action, it becomes necessary for the legislature to act by means of laws and thus possible to ascertain and enforce legal constraints on executive officers. The exercise of the judicial power by Article III courts reinforces the rule of law by providing an independent mechanism to ensure compliance with the law.[137]

Legislative delegations are an inherent consequence of the separation of powers precisely because the Congress only has the power to make the laws. While most people obey most laws most of the time, the use of the legislative power to make laws is not ordinarily sufficient, standing alone, to ensure compliance. The legislature must enlist the executive and judicial branches as the means of effectuating its legislative ends.[138] Moreover, because language is ambiguous and because it is impossible to anticipate the virtually limitless issues that may arise under a statute, Congress cannot legislate with sufficient specificity to remove all discretion from the application of the laws. Thus, legislation necessarily carries with it a degree of delegated power and discretion, which is exercised by the executive in the enforcement and administration of the law and by the judiciary in the interpretation and application of the law.[139] The interaction of the legislative, executive, and judicial powers may take a variety of forms, and the selection among them rests with Congress in the first instance.[140]

Delegations to the executive are particularly varied in form. At the core of the executive power is the power to investigate and prosecute violations of the law, with the criminal law serving as a paradigm example. But Congress may also delegate to the executive branch powers that more closely resemble the legislative or judicial power. Thus, for example, in the implementation of many regulatory programs, administrative agencies exercise authority to promulgate subsidiary rules and regulations that look like statutes and have legally binding effect. Likewise, agencies often conduct adjudicatory hearings in which they find facts and interpret and apply the law to resolve disputes, which closely parallels the functions of the courts. With the rise of the administrative state, the proliferation and powers of administrative agencies have strained both the political and legal dimensions of the separation of powers.

Delegations to the judiciary are perhaps less varied, but no less important. The principal function of courts is to resolve cases and controversies arising under the law, and the delegation to the judiciary of authority to resolve such disputes follows nearly automatically from the adoption of legislation. This delegation of judicial authority includes not only the resolution of criminal prosecutions and private causes of action, but also review of the actions of executive branch officials to ensure compliance with the law.[141] Because no statute is without ambiguity and because the power to find facts ultimately is the power to determine the outcome, jurisdiction to resolve cases and controversies by its very nature includes significant policymaking power and discretion. Nonetheless, the resolution of cases and controversies is so clearly within the judicial power contemplated by Article III that the statutory delegation of authority to the judiciary often goes unremarked. By way of contrast, the delegation to the judiciary of the power to make binding subsidiary rules concerning the adjudication of cases within its jurisdiction is more problematic, because such rulemaking does not resolve a particular case or controversy. The Court has nonetheless upheld the delegation of rulemaking authority to the judiciary, when it relates to the internal workings of the courts themselves.[142]

Delegation is necessary under separation of powers principles, but separation of powers also implies that Congress may not delegate the legislative power itself to either the executive or the judiciary, or to anyone else for that matter. This principle arguably follows from the Vesting Clause insofar as Congress, having been vested with the legislative power, may not assign that power to anyone else.[143] It is also an inescapable inference from the constitutional structure of separation of powers, because the delegation of legislative power would circumvent the political and structural constraints under which Congress operates and combine the legislative power with the other powers of government.[144] The difficulty, of course, lies in distinguishing between the necessary and proper delegation of executive and judicial power and the impermissible delegation of the legislative power itself.

Clinton v. City of New York (1998), the line item veto case, is an excellent illustration. Under the Line Item Veto Act, the President was authorized to "cancel" specific items of appropriation or "limited tax benefits" upon making specified findings. Cancellation would prevent the affected provision "from having legal force or effect." The Court concluded that, in both legal and practical effect, the statute delegated to the President the power to amend statutes by repealing some of their provisions. Such an amendatory power departed from the prescribed procedure of Article I and was therefore unconstitutional. Although the Court's analysis focused on the violation of constitutional procedures, its reasoning rests on the critical premise that the power to amend by partial repeal is legislative in character and therefore cannot be delegated to the President.[145] Thus, for example, the Court emphasized the amendatory character of the power delegated by the Line Item Veto Act to reject analogies to cases upholding delegated authority and to the traditional presidential discretion to decline to spend appropriated funds.

The question whether Congress has impermissibly delegated the legislative power itself arises most frequently under the so-called nondelegation doctrine, which applies when parties challenge the delegation of discretionary authority to the President, administrative agencies, the judiciary, or other entities. The Court has recognized that the delegation of discretion is inevitable and that it would be impractical and undesirable to require Congress to spell out every detail in a statutory scheme. At the same time, at some point, the delegation of discretion becomes so broad and open-ended that it is the delegation of the legislative power itself. Thus, the critical issue under the nondelegation doctrine is how to distinguish permissible delegations of executive and judicial authority from the impermissible delegation of the legislative power. The Court currently makes this determination using the "intelligible principle test," whose application is informed by various additional considerations.

The Intelligible Principle Test

The controlling test for a violation of the nondelegation doctrine is the intelligible principle test, which was articulated in J.W. Hampton, Jr. & Co. v. U.S. (1928). The test requires that legislation must contain a statutory standard (the "intelligible principle") governing the exercise of delegated authority. As discussed in Part I, before Hampton, the Court had upheld delegations using two rationales. First, in some cases, typically concerning foreign relations or trade, the Court had upheld statutes whose provisions would be effective only upon a presidential finding that a given contingency had arisen.[146] Although such statutes thus delegated to the President discretion to decide when and whether legislation would take effect, they did not violate the nondelegation doctrine because Congress had decided what the policy was and what contingency would trigger it. Second, in other cases, the Court had upheld the delegation of discretionary authority on the theory that the executive was merely "filling in the details" of the statutory scheme.[147] In Hampton, the Court upheld the statute at issue, which authorized the President to raise tariff rates above statutory levels when necessary to equalize differential costs of production. After a fairly extensive review of precedent, including both kinds of cases, the Court summarized the doctrine by stating that "if Congress shall lay down by legislative act an intelligible principle to which the person or body authorized to fix such rates is directed to conform, such legislative action is not a forbidden delegation of legislative power."

Since Hampton, the Court has consistently applied the intelligible principle test regardless of the form of the delegation. The test is generally understood to require that legislative delegations incorporate a standard to guide and control agency discretion. The role of this requirement was described by (then) Justice Rehnquist in his influential Benzene concurring opinion:

As formulated and enforced by this Court, the nondelegation doctrine serves three important functions. First, and most abstractly, it ensures to the extent consistent with orderly governmental administration that important choices of social policy are made by Congress, the branch of our Government most responsive to the popular will. . . . Second, the doctrine guarantees that, to the extent Congress finds it necessary to delegate authority, it provides the recipient of that authority with an "intelligible principle" to guide the exercise of the delegated discretion. . . . Third, and derivative of the second, the doctrine ensures that courts charged with reviewing the exercise of delegated legislative discretion will be able to test that exercise against ascertainable standards.[148]

This explanation of the nondelegation doctrine reflects an underlying conception of the legislative power as the power to make critical choices of policy through the adoption of legal standards. In collective action terms, these policy choices establish the course of collective action for the nation, expressed in the form of laws establishing the "ends" of public policy and the "means" to achieve them. The intelligible principle or standard is the "end" that must be determined by the legislature, and the delegation of authority to act pursuant to that standard is the means for achieving it.

The leading case finding a violation of the intelligible principle test is A.L.A. Schechter Poultry Co. v. United States (1935), which invalidated provisions of the National Industrial Recovery Act authorizing industry groups to adopt codes of "fair competition," subject to approval by the President.[149] None of the statutory provisions suggested as standards provided the requisite intelligible principle.[150] First, the statutory concept of fair competition was too open-ended and could encompass any rule an industry group might choose, in part because it was not connected to the common law concept of unfair competition, which had a judicially defined content. Second, the statute required that the codes must further legislative purposes expressly set forth in its text, but these purposes were so broad and varied that they left to the industry groups and the President discretion to adopt whatever codes they deemed desirable for the benefit of a given industry. Finally, the President could only approve a code if the industry group proposing it was representative and if the codes were not designed to promote monopolies or oppress small businesses, but the former requirement related only to the status of individual groups and the latter did not significantly constrain the range of policy choices available to industry groups and the President.

Although it predates the Court's "New Deal switch," *Schechter Poultry* remains the paradigm example of improper delegation,[151] and the Court has never repudiated or overruled it. Instead, subsequent cases have consistently cited *Schechter Poultry* as good law, but just as consistently distinguished it, finding in challenged legislation sufficient standards to satisfy the intelligible principle test. Some of these cases involved relatively broad standards resembling the fair competition standard found insufficient in *Schechter Poultry*. In National Broadcasting Co. v. United States (1943), for example, the Court upheld the delegation of power to the FCC to issue licenses to and regulate radio stations under a "public interest, convenience and necessity" standard.[152] Likewise, in Yakus v. United States (1944), the Court upheld the delegation of authority to fix maximum prices that were "fair and equitable" in response to wartime inflation or the threat of wartime inflation.[153] Thus, notwithstanding *Schechter Poultry*, a very general standard is sufficient to satisfy the intelligible principle test and it is not necessary for Congress to provide a "determinate criterion" for the exercise of administrative discretion.[154]

In view of precedent sustaining such standards, it is hardly surprising that more recent nondelegation cases have had little difficulty in concluding that statutes satisfy the intelligible principle test. This situation was summarized aptly in Whitman v. American Trucking Associations (2001), the Court's most recent decision rejecting a nondelegation challenge:

> In the history of the Court we have found the requisite "intelligible principle" lacking in only two statutes, one of which provided literally no guidance for the exercise of discretion, and the other of which conferred authority to regulate the entire economy on the basis of no more precise a standard than stimulating the economy by assuring "fair competition." [citing Panama Refining Co. v. Ryan (1935) and *Schechter Poultry* (1935)] We have, on the other hand, upheld the validity of § 11(b)(2) of the Public Utility Holding Company Act of 1935 . . . which gave the Securities and Exchange Commission authority to modify the structure of holding company systems so as to ensure that they are not "unduly or unnecessarily complicate[d]" and do not "unfairly or inequitably distribute voting power among security holders." [citing American Power & Light Co. v. Securities and Exchange Commission (1946)] We have approved the wartime conferral of agency power to fix the prices of commodities at a level that "'will be generally fair and equitable and will effectuate the [in some respects conflicting] purposes of th[e] Act.'" [citing *Yakus* (1944)] And we have found an "intelligible principle" in various statutes authorizing regulation in the "public interest." [citing *National Broadcasting Co.* (1943) and New York Central Securities Corp. v. United States (1932)] In short, we have "almost never felt qualified to second-guess Congress regarding the permissible degree of policy judgment that can be left to those executing or applying the law." [quoting Justice Scalia's dissent in Mistretta v. United States (1989)]

Thus, while some scholars have advocated a reinvigoration of the nondelegation doctrine[155] and the Court continues to insist that Congress may not delegate the legislative power,[156] Congress has little difficulty providing sufficient standards to satisfy the intelligible principle test.[157]

Although the Court has not invalidated statutes under the nondelegation doctrine since *Schechter Poultry*, the doctrine has had a significant influence on the construction of some challenged statutes. The search for standards often requires that the courts look beyond the text of the statute. Thus, in many cases, the Court has relied on the purposes of a statute to impart meaning to its standards[158] or read standards narrowly in light of the history and regulatory context of the legislation.[159] Of course, there is nothing extraordinary about reading a statute in light of its purposes, history, and context, even if some members of the Court would adhere to a strict textual approach. Nonetheless, the nondelegation doctrine reinforces and encourages this approach as a means of ensuring that there are sufficient statutory standards to satisfy the intelligible principle test.

In some cases, moreover, the nondelegation doctrine has been invoked to justify particularly tortured interpretations under the "constitutional avoidance" canon of statutory construction, which states that ambiguous statutes should be construed to avoid constitutional questions. While this rule of construction has its limits,[160] in conjunction with the intelligible principle test, it virtually invites courts to construe ambiguous statutes narrowly to provide a sufficient standard. Two particularly striking examples of reliance on the nondelegation doctrine to support a narrowing construction are National Cable Television Association, Inc. v. United States (1974) and Industrial Union Dept., AFL-CIO v. American Petroleum Institute (*Benzene*) (1980).

In *National Cable Television Association*, the Court upheld a statute authorizing agencies to impose fees for services pursuant to a standard requiring fees "to be fair and equitable taking into consideration direct and indirect cost to the Government, value to the recipient, public policy or interest served, and other pertinent facts."[161] Observing that "the hurdles revealed in [*Hampton* and *Schechter Poultry*] lead us to read the Act narrowly to avoid constitutional problems," the court held that "[t]he phrase 'value to the recipient' [was] the measure of the authorized fee." A companion case, Federal Power Comm'n v. New England Power Co. (1974), relied on this narrowing construction to reject the assessment of industry-wide fees based on the general economic benefits of a regulatory regime. These results are very difficult to square with the statutory text, which lists value to the recipient as only one of several relevant considerations. One complicating factor in both *National Cable Television Association* and *New England Power Co.* was the question whether such fees constituted a "tax," and there are some suggestions in both opinions that Congress's ability to delegate the power to tax is more constrained than other powers. As will be discussed below, however, the Court has since expressly rejected any such suggestion.[162]

In the *Benzene* decision, a plurality of the Court relied in part on the nondelegation doctrine to support a creative interpretation of the Occupational Safety and Health Act's provisions concerning exposure to toxic chemicals in the workplace. Under the Act, the Occupational Safety and Health Administration (OSHA) is authorized to promulgate worker health and safety standards imposing requirements "reasonably necessary or appropriate to provide safe or healthful employment and places of employment." In promulgating toxic chemical standards, moreover, OSHA was directed to set "the standard which most adequately assures, to the extent feasible, on the basis of the best available evidence, that no employee will suffer material impairment of health or functional capacity even if such employee has regular exposure to the hazard dealt with by such standard for the period of his working life." The plurality concluded that these provisions required OSHA to find, as a prerequisite to adopting a standard, that exposure at prohibited levels poses a "significant risk" to worker health and safety.

This requirement is nearly impossible to derive from the language quoted above, even supported by the plurality's somewhat strained legislative history arguments.[163] Thus, the plurality also relied on the nondelegation doctrine and the canon of constitutional avoidance:

If the Government was correct in arguing that neither § 3(8) [defining standards] nor § 6(b)(5) [concerning toxic chemicals] requires that the risk from a toxic substance be quantified sufficiently to enable the Secretary to characterize it as significant in an understandable way, the statute would make such a "sweeping delegation of legislative power" that it might be unconstitutional under the Court's reasoning in [*Schechter Poultry*] and [*Panama Refining Co.*]. A construction of the statute that avoids this kind of open-ended grant should certainly be favored.

One curious feature of the plurality's reliance on the nondelegation doctrine was its description of the reason why a contrary construction might violate the doctrine. Rather than focusing on whether the statute would lack a sufficient standard to satisfy the intelligible principle test, the plurality expressed concern that without a significant risk requirement, the statute "would give OSHA the power to impose enormous costs that might produce little, if any, discernible benefits." This concern seems more a matter of the substantive rationality of regulation than of excessive delegation.[164]

Although a judicial narrowing construction may save a statute that would otherwise lack sufficient standards, an administrative narrowing construction cannot. There was considerable support for administrative narrowing to avoid nondelegation problems, including a leading commentator[165] and some lower court decisions, such as an influential opinion authored by Judge Harold Leventhal[166] and the lower court decision in *American Trucking*.[167] The Supreme Court, however, squarely rejected this suggestion in *American Trucking*:

The idea that an agency can cure an unconstitutionally standardless delegation of power by declining to exercise some of that power seems to us internally contradictory. The very choice of which portion of the power to exercise—that is to say, the prescription of the standard that Congress had omitted—would itself be an exercise of the forbidden legislative authority. Whether the statute delegates legislative power is a question for the courts, and an agency's voluntary self-denial has no bearing upon the answer.

Put differently, while an agency's self-created standards might constrain its discretion and provide a basis for judicial review—thus satisfying the rule of law component of the nondelegation doctrine—it fails to satisfy the political component of the nondelegation doctrine, because it is the agency that is determining the ends of public policy by choosing the standard.

The real significance of the nondelegation doctrine lies not so much in its application to invalidate or construe narrowly otherwise excessive legislative delegations, but rather in its expression of the basic structure of separation of powers. Even open-ended standards reflecting such broad goals as controlling inflation by price controls, allocating broadcasting licenses to further the interests of listeners, or providing a safe workplace represent critical policy choices by the legislature.

The legislature can be held politically accountable for those choices.[168] Likewise, even a broad standard guides and constrains an agency's policy discretion and provides a basis for judicial review. As explained by the Court in American Power & Light Co. v. Securities and Exchange Commission (1946):

> Necessity therefore fixes a point beyond which it is unreasonable and impracticable to compel Congress to prescribe detailed rules; it then becomes constitutionally sufficient if Congress clearly delineates the general policy, the public agency which is to apply it, and the boundaries of this delegated authority. Private rights are protected by access to the courts to test the application of the policy in the light of these legislative declarations.

In the final analysis, the nondelegation doctrine remains good law. Exercise of the legislative power must and routinely does include standards limiting delegated discretion, even if those standards are often quite broad. The courts reinforce the requirement by identifying and construing statutory standards and by the possibility of invalidating statutes in extreme cases.

Factors Affecting the Intelligible Principle Test

As reflected in the foregoing discussion, the intelligible principle test, which requires that statutes contain a meaningful standard to guide and control delegated authority, is the generally applicable test for the nondelegation doctrine. The application of this test, however, may be affected by various factors, whose presence or absence may alter the specificity of the standard necessary to satisfy it. At various points over the history of the doctrine, the Court has suggested that a wide variety of factors may affect the specificity of required standards, including the scope of the delegated authority, the recipient of the delegated authority, the particular legislative power delegated, the procedures that apply to the exercise of delegated authority, and the individual interests affected by the delegated authority. As a result of the most recent doctrinal developments, some of these factors have taken on increased importance, while others have been rejected or receded into the background. Overall, both the theoretical relevance and practical significance of these other factors are far less clear than the basics of the intelligible principle test.

As a result of Whitman v. American Trucking Associations (2001), it now appears that more specific standards are required to constrain broader delegations. Although this idea may have been implicit from prior cases, it had never been expressly incorporated into the application of the intelligible principle test. Nonetheless, the Court in *American Trucking* stated matter-of-factly that "[i]t is true enough that the degree of agency discretion that is acceptable varies according to the scope of the power congressionally conferred."[169] Notwithstanding its intuitive appeal, this principle is difficult to tease out of the Court's prior decisions. The Court in *American Trucking* cited two decisions, Loving v. United States (1996) and United States v. Mazurie (1975), both of which address a different aspect of the nondelegation doctrine and neither of which discuss the scope of delegated authority.[170] In the absence of express authority, one might draw support from the general pattern of decisions,[171] but the results cannot easily be reconciled in those terms. Only two cases invalidate statutes as lacking standards, and they involved similar statutory standards applied to delegations of widely differing scope. *Schechter Poultry* certainly involved the delegation of very broad authority and the breadth of this authority arguably affected the Court's decision, but *Panama Refining* invalidated a much narrower grant under substantially similar standards.[172] The *Benzene* plurality's reference to OSHA's "power" to impose enormous costs without producing much benefit might reflect this principle, but it is by no means explicit.[173]

Whether or not this reasoning in *American Trucking* breaks new ground, it is the most explicit statement by the Court of the interaction between the scope of authority and the specificity of standards under the intelligible principle test. Assuming the principle is followed in other cases, it establishes an inverse relationship between the scope of delegated authority and the breadth of standards. The broader the delegated authority, the more specific the standards governing it must be. Conversely, the narrower the authority, the more open-ended the standards governing it may be. This relationship certainly makes intuitive sense, but it remains to be seen whether its adoption will have any practical impact in terms of invalidating or narrowing broad legislative delegations subject to open-ended standards.

A recent decision that may be instructive is Gonzales v. Oregon (2006), in which the Court held that the Controlled Substances Act did not authorize the attorney general to prohibit doctors from prescribing drugs for purposes of physician-assisted suicide, which had been recently authorized under an Oregon statute. The attorney general was asserting broad authority to regulate the practice of medicine, which under the reasoning of *American Trucking* would require a more specific statutory standard. Gonzales v. Oregon therefore presented an opportunity for the Court to rely on the nondelegation doctrine to support its construction of the statute (as the plurality did in *Benzene*). But the Court in Gonzales v. Oregon made no mention of the nondelegation doctrine at all, suggesting that the doctrine has little remaining force as a limit on delegated power. On the other hand, the statutory interpretation issue may have been sufficiently clear that such an argument would have been superfluous.

A second consideration that affects the specificity of standards necessary to satisfy the intelligible principle test is the recipient of the delegated power. Possible recipients include the other branches of government, some subunit of Congress itself, other political entities (including states, municipalities, and Indian tribes), or private actors. The character of the recipient might justify a relaxation of standards when the recipient of delegated authority is another governmental body that possesses independent authority in the field. Conversely, delegations to private parties pose particular problems that may warrant more careful scrutiny under the nondelegation doctrine.

The most well-known example of recipient-based relaxation of the intelligible principle test is United States v. Curtiss-Wright (1936), which upheld the delegation to the President of authority to block international arms shipments upon a determination that they would aggravate a regional conflict. The Court was willing to assume without deciding that, if it had concerned domestic matters, the delegation would be unconstitutional under the then-recent decision in *Schechter Poultry;* it reasoned, however, that broader delegations to the President were permissible in the foreign relations context. As the Court explained,

[W]e are here dealing not alone with an authority vested in the President by an exertion of legislative power, but with such an authority plus the very delicate, plenary and exclusive power of the President as the sole organ of the federal government in the field of international relations—a power which does not require as a basis for its exercise an act of Congress. . . .[174]

More recently, in Loving v. United States (1996), the Court used similar reasoning to uphold the delegation to the President of the power to determine aggravating factors in capital court-martial cases. Referring to the President's constitutional authority as commander-in-chief, the Court stated simply that "the same limitations on delegation do not apply 'where the entity exercising the delegated authority itself possesses independent authority over the subject matter. . . .' "[175]

Although the President's constitutional powers are the most prominent example of reliance on independent authority to justify broader delegations, this kind of reasoning has also arisen in other contexts. In United States. v. Mazurie (1975), for example, the Supreme Court upheld a delegation to Indian Tribes based on this rationale. Citing *Curtiss-Wright* for the general proposition that broader delegations are permissible when the recipient has independent authority, the Court emphasized that "Indian tribes are unique aggregations possessing attributes of sovereignty over both their members and their territory . . . ; they are 'a separate people' possessing 'the power of regulating their internal and social relations'. . . ." In addition, many state supreme courts have upheld legislative delegations to local governments (which have legislative power under home rule provisions of their constitutions) that might otherwise have violated the nondelegation doctrine.[176]

By analogy to these cases, one might argue that federal statutes delegating broad authority to the states would be constitutionally permissible because the states exercise independent legislative authority.[177] The Court, however, has consistently maintained that Congress may not delegate legislative power to the states, even as it has upheld statutes having precisely that effect. In Cooley v. Board of Wardens (1852), for example, the Court announced broadly that if the power to regulate commerce is exclusive, "Congress cannot re-grant, or in any manner reconvey" that power to the states, but the Court nonetheless upheld a federal statute incorporating by reference the piloting laws of the states, including laws adopted after its passage. In subsequent cases, the Court has upheld statutes with similar effect. In Wilkerson v. Rahrer (1891), the Court upheld federal legislation subjecting alcoholic beverages to state police power legislation that would otherwise violate the Commerce Clause. The Court in *Rahrer* insisted that Congress could not "transfer legislative powers to a state," but concluded that the law in question simply removed a barrier to the exercise of the state's police powers and rejected any analogy to state legislation delegating authority to local government units.

These cases involved the particular problem of congressional authorization of state laws that would otherwise violate the "dormant" Commerce Clause, and therefore presented distinctive issues. In United States v. Sharpnack (1958), how-ever, the Court applied similar reasoning in a different context. *Sharpnack* upheld a federal statute incorporating state and local criminal laws, making them binding in federal enclaves. Although the statute incorporated future state and local laws, thereby effectively permitting the state and local governments to legislate criminal offenses on federal enclaves, the Court insisted that this was not an impermissible delegation of authority to the state and local governments: "Rather than being a delegation by Congress of its legislative authority to the States, it is a deliberate continuing adoption by Congress for federal enclaves of such unpre-empted offenses and punishments as shall have been already put in effect by the respective States for their own government." In all these cases, the effect of the federal statute was to afford states standardless discretion with respect to certain local regulations that would otherwise be preempted by federal authority. Perhaps the best way to understand them would be to recognize that, in some areas where the federal and state legislative powers overlap, Congress may delegate authority to states.

The foregoing discussion deals with the *relaxation* of the intelligible principle test, but the test is apparently applied *more strictly* when the delegation is to pri-vate persons or entities. Such delegations present especially serious problems because of the potential conflicts of interest involved and the private recipient's lack of political accountability. Thus, for example, *Schechter Poultry* emphasized the fact that responsibility for the development of industry codes rested on private industry groups, and another New Deal era case, Carter v. Carter Coal Co. (1936), characterized delegations to private persons as "delegation in its most obnoxious form." Subsequent cases often distinguished *Schechter Poultry* partly on that ground.[178] While these Supreme Court precedents indicate that delegations to pri-vate individuals are suspect under the federal Constitution, most of the case law on this issue is found in state courts, because this type of delegation is more common at the state level.[179] These state cases suggest that some kinds of private delega-tions, such as those making a regulation contingent on the approval of a majority of those affected and certain kinds of occupational licensing, are permissible.[180]

Special issues also arise when Congress delegates authority to its own officials or to some subunits of the legislature.[181] As suggested by *Chadha*, the problem in such cases is not that Congress cannot exercise the legislative power, but that when it exercises the legislative power it must generally follow the bicameralism and presentment requirements of Article I. Conversely, the improper delegation of legislative authority in *Chadha* could not have been cured by providing standards—although the absence of standards is, in my view, the best explanation of why the legislative veto in that case was to be regarded as a legislative act.

Statutory standards governing the exercise of the veto would have converted it into an executive (or perhaps judicial) act, but these powers cannot be vested in Congress.[182] Subunits and officials of Congress, however, can and do exercise significant deliberative powers that will be discussed separately later in this book.

Another potentially significant factor affecting the application of the intelligible principle test is the particular type of power delegated. Some of the earliest discussions of the nondelegation doctrine suggest that delegation of minor powers is permissible but that delegation of unspecified major powers is precluded.[183] Nonetheless, under current doctrine, it would appear that such arguments are foreclosed. The idea of nondelegable powers has been most directly addressed in regard to the power to tax, where the principle of "no taxation without representation" gives it an additional appeal.[184] The Court's reasoning in National Cable Television Association, Inc. v. United States (1974) might be read to imply that the power to tax is nondelegable insofar as the Court distinguished between taxes and fees and imposed a narrowing construction on the statute that limited the agency to imposing fees for actual services provided.[185] In Skinner v. Mid-America Pipeline Co. (1989), however, the Court explicitly rejected this understanding of *National Cable Television Association*, stating flatly that it found "no support" for the contention that "the text of the Constitution or the practices of Congress require the application of a different and stricter nondelegation doctrine in cases where Congress delegates discretionary authority to the Executive under its taxing power."[186]

While *Skinner* squarely forecloses an argument for stricter standards for the taxing power, similar arguments could conceivably succeed with respect to other powers. For example, one might plausibly argue that there are stricter limits on delegating the power to declare war.[187] It is clear that the Framers were particularly concerned with limiting the power to declare war and consciously vested it in Congress to ensure that such action would not be taken lightly. It also seems that the power to *declare* war cannot easily be divided into a legislative component making the policy and an executive component implementing that policy. Declaration is an "on/off" switch; the executive power, once war is declared, is the power to conduct the war as commander-in-chief. Against these arguments, however, it could be argued that the more relaxed standard suggested by *Curtiss-Wright* should apply, because the power delegated concerns an area in which the President has substantial independent constitutional authority.[188]

In relation to the war power, it would be important to distinguish between the delegation of authority to the President to go to war against a particular country upon specified findings (the contingency model) and the delegation of an ongoing and general power to declare war when the President determines it to be desirable under standards specified by Congress. In the former example, for which there may be some historical precedent, Congress has at least made the policy decision that war against a specified enemy is justified if certain contingencies are true. In the latter example, for which there are no historical examples, Congress has left the selection of the enemy and the specific circumstances that warrant war to the

President. Also, under *American Trucking*, this kind of authority is particularly broad and therefore would arguably require a stricter standard. The recent action of Congress delegating authority to President Bush to initiate military operations in Iraq under specified conditions, were it to come before the courts in a justiciable form, would of course provide an excellent test case for the delegation of the power to declare war.[189] Given the history of constitutional litigation to test the validity of armed conflict during the Vietnam War, however, it seems that this issue, while fascinating in theory, is unlikely ever to be resolved in practice.[190]

Overall, treating some legislative powers as more important than others, and therefore as less delegable, is inherently problematic. Pursuing this line of analysis would require the courts to determine which legislative powers are "major powers" and why. It may be intuitive to say that the taxing power or the war power is more important than, say, the power to create post roads (for delivery of mail), but there is little in either the text or the history of the Constitution to justify such a distinction or to provide guidance as to which powers are less delegable than others. In view of these difficulties, which were noted by the Court in *Skinner*, it seems unlikely that the Court will move toward recognizing the particular power delegated as a significant consideration for the application of the nondelegation doctrine.

Two final considerations suggested by *Schechter Poultry* also may affect the degree of specificity in the standards required by the nondelegation doctrine. The first of these is agency procedures or, more precisely, the lack thereof. The absence of procedures governing the formulation of the industry codes authorized in *Schechter Poultry* was noted by the Court,[191] which distinguished the FTC on the grounds that it was subject to procedural safeguards but that "[i]n providing for codes, the National Industrial Recovery Act dispenses with this administrative procedure and with any administrative procedure of an analogous character." Conversely, the Court relied on the incorporation of procedural safeguards to distinguish *Schechter Poultry* in subsequent cases.[192] While the precise relevance of procedures to the intelligible principle test is not entirely clear, procedural safeguards are an essential rule of law safeguard, because they provide a check against error and abuse in the application of the law and they generate a record on the basis of which the courts can review an agency's compliance with statutory standards.[193] In an intuitive sense, it seems self-evident that discretionary administrative action under a given standard is more constrained when it is subject to procedural safeguards than when it is not.

Nonetheless, if a statute truly lacks an intelligible principle, it is hard to see how procedures could save it.[194] In particular, procedural safeguards do not address the underlying political dimension of the nondelegation doctrine. If Congress has not made the basic policy decision, procedural constraints on an agency's basic policy decision do not solve the problem. Perhaps this is why few recent cases rely on procedures in their application of the nondelegation doctrine. Indeed, the reasoning in *American Trucking*, which rejected the notion that an agency's own narrowing construction could save a statute that would otherwise

violate the nondelegation doctrine, arguably forecloses reliance on agency procedures to sustain an otherwise unconstitutional delegation.

Like the lack of procedural safeguards, the fact that violation of industry codes
was made a crime figured into the Court's reasoning in *Schechter Poultry* and in
subsequent cases distinguishing it.[195] Insofar as this reasoning suggests that the
power to define crimes is quintessentially legislative and cannot be delegated,[196] it
appears to be incompatible with the reasoning in *Skinner*. An alternative rationale, however, would be that it is the imposition of a greater burden on individual
liberties that justifies requiring a more specific standard. This rationale could
draw support from such cases as Hampton v. Mow Sun Wong (1976) and Kent v.
Dulles (1958), which narrowly construed statutory delegations of authority to
preserve individual liberties.[197]

The Court acknowledged this issue without resolving it in Touby v. United
States (1991). The statute in *Touby* was the Controlled Substances Act, which
authorized the attorney general to make possession of a drug a federal crime by
placing it on a "schedule" of controlled substances based on a determination that
the drug was an "imminent hazard to the public safety." The defendants in the
case, who challenged the statute as an improper delegation, argued that "something more than an intelligible principle" was required because "regulations of
this sort pose a heightened risk to individual liberty." Acknowledging that "[o]ur
cases are not entirely clear as to whether more specific guidance is in fact
required," the Court found it unnecessary to clarify the issue because the statute
"passe[d] muster even if greater congressional specificity is required in the criminal context." In Gonzales v. Oregon, another case involving the Controlled
Substances Act, the Court did not even mention the nondelegation doctrine in
holding that the Act did not grant the attorney general authority to proscribe the
use of drugs for physician-assisted suicide, thereby making the prescription of
drugs for that purpose a criminal violation of the Act. The significance of this
omission is difficult to assess, but it may suggest a continued reluctance to
address the criminal sanctions issue. Thus, it remains to be seen whether criminal
sanctions or other burdens on individual rights will be incorporated into the application of the intelligible principle test.

In sum, then, the intelligible principle test and its requirement of standards is
the generally applicable test in nondelegation cases, but the specificity of the
required standard may be affected by a variety of considerations. First, the greater
the scope of the power, the more specific the standards must be to satisfy the test.
Second, when the recipient of the delegated authority has independent power in
the field, lesser standards may satisfy the intelligible principle test, but delegation
to private parties may be precluded or require greater specificity. Third, greater
standards may be required when Congress delegates authority to make conduct a
crime or in other areas in which personal liberties are at stake. Conversely, the
Court appears to have firmly rejected the idea that more open-ended standards
will satisfy the intelligible principle test if the agency itself narrows them, and
(for similar reasons) the continued relevance of procedural safeguards is in doubt.

The Nondelegation Doctrine and the Federal Legislative Power

The nondelegation doctrine and its intelligible principle test not only are important constitutional doctrines in their own right, but also shed light on the federal legislative power in a more fundamental sense. As we have seen, the interpretation and application of the Necessary and Proper Clause reflect a basic understanding of the federal legislative power as the power to identify the ends of governmental (collective) action within the fields of the enumerated powers and to choose the means of achieving those ends. The nondelegation doctrine resonates with and amplifies this basic understanding. The elucidation of necessary and proper legislation has been dominated by federalism concerns surrounding the principle of enumerated power; that is, the "federal" component of the federal legislative power. The nondelegation doctrine, by way of contrast, presents few federalism concerns and focuses on the separation of powers component of the federal legislative power.

Under separation of powers, the legislative power includes the power, through the enactment of laws, to specify the ends and means of public policy, but it does not include the executive power to administer and enforce those laws or the judicial power to resolve cases arising under them. In collective action terms, the vesting of legislative power in Congress reflects the antecedent collective agreement to rely on a representative institution and deliberative process to reach agreement on further collective action within specified areas. While this structure reduces the transaction costs that would otherwise prevent agreement, it also creates—from the perspective of individual members of the collective—agency costs; the interests of Congress are not perfectly aligned with the interests of the members of the collective as a whole (the "people"). The Constitution imposes two principal kinds of constraints to reduce these agency costs: political accountability and the rule of law. Separation of powers and the nondelegation doctrine are integral to both types of constraints.

Because it exercises the power to determine the ends and means of collective action, the Framers designed Congress as the most politically accountable branch of the federal government. The nondelegation doctrine reflects the commonsense conclusion that the legislative power must be exercised by Congress itself for political accountability to function effectively. In collective action terms, delegation by Congress of the legislative power increases agency costs by creating two levels of the principal-agency relationship, one between the members of the collective and Congress and one between Congress and the administrative agency or other body receiving the delegated authority. Thus, two-level principal-agency relationships increase the likelihood that the ultimate decisionmaker's incentives will diverge from the interests of the people.

This problem is compounded by the fact that the two-level principal-agency relationship dilutes the effectiveness of political controls on Congress. Political accountability is an imperfect means of policing agency costs, because legislators infrequently stand for election and, when they do, the legislators' electors must simultaneously cast judgment, with imperfect information, over a number of legislative actions taken by their representatives during the preceding term of office. For particularly controversial issues, legislators have especially strong incentives to delegate decisionmaking responsibility to avoid even this imperfect accountability. It is small wonder, then, that (notwithstanding the acceptance of broad standards) the Court continues to insist that Congress must make the initial policy decision—reflected in the form of statutory standards—when it delegates authority.

Nonetheless, under separation of powers and the rule of law, our basic understanding of the legislative power as the power to determine ends and means implies that the legislature must delegate authority. Once the legislature makes an initial decision concerning the ends and means of collective action, it must rely on the executive and judicial branches of government to implement its enactments. In other words, separation of powers necessarily entails the use of the executive and judicial branches of government and specifically contemplates a particular kind of two-level principal-agency relationship. Conceptually, separation of powers relies on the agency costs that arise between the legislature and the executive or judicial branches as a mechanism for reducing the agency costs that arise between the people and the legislature. Because these branches are independent of Congress, it cannot directly control them. While the executive and judicial branches are less politically accountable than the legislature, however, they are bound by legislative enactments and thus accountable to the rule of law. Indeed, the separation of powers makes it possible for the legislature itself to be bound by the rule of law.

At the core of these arrangements lies the requirement that legislation must contain standards. Standards embody the legislature's choice of the ends and means of collective action. Thus, requiring standards reinforces the political accountability of the legislature. Equally important, statutory standards establish the rule of law foundations on which further executive and judicial action is based. This analysis suggests that the legislative power to choose the ends and means of collective action is exercised by adopting statutory standards to which both the members of the collective and the collective's own institutions are bound. The legislative power over the means of public policy encompasses the delegation of executive and judicial power to implement these statutory standards. The authority so delegated must be exercised in conformity with those standards. While this basic model accounts for the exercise of federal legislative power and the delegation of authority, a final aspect of the federal legislative power—the deliberative legislative powers—confound the model and require further assessment.

DELIBERATIVE POWERS

The deliberative powers of Congress, including the powers to conduct investigations and hold hearings, to subpoena witnesses and documents, and to sanction individuals for contempt, raise a distinctive set of issues. As we have seen, both the Necessary and Proper Clause and the nondelegation doctrine reflect a core understanding of the federal legislative power; it is the power to determine the ends of public policy and the means of achieving them through the enactment of necessary and proper laws. Deliberative legislative powers do not fit easily within this core understanding because their exercise by Congress is not limited to the enactment of laws. Thus, while the deliberative powers are defensible as a matter of institutional necessity, they may be implemented by means other than enactment of necessary and proper laws subject to the usual requirements of bicameralism and presentment. Likewise, deliberative powers encompass actions that are executive and judicial in form and thus seem to violate the usual separation of powers principles constraining Congress. These features of the deliberative powers create theoretical and practical difficulties that are well-illustrated by the recent high-profile case of Terry Schiavo.[198]

Ms. Schiavo was in a persistent vegetative state for a number of years. Her husband, citing Ms. Schiavo's expressed wishes, sought to terminate life-sustaining treatment over the objections of her parents. When the Florida courts ruled in favor of Ms. Schiavo's husband and approved termination of treatment, the case became a political football. Eventually, Ms. Schiavo's parents turned to Congress for assistance and the House Committee on Government Reform scheduled a hearing, which was to be held at the hospice where Ms. Schiavo was located. The committee issued subpoenas to Mr. Schiavo, the attending physicians and the hospice director, and Ms. Schiavo herself requiring them to appear at the hearing and bring "all medical and other equipment that provides nutrition and hydration to Theresa Schiavo—in its current and continuing state of operations."[199] The general counsel to the House of Representatives then filed an emergency petition with the Florida Supreme Court seeking an order directing the lower court to modify or stay its order directing the termination of treatment. The petition asserted that the issuance of the subpoenas was within the authority of Congress to conduct investigations and that compliance with the lower court's order to terminate treatment would prevent compliance with the subpoenas, placing the parties subject to the subpoenas in violation of the criminal law and in contempt of Congress. The Florida Supreme Court dismissed the petition for lack of jurisdiction and because it was moot.[200]

The issues raised by the investigation and subpoenas never came to a head,[201] but it is clear that the purpose of the subpoenas was to effect a change in the legal rights and duties of private parties outside of Congress by requiring treatment to continue at least until the hearing was complete. This effect would have been accomplished through the action of a House Committee without bicameralism and presentment (or even the approval of either chamber as a whole) and would have involved the committee's performance of functions normally performed by the executive and judicial branches. Likewise, there were few, if any, procedural or other safeguards to protect the rights of the affected parties. The point here is not to fully analyze the Schiavo case, but rather that it raises, in dramatic fashion, some fundamental questions concerning the deliberative powers. What is the source of Congress's authority to take such an action? What kind of connection would such an action have to the exercise of the legislative power to enact laws? What are the limits of this kind of deliberative power? The answers to these and related questions will be addressed in this section.

Deliberative Powers and the Deliberative Process

The deliberative powers reflect the institutional need of Congress to provide for its own deliberations. As a legislative body with the power to enact laws, Congress must employ some process through which it considers and acts on matters within its authority. Key steps in this process include gathering and assessing information relevant to policy issues, debating the merits of proposed action, negotiating and compromising among legislators, and fine-tuning statutory language. Article I, section 5, of the Constitution authorizes the House and Senate to choose their respective officers (except that the Vice President is constitutionally designated as the presiding officer in the Senate), to be the sole judge of their members' elections and qualifications, and to determine the rules for their proceedings, punish members for disorderly conduct, and expel members. These provisions offer few specifics about the deliberative process, instead leaving its development primarily to Congress. As the role and power of the federal government expanded, the deliberative process of Congress has evolved and its associated institutional apparatus has grown substantially. The details of the deliberative process in Congress need not be canvassed here, but certain key features should be highlighted.

First, each chamber has a complex set of parliamentary rules that govern its proceedings. Although there are common features to both sets of procedures, there are also important differences. In the House of Representatives, for example, there are no standing rules governing the debate of particular bills, so that each bill must be considered under its own, specifically approved, rule. In the Senate, by way of contrast, the standing rules provide for unlimited debate on any measure, which can only be terminated by a two-thirds vote, which is the source of the "filibuster."[202] The arcane rules governing deliberations provide opportunities for strategic maneuvering in enacting or blocking legislation and those with sophisticated understanding of the rules have an advantage in the deliberative process. More generally, the internal rules of deliberation have a significant effect on what legislation will eventually be adopted.[203] As is common in parliamentary bodies, moreover, disputes concerning rules and their application commonly arise, and the authority to resolve these disputes is a significant source of power for legislative leaders.

Second, there are in each chamber a number of standing and special committees (each of which may have multiple subcommittees) in which most of the important work on legislative proposals is done most of the time. Committees conduct investigations and hold hearings on proposed legislation or oversee agencies and the administrative implementation of legislation that has been enacted. Most legislation must be worked by a committee, which will consider amendments, "mark up" the bill by carefully reviewing its language, and ultimately have a great deal of control over whether particular bills are ever considered by the chamber as a whole. There are important practical advantages of this committee system. Most immediately, it permits each chamber to make progress on multiple legislative proposals simultaneously in different committees. Equally important, because committees specialize in particular fields and tend to be composed of legislators with a particular interest in the area, committees develop expertise on certain legislative subjects. At the same time, however, committees have become power centers in which powerful members may block legislation, a great deal of behind-the-scenes lobbying may take place, and the deliberative process may be distorted.

Third, each House has substantial authority regarding the recognition and discipline of its own members, much of which is explicit. This authority begins with the power to determine the elections and qualifications of its members, that is, to decide whether a member has been properly elected.[204] Each House may punish its members for "disorderly [b]ehavior" and, if two-thirds of the members agree, expel a member. The power to expel a member is particularly significant insofar as it permits Congress to override the results of an election, potentially frustrating the wishes of the state or district which the member serves.[205] Both Houses have been called on to exercise their certification and disciplinary authority with some frequency.[206]

Finally, as the volume of legislative and other congressional activity has increased, so has the surrounding bureaucracy. First, the legislature has a substantial support staff, including some who work for individual legislators and others who work for committees. Second, there are a number of legislative agencies, such as the General Accounting Office and the Library of Congress, that perform important functions that assist the deliberative process. Third, to assist with the preservation of order within the House and Senate, each has a sergeant-at-arms, who acts as the chief law enforcement officer for his or her respective chamber and serves additional practical and ceremonial functions. As we shall see, the sergeant-at-arms (or his or her agents) fulfills the executive function in implementing many of the deliberative powers of Congress.

As the foregoing discussion suggests, for the most part, the deliberative powers concern the internal institutional operations of Congress. To the extent that they do so, their exercise is relatively uncontroversial and either expressly authorized by Article I or inherent in a legislative body as a matter of institutional necessity. But, as the Schiavo case suggests, the deliberative powers can be used to affect parties and activities beyond the confines of Congress. First, to support deliberation concerning proposed legislation or other matters within its authority, Congress (or congressional committees) may conduct investigations and, in aid of those investigations, compel the testimony of witnesses and the production of documents. It may also find people who fail to appear and testify or who fail to provide documents in contempt of Congress and have them imprisoned without the benefit of a statute, an executive prosecution, or judicial trial. Second, and independently of the deliberation of any particular matter, Congress may use the contempt power as a means of institutional self-protection, to remove obstructions to its deliberations, prevent and deter bribery, and otherwise prevent interference with its deliberations.

These deliberative powers, moreover, may be exercised either by means of statute, which appears to be the modern practice,[207] or by means of independent action by either house or even by a committee of either house.

Statutory provisions concerning the deliberative powers arguably fall within the scope of the Necessary and Proper Clause. Certainly, gathering information about a given problem is an appropriate step in making policy concerning it, and hearings aided by compulsory process is a reasonable way for a legislative body to gather information. Likewise, the contempt power is arguably necessary to preserve the institutional integrity of Congress and thereby enable it to make policy that furthers the public interest. Unlike other applications of the Necessary and Proper Clause, however, statutes implementing such deliberative powers are not related to a particular exercise of a particular enumerated power (or powers). Instead, they are general statutes facilitating congressional exercise of the enumerated powers generally. It is unclear why this distinction should matter and the distinction has made little difference to the Court.[208] Nonetheless, because the Necessary and Proper Clause only authorizes Congress to enact legislation, the Clause cannot provide a sufficient constitutional basis for the exercise of deliberative powers by committees or either chamber standing alone.[209]

As discussed in Part I, the lack of a solid textual foundation did not prevent early Congresses from asserting deliberative powers by means other than legislation or early Supreme Court decisions from approving such assertions. Proponents of the deliberative powers relied on historical analogy to the practices of other legislative bodies, including Parliament and state legislatures. Unlike these other legislative bodies, however, Congress is a legislature of enumerated powers, which draws into question the assertion of deliberative powers that are not expressly granted. And while there was a tradition of separation of powers in England on which the Framers drew, Congress is subject to a written constitution with separation of powers provisions that would appear to limit its deliberative powers in ways that Parliament's powers were not.[210] These differences were not lost on early opponents of deliberative legislative powers. To the extent that historical analogies for deliberative federal powers ultimately carried the day, they suggest that Congress was meant to possess the powers ordinarily exercised by legislative bodies, even if the subject areas in which those powers could be exercised were limited.

Nonetheless, historical analogy remains an incomplete explanation for ascribing to Congress deliberative powers that cannot be found in the text of the Constitution and that appear to conflict with the basic structure of separation of powers. Ultimately, the justification for deliberative powers that carried the day was institutional necessity. With respect to investigations and the powers that grow out of them, Congress's responsibility for making policy requires that it have accurate information on which to base those policies. Thus, the "power to secure needed information by such means has long been treated as an attribute of the power to legislate."[211] Likewise, the contempt power was seen as essential to the institutional integrity of Congress to remove obstructions to its deliberative processes. As explained by Justice Joseph Story in his Commentaries on the Constitution:

The main object is to secure a purity, independence, and ability of the legislature adequate to the discharge of all their duties. If they can be overawed by force, or corrupted by largesses, or interrupted in their proceedings by violence, without the means of self protection, it is obvious, that they will soon be found incapable of legislating with wisdom or independence.[212]

The critical question is why it is necessary or appropriate to depart from the usual separation of powers model in the exercise of these powers.

As noted previously, Congress can and does exercise the deliberative powers by means of legislation that is implemented and applied by the executive and the judiciary.[213] For example, many statutes contain directives to executive or judicial institutions to gather information and report to Congress. Likewise, dissatisfied with the effectiveness of contempt sanctions in compelling testimony or documents under some circumstances, Congress adopted a statute in 1857 that makes it a crime to refuse to testify, produce documents, or answer pertinent questions before a duly authorized congressional investigation.[214] The federal bribery statute, moreover, also applies to bribes involving members of Congress.[215] Nonetheless, it has been clear since Anderson v. Dunn (1821) that Congress may exercise its deliberative powers without enacting a statute, by action of either the House or the Senate alone and, in some instances, by the action of a committee of either chamber. Indeed, the Court has explicitly rejected the suggestion that the enactment of statutes divests Congress or either house of the authority to sanction contumacious behavior, stating broadly that "congress could not divest [sic] itself, or either of its houses, of the essential and inherent power to punish for contempt, in cases to which the power of either house properly extended. . . ."[216]

Deliberative Powers in Collective Action Perspective

As with other aspects of the federal legislative power, the collective action perspective offers important insights into the deliberative powers. From that perspective, the essential character of the legislative power is that it permits a representative body to act by majority vote to determine the ends and means of public policy, thus avoiding the insurmountable transaction costs that would otherwise prevent collective action. For individual members of the collective, however, this delegation of authority creates agency costs that may lead to errors and abuse. Both the requirement of bicameralism and presentment and the structure of separation of powers respond to this agency cost problem. Bicameralism and presentment make it more difficult to reach decisions by requiring institutions representing different constituencies to concur in the decision. Separation of powers requires the executive and judiciary to participate in the enforcement and application of legislation, consciously incorporating agency costs (from the perspective of Congress) to provide a further check on errors and abuse. Thus, to the extent that the deliberative powers can be exercised without bicameralism and presentment or separation of powers, the transaction costs of congressional action are substantially reduced. Similarly, to the extent that deliberative powers can be exercised without the involvement of the executive or the judiciary, agency costs (from the perspective of Congress) associated with executive and judicial implementation of the exercise of deliberative powers are avoided. The question then becomes whether the institutional interests of Congress cited in support of the deliberative powers justify these exceptions from structural requirements that the Framers built in to the Constitution.

These departures from structural requirements are relatively easy to defend insofar as the deliberative powers are exercised to gather the information on which to base legislative action, which would encompass the deliberative powers to conduct investigations, to compel testimony and production of documents, and to enforce related orders through contempt. Having as complete and accurate information as possible on which to base legislative policy judgment is of critical importance. As the Court recognized in McGrain v. Daugherty (1927), "[a] legislative body cannot legislate wisely or effectively in the absence of information respecting the conditions which the legislation is intended to effect or change." In a larger sense, control of the information that flows to Congress carries with it the ability to profoundly influence the direction of congressional policy judgments. The transaction costs associated with requiring Congress to follow bicameralism and presentment every time it needs information or seeks to compel testimony and documents at hearings would bring legislative deliberations to a standstill. Conversely, a general statutory framework for information gathering—one that incorporated executive and judicial action—would make Congress dependent on the other branches for information, arguably compromising its core legislative functions. This possibility is particularly problematic when, as is often the case, the legislative and executive (or judicial) branches are controlled by opposing parties.

In this respect, there is a critical difference between requiring the involvement of the executive and judiciary in the enforcement and application of laws already enacted and requiring a similar involvement at the information-gathering stage. The executive and judicial role in implementing statutes gives these branches some ability to frustrate congressional policies and to affect interstitial policy within the realm of delegated discretion, but not to control or direct the antecedent policy choice that determines the course of collective action, which is the function reserved to Congress. Insofar as the ability to control information effectively includes the ability to determine the direction of decisions based on that information, congressional dependence on executive and/or judicial actors for information arguably affords the other branches too much power to control the antecedent policy choices that belong to Congress. Of course, for reasons of expertise and efficiency, Congress will often enlist the aid of the other branches, especially the executive branch, in gathering and analyzing information. The important point is that there may be situations and circumstances in which the need for Congress to get its own information—unfiltered by the interests of the other branches—is paramount.[217] Put differently, the information-gathering aspects of deliberative powers go to the core legislative function of determining the ends and means of collective action.

Conversely, notwithstanding the potential effect on the rights and duties of parties outside Congress, deliberative powers present at most a minor threat to the basic structure of separation of powers because they cannot be used to effectuate broad policy choices concerning collective action without the enactment of legislation that complies with bicameralism and presentment. Investigations and surrounding orders may of course have an influence on public opinion or agency action, but this effect is much more limited than the enactment of laws. It is likewise true that particular individuals may be dramatically affected, even imprisoned, pursuant to the deliberative powers. But as we shall see this impact is constrained to some degree through judicially enforceable limits, including both intrinsic limits growing out of the deliberative powers themselves and external limits arising from constitutional rights such as due process. In view of the importance of information to the fundamental legislative responsibilities of Congress, this limited ability to affect outside parties without bicameralism and presentment and without enlisting the aid of the executive and judiciary is arguably justified.

Outside of these information-gathering functions, the exercise of the deliberative contempt power to address other obstructions or threats to legislative deliberations, such as physical obstructions, bribery, and libel, is much more difficult to justify. As explained by Justice Story, above, the institutional justification for these exercises of the deliberative powers relates to the independence and integrity of the decisional process itself. Such uses of the contempt power present a form of institutional self-defense, and in that sense serve a similar function to legislative immunities. The critical question is whether the need to respond to such obstructions justifies permitting Congress to act by means other than statutes and without the ordinary participation of the executive and the judiciary. At most, such action is justified to remove an immediate threat to the deliberative process under a kind of necessity rationale similar to that which applies in the context of individual self defense.

The most obvious case for use of legislative contempt as a form of institutional self-defense comes in dealing with physical obstructions to legislative deliberations. Several instances in which contempt sanctions were issued for assaults on members of Congress or its officers or other forms of physical obstructions are cited approvingly in Marshall v. Gordon (1917),[218] but the Court has not directly addressed congressional authority to exercise contempt powers to remove physical obstructions.[219] Nonetheless, the Court's decision in Groppi v. Leslie (1972) provides a useful illustration. The petitioner in *Groppi* led a group of protesters who occupied the chamber of the state assembly, and two days later the assembly passed a resolution finding him in contempt and ordering his imprisonment for (the lesser of) six months or the duration of the session.[220] The Court granted his petition for writ of habeas corpus because the lack of notice and opportunity to be heard on the contempt sanction had denied the petitioner due process, but the

Court clearly indicated that the legislature had the power to sanction the conduct in question with contempt. Moreover, the Court recognized that "[t]he potential for disrupting or immobilizing the vital legislative processes of State and Federal Governments that would flow from requiring a full blown legislative 'trial' prior to the imposition of punishment for contempt of the legislature is a factor entitled to very great weight. . . . " At least when dealing with an ongoing physical obstruction or disruption of deliberations, permitting immediate action by the house or committee adversely affected is defensible.

The connection between the contempt power and the integrity of the deliberative process is also clear when Congress exercises the contempt power to deal with bribery or attempted bribery, although the need to exercise that power without bicameralism and presentment or separation of powers constraints is questionable. Congress is a representative body whose members are politically accountable to their respective constituencies. Political accountability is the means through which the "people," as principal, oversee the actions of Congress acting as the agent of the collective. Bribery compromises that principal-agency relationship; it means that the legislator accepting the bribe is serving a different principal. In this sense, bribery is a fundamental threat to the institutional integrity of Congress which, like distorted information, affects the initial antecedent policy choice concerning the ends and means of collective action.

Nonetheless, the justifications for permitting a departure from the usual process of enacting legislation to be enforced and applied by the executive and judiciary seem less persuasive here than in the context of information gathering or removing immediate obstructions. Bribery is an unlikely vehicle for executive or judicial branch efforts to influence legislative policy. Thus, dependence on the other branches to enforce statutory provisions against bribery or obstruction of Congress presents fewer risks to the decisional processes of Congress than informational dependency. Indeed, by the end of the nineteenth century, Congress had adopted a bribery statute that has become, for all practical purposes, the exclusive means of punishing bribery of Congress. The use of direct contempt sanctions to punish bribery or attempted bribery is all but unheard of today.[221] Departure from the separation of powers framework is also particularly problematic insofar as contempt sanctions for bribery duplicate criminal prosecutions, but they do so without the structural or procedural safeguards that accompany them.[222]

It is unclear what other obstructions or threats to the integrity and independence of Congress might provide a constitutionally sufficient basis for the exercise of the contempt power. One possibility, suggested by Marshall v. Gordon (1917), is libel, which in extreme cases might be said to undermine or threaten the integrity and independence of congressional deliberations. As will be discussed more fully below, *Marshall* concluded that a district attorney's published letter sharply criticizing a congressional investigation was an insufficient basis for the House of Representatives to find its author in contempt and order him imprisoned, but the Court did not totally foreclose the possibility of libel as the basis of contempt.

Allowing Congress to sanction for contempt on the basis of libel, however, would be highly problematic. Libelous attacks damage the reputation of Congress or its members, thus lowering public confidence in the process, but any impact on any particular policy decision of Congress is speculative at best.[223] Perhaps fear of such attacks would affect some members' decisions, causing them to avoid controversial positions, but it is hard to see that this risk is so great as to justify a departure from bicameralism and presentment or separation of powers, especially in light of the very real threat that Congress might abuse this power. Historical experience has certainly taught us that those in power in government tend to view any criticism as libelous and may abuse their power to punish their most vocal critics. That, in significant respects, is why freedom of speech and press is enshrined in the First Amendment and why the prosecution of seditious libel is widely thought to violate those rights.[224] Given the threat to these First Amendment values, the removal of structural and procedural restraints on congressional action to punish its critics is at the very least problematic. It is hardly surprising, therefore, that the Court was skeptical of such claims in *Marshall*.

In sum, the deliberative legislative powers of Congress are constitutionally defensible as inherent powers implied by institutional necessity. Nonetheless, these powers remain anomalous, particularly insofar as they may be exercised directly by either the House or Senate standing alone or even by a committee of either chamber, which circumvents bicameralism and presentment and separation of powers. Perhaps in response to these difficulties and as suggested by the foregoing discussion, the Supreme Court has imposed significant constitutional limits on the exercise of the deliberative powers. Some of these limits are intrinsic, in the sense that they grow out of the Court's understanding of the source and character of the deliberative powers themselves. In addition, extrinsic constitutional restrictions, such as due process and the First Amendment also limit the exercise of the deliberative powers. Judicial involvement in these cases, however, is complicated by constitutional provisions concerning legislative immunity, which affect the procedural context of judicial review as well as its scope. The following sections analyze these issues in greater detail.

Intrinsic Limits on Deliberative Powers

While the Supreme Court has recognized deliberative legislative powers that derive from the institutional necessities of Congress, the very nature of and rationale for deliberative powers carry with them intrinsic limitations. Like the Necessary and Proper Clause, these powers do not exist as independent sources of authority but rather by virtue of their relationship to particular institutional demands, and this relationship must be established to sustain their exercise. To the extent that the exercise of deliberative powers does not follow bicameralism and presentment and compromises the usual separation of powers framework, the Court has, in some cases at least, been far less deferential to congressional judgments concerning the exercise of deliberative powers than it has been in applying the *McCulloch* test for the Necessary and Proper Clause. First, the Court has at times required a particularly strong showing of institutional necessity to justify the exercise of the deliberative powers. Second, the deliberative powers, particularly the contempt power, are limited to the "least possible power" needed to satisfy the demands of institutional necessity.

The required showing of institutional necessity has been addressed most frequently in the context of congressional investigations, subpoenas, and related contempt actions. Beginning with Kilbourn v. Thompson (1880), the Court has consistently held that investigations must bear some relationship to legislative action within the scope of congressional authority and that Congress lacks the authority to conduct investigations for their own sake or solely to expose conduct. In *Kilbourn*, the plaintiff brought a false imprisonment action claiming that the House of Representatives lacked the authority to order his imprisonment for refusing to answer questions or produce documents as required by subpoenas issued pursuant to a committee investigation.[225] The Court began its analysis by reviewing the basis of the contempt power and concluding that Congress had "the right to compel attendance of witnesses, and their answer to proper questions, in the same manner and by the use of the same means that courts of justice can in like cases." But, the Court continued, this power was limited:

Whether the power of punishment in either House by fine or imprisonment goes beyond this or not, we are sure that no person can be punished for contumacy as a witness before either House, unless his testimony is required in a matter into which that House has jurisdiction to inquire, and we feel equally sure that neither of these bodies possesses the general power of making inquiry into the private affairs of the citizen.[226]

The investigation in *Kilbourn*, which related to a controversial bankruptcy settlement involving a real estate pool in which the United States was a creditor, "assumed a power which could only be properly exercised by another branch of the government, because it was in its nature clearly judicial." In particular, there was no suggestion of any final legislative action by Congress as a result of the investigation, which therefore appeared to be a "fruitless investigation into the personal affairs of individuals."

The *Kilbourn* requirement does not mean, however, that investigations must be linked to specific legislative proposals; it is sufficient that the investigation be related to a subject on which Congress might legislate. In McGrain v. Daugherty (1927), for example, the Court rejected a habeas petition challenging the petitioner's incarceration pursuant to a "process of attachment" issued by the Senate. The investigation concerned the conduct of litigation under the Sherman Act by the then attorney general of the United States, who had been accused of mishandling or failing to prosecute antitrust violations. The witness in question was the brother of the attorney general, who refused to testify and, following his incarceration, challenged the authority of the Senate to conduct the investigation. After addressing various preliminary arguments, the Court engaged in an extensive review of the historical and judicial precedents for the deliberative powers of Congress, which it interpreted as establishing two basic principles:

[T]he two houses of Congress, in their separate relations, possess, not only such powers as are expressly granted to them by the Constitution, but such auxiliary powers as are necessary and appropriate to make the express powers effective; and the other, that neither house is invested with 'general' power to inquire into private affairs and compel disclosures, but only with such limited power of inquiry as is shown to exist when the rule of constitutional interpretation just stated is rightly applied.

The Court then concluded that the subpoena to the witness "was to obtain information in aid of the legislative function," reasoning that the subject was one "on which legislation could be had" and that "the subject-matter is such that the presumption should be indulged that this was the real object."

A related point is that committees or subcommittees may exercise authority to compel testimony or production of documents only pursuant to a valid delegation by the respective houses, and this delegation in turn limits the authority of the committee or subcommittee. Thus, for example, in Gojack v. United States (1966), the Supreme Court reversed a conviction under a statutory provision making it a crime to refuse to testify or provide documents to a congressional investigation,[227] because the particular subcommittee investigation pursuant to which the witness had been called was never approved by the entire committee, as required by the committee rules.[228] Likewise, a properly authorized committee investigation must be alleged in the indictment.[229] Indeed, even when the underlying investigation is proper, a conviction under the statute cannot be sustained unless the questions or documents at issue are shown to be pertinent to the investigation.[230] In some cases, moreover, the Court has narrowly construed the scope of an authorized investigation to avoid constitutional difficulties or held that the authority to investigate was so vague as to deny due process.[231]

These requirements have both constitutional and statutory dimensions. In many cases,[232] the Court has treated a refusal to answer a question that is relevant to a valid investigation as an essential element of a statutory offense, because the statute refers to being summoned under the "authority of either House" and refusing to answer "any question pertinent to the question under inquiry."[233] As the Court observed in Deutsch v. United States (1961), however, there is a constitutional dimension as well. This interest relates to the right of a witness to know that his or her conduct is prohibited, which implies that "the pertinency of the interrogation to the topic under the congressional committee's inquiry must be brought home to the witness at the time the questions are put to him."[234] The main difference between these two manifestations of the general requirement is that, to invoke the constitutional ground, a witness must apparently object to the pertinency of the question to a valid investigation at the time of the questioning (thus permitting Congress to "bring home" its pertinency), while no contemporaneous objection must be made to raise the statutory issue.[235]

In general it is relatively easy to establish that investigations pertain to matters within congressional authority,[236] but there is no shortage of cases finding an insufficient basis for contempt sanctions or criminal convictions because questions are insufficiently related to proper investigations. The latter conclusion was particularly common in relation to the "McCarthy Hearings," which will be discussed further below. Investigations and related actions are within the deliberative powers so long as (1) the subject matter relates to a matter on which Congress might take action within its constitutional authority, including matters other than enactment of statutes, such as confirmation of appointments or impeachments; (2) the object of the investigation is not excessively vague or open-ended; and (3) the investigation is properly authorized with sufficient clarity pursuant to the applicable internal rules of Congress. In most instances, these requirements present few obstacles to congressional investigations and subpoenas, or the exercise of the contempt power to enforce them. Applying these rules to the Schiavo case, for example, would seem to support the issuance of subpoenas unless there is some defect in the committee's authorization.

There is far less authority concerning the use of the contempt power for purposes of institutional self-defense in response to physical obstructions, bribery, or libel. Such authority as does exist tends to confirm the power, but it also suggests significant limits. In this regard, it may be important to distinguish between direct action by either house and prosecutions pursuant to statutory provisions.

Congress appears to have the power to punish physical obstructions to its deliberations, even if there is no authority directly on point. In Groppi v. Leslie (1972), the Court addressed a state legislature's imposition of criminal contempt citations in response to the occupation of one of its chambers, confirming the power of the legislature to take this action but ultimately holding that the procedures used violated due process. In the course of its analysis, the Court observed that "[a] legislature, like a court, must, of necessity, possess the power to act 'immediately' and 'instantly' to quell disorders in the chamber if it is to be able to maintain its authority and continue with the proper dispatch of its business." The Court reasoned further that once the emergency has passed, the legislature retains an interest in deterring disruptions that supports "giving notice and bringing the contemnor before the body and giving opportunity to be heard before being declared and sentenced." Although the case dealt with a state legislature, the Court's reasoning did not suggest that it regarded the contempt power of state legislatures to differ from that of Congress.[237]

Likewise, the power of Congress to punish bribes or attempted bribes has been clear since Anderson v. Dunn (1821). Today, bribes and attempted bribes are generally punished by means of the bribery statute,[238] whose constitutionality is well accepted. It also seems reasonably clear that prosecutions under bribery statutes are valid without specific proof that the bribe or attempted bribe would, in fact, undermine the integrity of the deliberative process. Although there are few, if any, modern examples, it appears that Congress retains the power to sanction attempted bribery as contempt,[239] even if the exercise of that power is likely to be constrained by due process and other constitutional rights.

The ability of Congress to use the legislative contempt power to punish for libel, however, is by no means clear and, at a minimum, is sharply constrained. In Marshall v. Gordon (1917), which appears to be the only relevant case to be decided by the Supreme Court, a dispute arose between a congressional committee and the district attorney for the Southern District of New York (a federal official). The district attorney was investigating alleged antitrust violations by a member of the House of Representatives—apparently in relation to labor activities.[240] The member responded (on the House floor) by accusing the district attorney of misconduct and calling for an investigation. When a committee was formed and attempted to take evidence on the antitrust investigation, the district attorney responded by causing a story to be written in a daily newspaper accusing the congressional committee of attempting to penetrate and interfere with the grand jury's investigation of antitrust violations. The committee demanded that the author of the story identify his informant, at which point the district attorney wrote to the committee identifying himself as the source of the story and reiterating his charges against the committee "in amplified form in language which was certainly unparliamentary and manifestly ill-tempered, and which was well calculated to arouse the indignation not only of the members of the committee, but of those of the House generally." The House found the district attorney in contempt based on this letter and ordered him incarcerated.

The Supreme Court held that the lower court should have granted the district attorney's petition for writ of habeas corpus. After an extensive historical review of the contempt power of the House and Senate, the Court concluded that this power was narrowly confined to situations in which it was necessary "to prevent the right to exert the powers given from being obstructed and virtually destroyed."[241] The exercise of the contempt power in this case, however, could not be sustained on that basis. In light of the factual background, the Court reasoned:

[T]here is room only for the conclusion that the contempt was deemed to result from the writing of the letter, not because of any obstruction to the performance of legislative duty resulting from the letter, or because the preservation of the power of the House to carry out its legislative authority was endangered by its writing, but because of the effect and operation which the irritating and ill-tempered statements made in the letter would produce upon the public mind, or because of the sense of indignation which it may be assumed was produced by the letter upon the members of the committee and of the House generally.[242]

This narrow view of the contempt power was necessary to properly balance the legitimate institutional needs of Congress against the countervailing concerns of separation of powers and protection of individual rights. In view of *Marshall*, it is difficult to see how alleged libel of Congress could ever sufficiently obstruct legislative deliberations to justify contempt sanctions.

As the foregoing discussion indicates, one intrinsic requirement for the exercise of the contempt power is that it must be closely linked to the institutional needs of Congress. A related, but distinct limit is that, assuming a valid basis for its exercise, the contempt power encompasses only the "least possible power" necessary to accomplish its end. This limitation was recognized in the first decision upholding the power, Anderson v. Dunn (1821), in which the Court described the power as follows:

The present question is, what is the extent of the punishing power which the deliberative assemblies of the Union may assume and exercise on the principle of self-preservation? Analogy, and the nature of the case, furnish the answer—'the least possible power adequate to the end proposed;' which is the power of imprisonment. . . . And even to the duration of imprisonment a period is imposed by the nature of things, since the existence of the power that imprisons is indispensable to its continuance; and although the legislative power continues perpetual, the legislative body ceases to exist on the moment of its adjournment or periodical dissolution. It follows, that imprisonment must terminate with that adjournment.

This discussion suggests two components of the "least power" concept. The first is that punishment may not go beyond imprisonment, and the second is that imprisonment ends with the end of the legislative session.[243]

The limitation of the contempt power to imprisonment has proven to be of little practical significance. It means that more serious punishments are not permitted, but there has been little indication that Congress has sought more serious punishment. Conversely, this limitation would presumably permit less serious punishments, such as fines or public apologies.[244] In any event, research disclosed no cases for which the form of punishment pursuant to the contempt power was at issue.

The limitation of imprisonment to the duration of the legislative session, however, has proven to be highly significant in practice. Particularly when a contempt occurs near the end of the legislative session, exercise of the power is of limited practical effect or may be precluded altogether if the session ends before any action can be taken. Moreover, unless the contumacious behavior is repeated in the following session, Congress cannot sanction conduct that affected only the previous session. These obstacles to effective punishment prompted Congress to adopt a contempt statute in 1857, which was upheld in In re Chapman (1897). These concerns also presumably contributed to the use of the bribery statute rather than contempt sanctions to address bribery or attempted bribery of members of Congress. Prosecutions under these statutes have, by and large, replaced actions of either house to find parties in contempt.[245] Nonetheless, as noted previously, these statutes do not impair the ability of either house to punish for contempt.[246]

At its most extreme, the "least power" concept implies that Congress may exercise the contempt power only to remove obstacles or direct threats to the deliberative process, which might imply that the contempt power cannot be used for purposes of punishment after the obstacle or threat has been removed. The Supreme Court appeared to say as much in Marshall v. Gordon (1917), in which it observed that "from the very nature of the power it is clear that it does not embrace punishment for contempt as punishment, since it rests only on the right of self-preservation. . . ." In Jurney v. MacCracken (1935), however, the Court qualified this language and permitted punishment after the fact. The petitioner had been found in contempt after he initially claimed privilege and declined to produce papers demanded pursuant to a congressional investigation, permitted some papers to be removed or destroyed by clients, and later (when his claims of privilege were rejected) produced all papers that were within his possession and control. Relying on *Marshall*, he argued that because he had produced all papers that could be produced, there was no longer any obstruction to Congress and he could not be found in contempt "solely qua punishment." The Supreme Court disagreed, citing early examples in which Congress had found parties in contempt for past acts and reading the statements in *Marshall* "in light of the particular facts."

These intrinsic limits follow from the underlying character of deliberative powers and the institutional necessity rationale that supports them. Investigations must be justified as incidental to some legislative action that is within congressional authority, there must be clear and specific authority for committee or subcommittee action, and subpoenas and questions must be pertinent to the matter under inquiry. The traditional practice of direct contempt actions by the House or the Senate appears to have been largely replaced by prosecution pursuant to specific statutes, but the contempt power is retained by both houses. That power clearly extends to compelling compliance with lawful investigatory orders and questions, removing obstructions and disruptions of proceedings, and punishing bribery, but its use to punish libel of the Congress is of doubtful constitutionality. When the contempt power is exercised directly by either house, it is the least possible power necessary to accomplish the purpose involved, which is generally imprisonment for the duration of the contempt or until the close of the legislative session, whichever is first.

External Limitations

In addition to intrinsic limits, various individual rights impose external limits on the exercise of deliberative powers. These individual rights restrictions have become increasingly important as the deliberative power of Congress became well-established and the scope of congressional investigations expanded, particularly during the McCarthy era. As the Supreme Court put it in Watkins v. United States (1957), while "[p]rior cases, like *Kilbourn*, *McGrain*, and *Sinclair*, had defined the scope of investigative power in terms of the inherent limitations of the sources of that power," with the advent of expansive investigations like the McCarthy hearings, "the emphasis shifted to problems of accommodating the interest of the Government with the rights and privileges of individuals." In general terms, the individual rights constraints imposed on the deliberative powers can be grouped into three categories: general due process requirements, particular criminal procedure safeguards, and First Amendment freedoms. The limits imposed by these individual rights safeguards depend to a large extent on whether Congress exercises its contempt power directly or through a prosecution under the contempt statute.

Paradoxically, there are fewer individual rights protections when Congress acts directly than in a statutory prosecution.[247] When contumacious behavior occurs in the presence of a court, the court has traditionally had the authority to punish the contempt on the spot with few procedures, and a similar rule appears to apply to the exercise of the contempt power by either house of Congress.[248] In such cases, the absence of structural constraints is compounded by departures from ordinary rules of fundamental fairness—the sanctioning body acts as a judge in its own cause because it is vindicating its own interest and procedural safeguards are limited. Although basic requirements of notice and opportunity to be heard appear to apply to direct exercises of the contempt power by either House, these protections are a far cry from the full panoply of procedural safeguards that apply to criminal prosecutions. In prosecutions under the contempt statute, however, "the courts must accord to the defendants every right which is guaranteed to defendants in all other criminal cases."[249] Thus, cases arising under the contempt statute present a broader range of individual rights issues and the implications of those cases for direct contempt sanctions by either House remain unclear.

The most basic individual rights limitation on the deliberative powers is due process, which includes various components. First, under *Watkins* and its progeny, due process requires that the individual have adequate notice that his or her conduct is contumacious, an issue that arises most frequently in relation to the refusal to answer questions, which only constitutes contempt if the question is pertinent to a valid congressional investigation.[250] A related point is that due process may effectively require either house and any committee or subcommittee thereof to follow its own rules in conducting an investigation.[251] This requirement concerns the fairness of punishing the underlying conduct rather than the fairness of the means of determining guilt or innocence; unless the power of the committee to ask a question is clear, a witness is not "on notice" that his or her refusal to answer is contumacious behavior.[252] Thus, although the issue has typically arisen in the context of establishing an element of the statutory offense, a similar requirement would arguably apply in direct prosecutions.[253]

Second, under Groppi v. Leslie (1972), some kind of notice and opportunity to be heard is apparently required, except perhaps for the removal of immediate physical obstructions.[254] The case arose as a result of a demonstration staged on the floor of the state assembly to protest proposed cuts in social welfare programs. Two days after the demonstration, the assembly found one of the instigators of the demonstration guilty of criminal contempt, directing his confinement for a period of six months. The defendant, who was in jail at the time, received no notice or opportunity to be heard. This summary procedure, coming as it did after the need for immediate action to remove an ongoing disruption, violated due process. While *Groppi* indicates that some kind of notice and opportunity to be heard is ordinarily required, it clearly recognizes that a "full-blown legislative 'trial' " is not necessary, leaving unclear the content of the process due in legislative contempt proceedings. The Court has had no other recent occasions to address this issue because statutory prosecutions have largely replaced direct congressional actions.

In addition to these general requirements of due process, some particular Bill of Rights safeguards apply. For practical purposes, the most important of these is the Fifth Amendment privilege against self-incrimination, which is often invoked in the context of committee questioning involving potentially illegal conduct. This issue was addressed in a trilogy of cases decided on the same day in 1955.[255] The first of these cases, Quinn v. United States (1955), held that "[i]f an objection to a question is made in any language that a committee may reasonably be expected to understand as an attempt to invoke the privilege, it must be respected both by the committee and by a court in a prosecution. . . ."[256] In one of the companion cases to *Quinn*, the Court held that once the privilege against self-incrimination has been invoked, a waiver of that right cannot be lightly inferred,[257] and in the other, the Court held that abandonment of a claim of privilege over two years after the hearing took place did not excuse the failure of the committee to rule on it at the time the claim was asserted.[258] In all three cases, the government accepted that the privilege against self-incrimination, if properly asserted and maintained, would protect a witness's refusal to answer a question, but it challenged the sufficiency of the assertion or argued that the privilege had been waived. Set against the background of the McCarthy hearings, the Court's opinions reflected concern that invoking the privilege in response to questions about Communist Party affiliations or activities would likely damage a witness's reputation.[259]

The Court's recognition that the privilege against self-incrimination applies in the context of congressional investigations means that a witness properly asserting the privilege is not guilty of contempt for refusing to answer a question, even if it is pertinent to a valid investigation. Although this possibility might obstruct congressional investigations, that obstruction can be overcome by granting immunity pursuant to the "use immunity" statute, which explicitly applies to congressional investigations.[260] If use immunity is granted, the statute specifies that a witness "may not refuse to comply with the order on the basis of his privilege against self-incrimination; but no testimony or other information compelled under the order (or any information directly or indirectly derived from such testimony or information) may be used against the witness in any criminal case, except a prosecution for perjury, giving a false statement, or otherwise failing to comply with the order." The operation of this statute is illustrated by the famous case of Lieutenant Colonel Oliver North, who was brought before a congressional hearing in connection with the so-called "Iran-Contra Arms for Hostages" investigation. When he invoked the Fifth Amendment privilege against self-incrimination, Lieutenant Colonel North was granted immunity and gave dramatic testimony that made him something of a celebrity. He was later prosecuted and convicted for various criminal acts, but these convictions were overturned in large part because they were based on evidence derived directly or indirectly from his testimony.[261]

Various other rights pertaining to criminal prosecutions also apply to contempt actions, at least to some extent. First, in McGrain v. Daugherty (1927), the Court assumed that the requirements of the Fourth Amendment apply to an arrest warrant issued by the Senate upon finding that an intemperate letter was libelous and a contempt of Congress, although it concluded on the facts that the requirements of the Amendment had been met.[262] Second, in Russell v. United States (1962), the Court held that in a prosecution under the contempt statute, which explicitly requires the case to be referred to a grand jury for prosecution, constitutional requirements apply to the resulting indictment. In particular, the indictment must inform the accused, with reasonable certainty, of the nature of the accusation, which means that the indictment must identify the subject matter of the inquiry.[263] Third, although Sinclair v. United States (1929) held that in a statutory prosecution the pertinency of questions to a proper investigation was a question of law to be decided by the court,[264] that decision has been overruled (in a different context) and the right to trial by jury appears to attach.[265] Finally, notwithstanding In re Chapman (1897), which rejected the argument that the possibility of both direct contempt sanctions and criminal prosecution for the same conduct violated the prohibition of double jeopardy, direct contempt sanctions by Congress and prosecution under the statute for the same conduct would probably be unconstitutional.[266]

In addition to procedural rights deriving from due process or specific Bill of Rights provisions, the exercise of the deliberative powers also must respect substantive constitutional rights. Thus, for example, although there is no direct authority on point, Congress presumably could not use its deliberative powers in a manner that would violate equal protection or religious freedoms, such as by targeting racial or religious minorities without a compelling governmental interest. In practice, the only substantive rights that have been addressed by the Supreme Court in the contempt context are First Amendment rights, and once again the most significant cases arise from the McCarthy hearings. Questions concerning activities involving the Communist Party probed a witness's political views, expression, and associations, and thus implicated core political freedoms. As the Court observed in Watkins, "[t]he mere summoning of a witness and compelling him to testify, against his will, about his beliefs, expressions or associations is a measure of governmental interference," especially when "those forced revelations concern matters that are unorthodox, unpopular, or even hateful to the general public." Thus, in declining to answer such questions before congressional committees, witnesses often invoked the First along with the Fifth Amendment.

But as in other areas involving the tension between the anticommunist efforts of the time and the First Amendment, the Court provided, at best, inconsistent protection for these rights in the context of legislative investigations.[267] In United States v. Rumely (1953), the Court narrowly construed, on First Amendment grounds, the resolution authorizing a house committee to investigate lobbying activities. As a result of this narrowing construction, questions concerning the sales of certain books "of a particular political tendentiousness," which were put to the secretary of a political organization, were not pertinent to the authorized inquiry of the house committee, and the conviction of the secretary for refusing to answer them was invalid. Nonetheless, and more directly, in Barenblatt v. United States (1959), the Court held that inquiry into membership in the Communist Party did not violate the First Amendment right of association. Drawing on language in

Watkins, the Court essentially balanced the individual interest in political freedom against the government interest in investigating the Communist Party and its activities, concluding that "the balance between the individual and governmental interest here at stake must be struck in favor of the latter, and that therefore the provisions of the First Amendment have not been offended."[268]

For purposes of this book, the significance of individual rights limits on the deliberative powers lies not so much in the particular rights or the limits they impose, but rather in what they tell us about the deliberative powers in general and their relation to the legislative power. Although deliberative powers escape the usual bicameralism and presentment requirements and do not conform to the normal structure of separation of powers, they do involve the exercise of governmental authority and are subject to the individual rights protections imposed by the Constitution, including basic requirements of due process, some criminal procedure safeguards, and the First Amendment. While the Court has been fairly forceful in requiring criminal prosecutions under the contempt statute to meet basic requirements of procedural fairness, it has been reluctant to limit the authority of duly authorized congressional committees to inquire into matters within the scope of their investigations, even when doing so presents significant constitutional problems. This reluctance reflects a certain deference to the institutional prerogatives of Congress that also is reflected in the procedural context in which limitations on the deliberative powers can be asserted.

Institutional Prerogatives and the Limits of Deliberative Powers

As we have seen, Congress may exercise the deliberative powers directly, without relying on the cooperation of the executive branch to enforce or of the courts to adjudicate. The same institutional necessity that justifies direct congressional enforcement and adjudication also has important implications for the appropriate judicial role in enforcing limits on the deliberative powers. Judicial review of the deliberative powers requires the courts to delve into the deliberative processes of Congress in a way that may intrude into core legislative functions and compromise congressional independence. Various constitutional provisions and doctrines, however, protect Congress from such interference, including justiciability and related doctrines that prevent judicial review of some issues, congressional immunities that prevent or limit certain forms of judicial inquiry into legislative activities, and principles of deference that apply in even those instances in which judicial review is proper. These provisions and doctrines have implications for some cases involving the exercise of the deliberative powers.

To the extent that certain internal matters are reserved to the exclusive authority of the House, the Senate, or Congress as a whole, the exercise of deliberative powers may be nonjusticiable under the political question doctrine. In particular, if an issue is "textually committed" to congressional discretion (or the discretion of either house) or there are no "judicially discoverable and manageable standards" for reviewing its resolution by Congress, the issue presents a nonjusticiable political question.[269] Some constitutional provisions arguably constitute a "textual commitment" of certain decisions to the respective houses of Congress, including the powers to determine the elections, returns, and qualifications of members (Art. I, § 5, cl. 1); to determine the rules of proceedings and discipline members (Art. I, § 5, cl. 2); and the power of impeachment and to try impeachments (Art. I, § 2, cl. 5; and Art. I, § 3, cl. 6). Notwithstanding these provisions and the relative difficulty of judicially discovering and managing standards to govern the legislative process, the political question doctrine appears to have a relatively restrictive application, even as applied to the internal operations of Congress.

Three Supreme Court cases address the applicability of the political question doctrine to the deliberative powers of Congress. In Powell v. McCormack (1969), the Supreme Court invalidated the House of Representatives' refusal to seat Representative Adam Clayton Powell, Jr., based on alleged misconduct in prior sessions. While Article I expressly states that each house shall be "sole judge" of the qualifications of its members, the Court interpreted this language as limited to judging the so-called "standing qualifications" (age, citizenship, and residence) found in the text of Article I, which were exclusive and left no room for the imposition of additional qualifications. Likewise, in United States v. Munoz-Flores (1990), the Court declined to apply the political question doctrine to alleged violations of the Origination Clause (Article I, § 7, cl. 1), which requires that appropriations bills must originate in the House of Representatives. On the other hand, the procedures used by the Senate to try impeachments were deemed to present a political question in United States v. Nixon (1993).

A second doctrine, the enrolled bill doctrine, may also prevent courts from adjudicating issues related to the deliberative process. In Marshall Field & Co. v. Clark (1892), the Court refused to invalidate a statute on the basis of allegations that a section included in the version of the statute passed by the House and Senate was (apparently inadvertently) omitted from the bill certified by the leadership of the respective chambers and sent to the President (the "enrolled bill"). The Court refused to consider evidence in the respective journals of the House and Senate, reasoning instead that an enrolled bill carries "on its face a solemn assurance by the legislative and executive departments of the government . . . that it was passed by congress" and that "[t]he respect due to coequal and independent departments requires the judicial department to act upon that assurance, and to accept, as having passed congress, all bills authenticated in the manner stated." The enrolled bill doctrine, however, has been sharply criticized by some commentators and restricted or abandoned in many states. In United States v. Munoz-Flores (1990), the Court read *Marshall Field* narrowly, and concluded that the enrolled bill doctrine does not apply to claims that the adoption of legislation violated the Origination Clause, although Justice Scalia relied on the doctrine in a separate concurrence. To the extent that it remains valid, the enrolled bill doctrine would appear to prevent any challenge to legislation based on the failure of either chamber to follow its own rules for deliberations.

In practice, although the political question doctrine and the enrolled bill doctrine complicate efforts to review the exercise of deliberative powers, they have not prevented the Supreme Court from enforcing both intrinsic and extrinsic limits on those powers. In particular, as the previous review of the cases limiting the deliberative powers attests, the Court has often reviewed the exercise of the contempt power. At the same time, however, the procedures by which Congress deliberates have seldom been reviewed by the courts, particularly insofar as they relate solely to the internal institutional operations of Congress. In other words, the day-to-day exercise of the deliberative powers to govern the institutional operations of Congress is for all practical purposes not subject to judicial review, but the exercise of deliberative powers to rights outside of Congress itself ordinarily are.

Another potentially important limitation on judicial interference with the deliberative powers is legislative immunity, particularly the Speech or Debate Clause (Art. I, § 6, cl. 1).[270] The Clause has been interpreted as providing immunity for all legislative acts (not just "speech" and "debate"), which are defined broadly as things ordinarily done in the course of deliberation and eventual passage or defeat of legislation or other action within congressional authority and to provide protection for legislative staff or employees as well.[271] In general terms, the exercise of the deliberative powers constitutes a legislative act to which immunity attaches, but that immunity does not prevent all forms of judicial review. Instead, legislative immunity affects the form and timing of judicial review—it prevents or limits the ability of people affected by deliberative powers to sue members of Congress (and to some extent their staff) for the exercise of deliberative powers, but it does not prevent review on appeal from a contempt conviction or by means of a writ of habeas corpus.

Legislative immunity issues have arisen in several Supreme Court decisions involving exercise of the deliberative powers. In Kilbourn v. Thompson (1880), for example, the Court held that legislators were immune from suit for false imprisonment, but allowed the suit to go forward against the sergeant-at-arms and ultimately held that the plaintiff had been improperly found in contempt, because subpoenas he had disobeyed were not issued pursuant to a proper investigation.[272] *Kilbourn* implies that legislators are immune even when they act outside the scope of their authority, although legislative staff may not be.[273] More recently, however, in Doe v. McMillan (1973) the Court applied the Speech and Debate Clause to hold that members of a congressional committee and their staff could not be sued for invasion of privacy based on "[t]he acts of authorizing an investigation pursuant to which the subject materials were gathered, holding hearings where the materials were presented, preparing a report where they were reproduced, and authorizing the publication and distribution of that report."[274]

Kilbourn and *McMillan* involved suits for damages, but the Court extended immunity to other remedies in Eastland v. United States Servicemen's Fund (1975), which dismissed a suit to enjoin enforcement of subpoenas issued pursuant to a valid investigation.[275] *Eastland* indicated that the scope of judicial inquiry was "narrow" and that the courts " 'should not go beyond the narrow confines of determining that a committee's inquiry may fairly be deemed within its province.' "[276] *Eastland* does not mean that judicial review is entirely foreclosed by legislative immunity, a point that was made explicitly in a concurrence by Justice Marshall (joined by Justices Brennan and Stewart). If the witness asserts his or her objection before a committee and the objection is overruled, the witness may refuse to comply and raise a defense at a subsequent trial under the statute (or in a habeas petition if Congress directly imposes contempt sanctions). Nothing in the *Eastland* opinion suggests that immunity would prevent such challenges, because it approvingly cited a number of cases in which contempt sanctions were reviewed under such circumstances.

The application of immunity to a suit to enjoin the enforcement of a subpoena is, in my view, more problematic than immunity from suits for false imprisonment or invasion of privacy for two reasons. First, while it is true, as the Court observed in *Eastland*, that such an action may be used to delay and frustrate a legitimate legislative inquiry, suits for injunctive relief do not threaten the independence of legislators in the same way suits for damages would. Second, the absence of any means to test the validity of a subpoena (or a question asked at a hearing) puts the witnesses between a rock and a hard place. The witness can raise objections and refuse to answer, but if the witness is wrong, the contempt stands and punishment will be meted out. Alternatively, the witness can avoid the risk by complying, but perhaps at the cost of forfeiting his or her constitutional rights.

Justiciability doctrines and legislative immunity affect whether courts may hear cases involving the deliberative powers and may limit the form or timing of judicial review. Nonetheless, these doctrines apply only under narrow circumstances, and judicial review of the exercise of deliberative powers is seldom foreclosed altogether. When the courts do review the exercise of deliberative powers, the same institutional and separation of powers considerations that underlie justiciability limitations and legislative immunity also support deference to congressional judgments. Just how much deference is due, however, remains unclear. The Court has not clearly articulated a standard of review, such as the rational basis test, for the exercise of the deliberative powers, nor do the cases exhibit consistency in the degree of deference. Some cases, such as *Kilbourne*, Marshall v. Gordon, and a few McCarthy-era cases, accord little deference to congressional judgments concerning the necessity for exercising the deliberative powers. Other cases, however, suggest that Congress is entitled to deference and that courts should not second-guess congressional judgments. The uncertainty of the judicial response compounds the difficulties confronted by witnesses in deciding how to respond to legislative investigations.

NOTES

1. The seminal work on collective action is Mancur Olson, *The Logic of Collective Action* (1965), which spawned a burgeoning theoretical literature analyzing government from a collective action perspective. See generally James S. Coleman, *Individual Interests and Collective Action* (1986); Michael Hechter, *Principles of Group Solidarity* (1987); Mancur Olsen, *The Rise and Decline of Nations* (1982); David Reisman, *Theories of*

Collective Action (1990); Todd Sandler, *Collective Action: Theory and Applications* (1992); Thomas Schwartz, *The Logic of Collective Choice* (1986). The application of collective action theory to interstate relations, including federalism, is of relatively recent origin. For illustrative examples, see Clayton P. Gillette, "The Exercise of Trumps by Decentralized Governments," 83 *Va. L. Rev.* 1347 (1997); Richard E. Levy, "Federalism and Collective Action," 45 *U. Kan. L. Rev.* 1241 (1997).

2. See generally Ronald H. Coase, "The Problem of Social Cost," 3 *J.L. & Econ.* 1 (1960). The Coase theorem postulates that in the absence of transaction costs, legal rights will end up with their most valued user, regardless of their original allocation. This theorem recently has been challenged on the basis of social science literature suggesting that the price people will pay to obtain a good may be less than the price for which they are willing to relinquish it, a phenomenon known as the "offer-asking" differential, or "endowment effect." See generally, for example, Daphna Lewinsohn-Zamir, "The Choice Between Property Rules and Liability Rules Revisited: Critical Observations from Behavioral Studies," 80 *Tex. L. Rev.* 219 (2001).

3. Assume, for example, that parties A, B, and C each have property along a river. A, who occupies the most upstream location, uses the river to discharge chemicals from a plant, while B and C each fish further downstream. A's discharge of chemicals kills the fish. If the profit from the plant exceeds that of the combined profits from fishing, then an agreement could be reached if A would compensate B and C and share some of the net profit with them. Conversely, if the combined profits from fishing exceed that of the plant, then B and C could pay A to cease operating the plant.

4. The example in the previous note assumes an unrealistically small group. In practice, the number and types of uses of a river are much more numerous. If we imagine trying to get all those with a stake in the uses of the Mississippi River together to negotiate an agreement on the uses of the river that would maximize the total interests involved and compensate net losers, it is not difficult to see how transaction costs may form an insurmountable barrier to collective action on a large scale.

5. See generally Michael C. Jensen & William H. Meckling, "Theory of the Firm: Managerial Behavior, Agency Costs and Ownership Structure," 3 *J. Fin. Econ* 305, 308 (1976). Collective action also produces agency costs that operate in the other direction, insofar as the collective is also acting as the agent of its individual members. See, e.g., Lillian R. Bevier, "What Ails Us?" 112 *Yale L.J.* 1135, 1166 (2003) ("Modern representative government is a colossal collective action problem, beset by incalculable agency costs and pervasive informational asymmetries between citizens, well-organized groups, bureaucrats, and elected representatives.").

6. This is the essence of Hobbes's famous analysis of government in the Leviathan, hence the adjective "Hobbesian." See Thomas Hobbes, *Leviathan* (1651).

7. That it sometimes happens that a people spontaneously cooperate to repel an invasion or otherwise defend themselves in cases of imminent danger does not alter this general point. In extreme cases, the costs of noncooperation are sufficiently great to overcome the barriers to collective action. Once such emergencies pass, however, maintaining a collective defense or responding to more minor or localized threats will be impossible.

8. See generally, for example, Dan M. Kahan, "The Logic of Reciprocity: Trust, Collective Action, and Law," 102 *Mich. L. Rev.* 71 (2003).

9. See generally John Hart Ely, *Democracy and Distrust: A Theory of Judicial Review* (1980).

10. The interest of the state is typically defined by the individuals or groups with the political power to make policy, which, depending on the form of government, may or may not be representative of the collective as a whole. For purposes of the present analysis, the means through which the state defines "its" interests does not matter. However those interests are identified and fixed, the state pursues them on the international level in its relation to other states.

11. Recently, this perspective on international relations has found its way into the academic literature concerning international law. See generally Anne-Marie Slaughter, Andrew S. Tulumello, & Stephen Wood, "International Law and International Relations Theory: A New Generation of Interdisciplinary Scholarship," 92 *Am. J. Int'l L.* 367 (1998); Jeffrey L. Dunoff & Joel P. Trachtman, "Economic Analysis of International Law," 24 *Yale J. Int'l Law* 1 (1999).

12. See generally Richard E. Levy, "Federalism and Collective Action," 45 *U. Kan. L. Rev.* 1241 (1997).

13. For a detailed treatment of collective action under the Articles of Confederation and the suggestion that the "goods" achieved through it were not pure public goods, see Keith L. Dougherty, *Collective Action Under the Articles of Confederation* (2001).

14. Even though thirteen is a manageable number for some forms of collective action, it is still quite difficult to reach consensus among thirteen independent actors.

15. See Albert Hirschman, *Exit, Voice and Loyalty—Responses to Decline in Firms, Organizations and States* (1970). Hirschman's analysis was applied to the integration of Europe in an influential article by Joseph Weiler. See Joseph H.H. Weiler, "The Transformation of Europe," 100 *Yale L.J.* 2403 (1991).

16. For further discussion, see Robert van den Bergh, Michael Faure, & Jurgen Lefevere, *The Subsidiarity Principle in European Environmental Law: An Economic Analysis, in Law and Economics of the Environment* (Eide & van den Bergh eds., 1996); William W. Buzbee, "Recognizing the Regulatory Commons," 89 *Ia. L. Rev.* 1 (2003); Ken Kollman, John H. Miller, & Scott Page, "Decentralization and the Search for Policy Solutions," 16 *J. L. Econ. & Org.* 102 (2000); John Linarelli, "The Economics of Uniform Laws and Uniform Lawmaking," 48 *Wayne L. Rev.* 1387 (2003); Joel P. Trachtman, "Economic Analysis of Prescriptive Jurisdiction," 42 *Va. J. Int'l L.* 1 (2001).

17. The Virginia Resolutions approved by the Constitutional Convention as the blueprint for developing the Constitution provided that Congress was to have power "to legislate in all cases for the general interests of the union, and also in those to which the States are separately incompetent, or in which the harmony of the United States may be interrupted by the exercise of individual legislation." Similarly worded proposals provided the basis for the Committee on Detail's list of enumerated powers. See Max Farrand, 2 *The Records of the Federal Convention* 18 (Yale University Press rev. ed., 1937).

18. The Constitution also arguably expressly prohibits interstate tariffs in the Import Export Clause (Art. I, § 10, cl. 2), although to this point the Clause has been interpreted as limited to foreign imports and exports. See Christopher R. Drahozal, "On Tariffs v. Subsidies in Interstate Trade: A Legal and Economic Analysis," 74 *Wash. U. L.Q.* 1127 (1996).

19. See generally Richard E. Levy, "Federalism and Collective Action," 45 *U. Kan. L. Rev.* 1241, 1247–56 (1997) (discussion of foreign affairs, individual rights, and other federal powers).

20. This is not to say that the existence of clear geographic boundaries eliminates problems of interjurisdictional conflict. Even as to independent nation states, each of which possesses "complete" sovereignty over its clearly defined territory, overlapping

claims of power frequently arise, such as when the United States asserts authority to regulate and punish activities that take place in other countries but have adverse effects in the United States. In a federal system, such geographic overlaps among the member states are compounded by the allocation of power between the state and national governments according to subject matter.

21. This history is described in Part I of the book.

22. See, e.g., Hodel v. Virginia Surface Mining and Reclamation Ass'n, 452 U.S. 264, 276–77 (1981); Heart of Atlanta Motel v. United States, 379 U.S. 241, 262 (1964).

23. A notable exception is United States v. Darby, 312 U.S. 100 (1941), which held that Fair Labor Standards Act provisions imposing minimum wage and maximum hour requirements and concomitant recordkeeping requirements, were necessary and proper to a ban on shipping in interstate commerce goods manufactured by employees whose wages and hours violated the Act's requirements.

24. *Lopez*, 514 U.S. at 558–59; accord *Morrison*, 529 U.S. at 608–09.

25. See Hodel v. Virginia Surface Mining and Reclamation Ass'n, 452 U.S. 264, 276-77 (1982). Hodel first described the relevant inquiry as whether there is a rational basis for a congressional determination that an activity affected interstate commerce and whether the law is a reasonable means for addressing that effect. It then added, "Moreover, this Court has made clear that the commerce power extends not only to 'the use of channels of interstate or foreign commerce' and to 'protection of the instrumentalities of interstate commerce . . . or persons or things in commerce,' but also to 'activities affecting commerce.'" See also Perez v. United States, 402 U.S. 146, 150 (1971).

26. See *Lopez*, 514 U.S. at 556–59. The Court reviewed the case law, emphasizing that even the broadest reading of the commerce power recognized that it must be limited to preserve federalism and that trivial effects on interstate commerce are insufficient to sustain federal legislative authority. The Court then observed that it "has heeded that warning and undertaken to decide whether a rational basis existed for concluding that a regulated activity sufficiently affected interstate commerce." *Id.* at 557. The Court then quoted from several cases acknowledging that the commerce power has judicially enforceable limits before making the transition to the three categories of commerce power legislation with the prefatory sentence: "Consistent with this structure, we have identified three broad categories of activity that Congress may regulate under its commerce power." *Id.* at 558.

27. See David E. Engdahl, "The Necessary and Proper Clause as an Intrinsic Restraint on Federal Lawmaking Power," 22 *Harv. J. L. & Pub. Pol'y* 107 (1998); John T. Valauri, "The Clothes Have No Emperor Or, Cabining the Commerce Clause," 41 *San Diego L. Rev.* 405 (2004).

28. For this proposition, Justice Scalia cited United States v. Coombs, 37 U.S. (12 Pet.) 72, 78 (1838), as well as several other commerce power cases.

29. This discussion quoted the Federalist No. 33, at 204 (A. Hamilton) and cited to Lawson & Granger, "The 'Proper' Scope of Federal Power: A Jurisdictional Interpretation of the Sweeping Clause," 43 *Duke L.J.* 267, 297–326, 330–33 (1993).

30. Even as the Court read the scope of federal power narrowly, it rejected Madison's argument and adopted Hamilton's. See United States v. Butler, 297 U.S. 1, 65–66 (1936). *Butler* struck down the taxing and spending program in question, however, on the ground that it was in fact a regulatory program that interfered with the police powers of the states. Compare Bailey v. Drexel Furniture Co. (*The Child Labor Tax Case*), 259 U.S. 20 (1922).

31. The Court also struggled with the scope of necessary and proper legislation in connection with other fiscal powers. First, after initially invalidating the Legal Tender Act

of 1862, as beyond the scope of federal power in Hepburn v. Griswold, 75 U.S. (8 Wall.) 603 (1870), the Court reversed itself the very next term and upheld the Act in The Legal Tender Cases, 79 U.S. (12 Wall.) 457 (1871) (overruling *Hepburn*). See generally David P. Currie, *The First Hundred Years*, at 320–28 (critically analyzing *Hepburn*); Ajit V. Pai, "Congress and the Constitution: The Legal Tender Act of 1862," 77 *Or. L. Rev.* 535 (1998) (discussing debates over constitutionality of the Act). In a later case upholding the statutory abrogation of contractual obligations to pay in gold against a due process challenge, Norman v. Baltimore & Ohio Railroad Co., 294 U.S. 240, 303 (1935), the Court described federal power to regulate the currency as follows:

> The broad and comprehensive national authority over the subjects of revenue, finance, and currency is derived from the aggregate of the powers granted to the Congress, embracing the powers to lay and collect taxes, to borrow money, to regulate commerce with foreign nations and among the several states, to coin money, regulate the value thereof, and of foreign coin, and fix the standards of weights and measures, and the added express power "to make all laws which shall be necessary and proper for carrying into execution" the other enumerated powers.

32. See United States v. Butler, 297 U.S. 1 (1936); Bailey v. Drexel Furniture Co. (*The Child Labor Tax Case*), 259 U.S. 20 (1922).

33. Indeed, it is worth remembering that *McCulloch* itself upheld the national bank as necessary and proper to the exercise of the taxing and spending powers.

34. See, e.g., United States v. Kahriger, 345 U.S. 22 (1953) (overruled on other grounds, Marchetti v. United States, 390 U.S. 39 (1968)); United States v. Sanchez, 340 U.S. 42 (1950); Chas. C. Steward Machine Co. v. Davis, 301 U.S. 548 (1937); Sozinsky v. United States, 300 U.S. 506 (1937).

35. See *Kahriger*, 345 U.S. at 31 ("All the provisions of this excise are *adapted* to the collection of a valid tax.").

36. See Regan v. Taxation with Representation, 461 U.S. 540 (1983) (rejecting First Amendment and equal protection challenge to tax provision denying charitable exemption to most organizations engaged in lobbying activities).

37. *Dole* also suggested that a condition on receipt of federal funds might be unconstitutional if it is "so coercive as to pass the point at which 'pressure turns to compulsion,' " which may be a separate inquiry or may be part of the independent constitutional bar of state sovereignty, discussed earlier in connection with the no-commandeering rule and state sovereign immunity.

38. The unambiguous language requirement of *Dole*, at part two of the test, does not have antecedents in *McCulloch* and appears to be unique to the spending power, although there is a parallel requirement for abrogation of state sovereign immunity pursuant to the power to enforce the Fourteenth Amendment, which is discussed later in this part.

39. For critical analysis of *Sabri*, see Gary Lawson, "Making a Federal Case Out of It: Sabri v. United States and the Constitution of Leviathan," 2004 *Cato Sup. Ct. Rev.* 119 (2004).

40. In the commerce power area, by way of contrast, the Court had, in keeping with *Lopez* and *Morrison*, interpreted a statutory jurisdictional requirement narrowly to prevent potential federalism problems. See Jones v. United States 529 U.S. 848 (2000).

41. U.S. Const., Am. 14, § 5. Accord *id.* Am. 13, § 2 ("Congress shall have power to enforce this article by appropriate legislation."); *id.* Am. 15, § 2 (same). The same language is used in later amendments securing voting rights. See *id.* Am. 19, § 2; *id.* Am. 23, § 2; *id.* Am. 24, § 2; *id.* Am. 26, § 2.

42. Fitzpatrick v. Bitzer, 427 U.S. 445 (1976).

43. Most observers read the Court's pre-Oregon v. Smith cases as applying strict scrutiny to neutral laws that burdened free exercise in significant ways, but the Court in Smith read those cases narrowly. For criticism of Oregon v. Smith in relation to prior case law, see, e.g., Stephen L. Carter, "The Separation of Church and Self," 46 *SMU L. Rev.* 585 (1992); John Delaney, "Police Power Absolutism and Nullifying the Free Exercise Clause: A Critique of Oregon v. Smith," 25 *Ind. L. Rev.* 71 (1991); Douglas Laycock, "The Remnants of Free Exercise," 1990 *Sup. Ct. Rev.* 1 (1990); and Michael W. McConnell, "Free Exercise Revisionism and the Smith Decision," 57 *U. Chi. L. Rev.* 1109 (1990).

44. Some language in footnote 10 of Morgan emphasizing that Congress has no power to "dilute" Fourteenth Amendment rights might be read to support congressional authority to expand those rights. For discussion of this issue, see Jesse H. Choper, "Congressional Power to Expand Judicial Definitions of the Substantive Terms of the Civil War Amendments," 67 *Minn. L. Rev.* 299 (1982); William Cohen, "Congressional Power to Interpret Due Process and Equal Protection," 27 *Stan. L. Rev.* 603 (1975); and Matt Pawa, "Comment, When the Supreme Court Restricts Constitutional Rights, Can Congress Save Us? An Examination of Section 5 of the Fourteenth Amendment," 141 *U. Pa. L. Rev.* 1029 (1993).

45. For critical analysis of Tennessee v. Lane, see Robert A. Levy, "Tennessee v. Lane: How Illegitimate Power Negated Non-existent Immunity," 2004 *Cato Sup. Ct. Rev.* 161 (2004).

46. It also appears, though less clearly so, that this test is more stringent than *Lopez*, which seems to preclude regulation of individual instances of noncommercial activity absent a "jurisdictional nexus," but remains very generous to federal regulatory authority in other respects.

47. See Eldred v. Ashcroft, 537 U.S. 186, 217–18 (2003) (emphasizing the textual differences between the Fourteenth Amendment power and the power to grant patents and copyrights in refusing to extend the congruence and proportionality test to congressional authority under the Patent and Copyright Clause).

48. A number of cases decided around World War I also upheld broad congressional authority under the war power, typically emphasizing deference to congressional judgments about the need for a particular measure and occasionally relying specifically on the Necessary and Proper Clause and *McCulloch*. See Hamilton v. Kentucky Distilleries & Warehouse Co., 251 U.S. 146, 148–63 (1919) (upholding a ban on the sale of liquor in the vicinity of military establishments even though ban was adopted after armistice because the state of emergency had not ended); Dakota Cent. Telephone Co. v. South Dakota ex rel. Payne, 250 U.S. 163 (1919) (upholding congressional authority to provide for federal takeover of telephone lines); Northern Pac. R.R. v. North Dakota ex rel. Langer, 250 U.S. 135, 149–50 (1919) (upholding federal takeover of the railroads); McKinley v. United States, 249 U.S. 397 (1919) (upholding federal authority to ban brothels within the vicinity of military installations); Arver v. United States (*The Selective Service Cases*), 245 U.S. 366 (1918) (upholding federal authority to provide for a draft).

49. See, e.g., *Ex parte* Milligan, 71 U.S. (4 Wall.) 2, (1866) (holding that military trial of a civilian was impermissible).

50. Toth v. Quarles, 350 U.S. 11, 23 (1955) (quoting Anderson v. Dunn, 19 U.S. (6 Wheat.) 204 (1821), which is discussed below in connection with the deliberative powers of Congress).

51. See David P. Currie, *The Constitution in the Supreme Court: The Second Century, 1888–1986*, at 401 (1990).

52. In addition to *Toth*, see Kinsella v. Krueger, 351 U.S. 470 (1956) and Reid v. Covert, 351 U.S. 487 (1956), both of which initially upheld courts martial of a military

spouse and distinguished *Toth* on flimsy grounds, only to be reversed on reargument. Reid v. Covert, 354 U.S. 1 (1957) (reversing *Kinsella* as well).

53. Graham v. John Deere Co., 363 U.S. 1, 5 (1963).

54. See Feist Publications v. Rural Telephone Service Co., 499 U.S. 340, 346 (1991) ("Originality is a constitutional requirement.") Thus, for example, in the *Trade-Mark Cases*, 100 U.S. 82, 93–94 (1879), the Court held that the Clause did not authorize Congress to protect trademarks.

55. See, e.g., *Graham*, 363 U.S. at 6.

56. For example, after determining that the act in question complied with the limited times requirement of the Clause, the Court stated "we turn now to whether it is a rational exercise of the legislative authority conferred by the Copyright Clause. On that point, we defer substantially to Congress."

57. Most of the Court's copyright power analysis was devoted to rejecting arguments that the extension of existing copyrights violated various substantive requirements of the Clause, including the limited time requirement, the originality requirement, and the requirement that copyright promote the useful arts.

58. See Missouri v. Holland, 252 U.S 416 (1920) (upholding federal regulation of migratory birds as necessary and proper to a treaty with Canada even though such regulation would be beyond the scope of the commerce power under then prevailing doctrine); for general discussion see Nicholas Q. Rosenkranz, "Executing the Treaty Power," 118 *Harv. L. Rev.* 1867 (2005).

59. See, e.g., Jinks v. Richland County, S.C., 538 U.S. 456 (2003) (upholding federal statute of limitations as necessary and proper to the Article I power to establish inferior tribunals and Article III's vesting of jurisdiction in federal courts); Burlington Northern R.R. v. Woods, 480 U.S. 1, 5 n.3 (1987) ("Article III of the Constitution, augmented by the Necessary and Proper Clause of Article I, § 8, cl. 18, empowers Congress to establish a system of federal district and appellate courts and, impliedly, to establish procedural Rules governing litigation in these courts."); Hanna v. Plumer, 380 U.S. 460, 472 (1965) ("[T]he constitutional provision for a federal court system (augmented by the Necessary and Proper Clause) carries with it congressional power to make rules governing the practice and pleading in those courts, which in turn includes a power to regulate matters which, though falling within the uncertain area between substance and procedure, are rationally capable of classification as either.") (citing *McCulloch*); Wayman v. Southard, 23 U.S. (10 Wheat.) 1, 22 (1825) (reasoning that power to make laws for enforcement of federal judgments was necessary and proper to the jurisdiction of federal courts).

60. To be sure, the text is not inconsistent with the constitutive model insofar as the Clause references the "foregoing" powers. Nonetheless, a more logical phrasing for the constitutive model would be to use the Clause as an introductory phrase before the list of enumerated powers, such as "Congress shall have the power to enact necessary and proper laws to implement the following powers."

61. Thus, for example, Congress has legislative power to implement treaties, see Missouri v. Holland, 252 U.S 416 (1920), although treaties may also be self-executing and thus operate without legislative implementation. See Whitney v. Robertson, 124 U.S. 190 (1888). Insofar as the Clause attaches to some self-executing powers, the inference from the phrasing of the Clause is not a particularly strong one, even if the power to enact necessary and proper laws may be different as attached to legislative powers as opposed to powers of other departments. See Saikrishna B. Prakash & Michael D. Ramsey, "The Executive Power over Foreign Affairs," 111 *Yale L. J.* 231, 255–56 (2001) (arguing that Congress' power under the Necessary and Proper Clause to legislate in support of the

President's foreign affairs powers "is subject to a key limitation" in that "it must be exercised in coordination with, and not in opposition to, the President").

62. Eugene Gressman & Eric K. Gressman, "Necessary and Proper Roots of Exceptions to Federal Jurisdiction," 51 *Geo. Wash. L. Rev.* 495, 508 (1983).

63. Madison's defense was similar, although somewhat less explicit on this point.

64. In the process, the Court overruled Hammer v. Dagenhart (*The Child Labor Case*).

65. The Court's discussion, however, also reflects the constitutive model insofar as it stated that:

The power of Congress over interstate commerce is not confined to the regulation of commerce among the states. It extends to those activities intrastate which so affect interstate commerce or the exercise of the power of Congress over it as to make regulation of them appropriate means to the attainment of a legitimate end, the exercise of the power of Congress to regulate interstate commerce. (Citing *McCulloch*).

66. In particular, the power to prohibit goods in commerce based on the manner of the production coupled with the power to regulate production as necessary and proper to the enforcement of the prohibition arguably confers unlimited legislative authority on Congress. Thus, for example, Gerald Gunther famously referred to this aspect of *Darby*'s analysis as a "superbootstrap" that would permit the regulation of any activity without regard to an effect on commerce by means of an initial ban on interstate shipment and movement coupled with the necessary and proper direct regulation of the activity. See Gerald Gunther, *Constitutional Law* 143–44 (11th ed., 1985). More recent versions of this casebook have truncated and toned down the criticism somewhat. See Kathleen M. Sullivan & Gerald Gunther, "Constitutional Law" 149 (15th ed., 2004) (omitting characterization of *Darby*'s analysis as a "superbootstrap" and asking whether *Darby* permits regulation without regard to effects on commerce).

67. Specifically, the Court relied on the second category of commerce power authority listed in *Lopez*—the power to regulate and protect the instrumentalities of commerce.

68. (Emphasis added.) This statement reflects a rather broad conception of the content of the commerce power independent of the Necessary and Proper Clause. In contrast to *Darby*, which involved the regulation (by prohibition) of the actual interstate movement of goods, *Pierce County* relied on a protective rationale—the statute was intended to protect the instrumentalities of commerce (highways) and persons and things in commerce (i.e., using the highways). This strikes me as more appropriately characterized as legislation under the Necessary and Proper Clause.

69. In addition, some ends would be improper because they violate other constitutional provisions, such as due process. Compare Romer v. Evans, 517 U.S. 620 (1996) (reasoning that animus against a politically unpopular group is not a legitimate governmental purpose).

70. Thus, for example, Congress could only pursue noncommerce power ends through means that are squarely within the commerce power itself, such as the regulation of access to the channels and instrumentalities of commerce.

71. For example, federal legislation that violates individual rights is typically analyzed without reference to the *McCulloch* test. Nonetheless, the additional power model would have some implications for the reasoning behind state sovereignty–based restrictions on federal power, insofar as the Court could not rely on the *McCulloch* test to explain their application to matters falling within one of the specific enumerated powers, such as a coercive tax on states.

72. Elsewhere in the opinion, however, Chief Justice Marshall appears to equate the terms appropriate and conducive: "This could not be done by confiding the choice of means to such narrow limits as not to leave it in the power of Congress to adopt any which might be appropriate, and which were conducive to the end."

73. Notable examples include Hodel v. Virginia Surface Mining and Reclamation Ass'n, 452 U.S. 264 (1981) (upholding the Surface Mining Act's regulation of coal mining practices), Katzenbach v. McClung, 379 U.S. 294 (1964) (upholding the application of the Civil Rights Statute to a restaurant that received some food from interstate commerce but did not serve many customers in interstate commerce), and Wickard v. Filburn, 317 U.S. 111 (1942) (upholding application of grain production quotas to farmer's production of grain to feed his own livestock).

74. *Lopez* is discussed in greater detail *supra* text following note 22.

75. Without the ability to reason from cumulative or aggregate effects, Congress must apparently incorporate a jurisdictional requirement that links each instance of a noncommercial activity to interstate commerce or satisfy the Court that as a factual matter individual instances of an activity have a "substantial" effect on interstate commerce. See *Lopez* at 561–63; accord United States v. Morrison, 529 U.S. 598, 613–15 (2000).

76. In previous cases, the Court had often relied on the legislative record to confirm the reasonableness of a congressional determination that an activity substantially affects interstate commerce, while also emphasizing that such findings are not necessary. See, e.g., Katzenbach v. McClung, 379 U.S. 294, 299 (1964) ("As we noted in *Heart of Atlanta Motel* both houses of Congress conducted prolonged hearings on the Act. And, as we said there, while no formal findings were made, which of course are not necessary, it is well that we make mention of the testimony at these hearings the better to understand the problem before Congress and determine whether the Act is a reasonable and appropriate means toward its solution.").

77. This reasoning may be contrasted with Hodel v. Virginia Surface Mining and Reclamation Ass'n, 452 U.S. 264, 280–81 (1981), in which the Court rejected the argument that the rational basis test should not apply insofar as the federal law regulated land use, a local activity, stating that "[t]he denomination of an activity as a 'local' or 'intrastate' activity does not resolve the question whether Congress may regulate it under the Commerce Clause."

78. The congruence and proportionality test also applies under the Takings Clause, where it operates as a form of elevated scrutiny when the government exacts an easement or similar interest as a condition of granting a permit or license to build. See Dolan v. City of Tigard, 512 U.S. 374 (1994).

79. See Randy E. Barnett, "The Original Meaning of the Necessary and Proper Clause," 6 *U. Pa. J. Const. L.* 183 (2003); Randy E. Barnett, "Necessary and Proper," 44 *U.C.L.A. L. Rev.* 745 (1997); David E. Engdahl, "The Necessary and Proper Clause as an Intrinsic Restraint on Federal Lawmaking Power," 22 *Harv. J. L. & Pub. Pol'y* 107 (1998); Gary Lawson & Patricia B. Granger, "The 'Proper' Scope of Federal Power: A Jurisdictional Interpretation of the Sweeping Clause," 43 *Duke L.J.* 267, 297 (1993); and H. Jefferson Powell, "Enumerated Means and Unlimited Ends," 94 *Mich. L. Rev.* 651 (1995); see also Stephen Gardbaum, "Rethinking Constitutional Federalism," 74 *Tex. L. Rev.* 795 (1996) (arguing that special justifications should be required when Congress preempts state regulation of local activities because of their effect on interstate commerce).

80. Sabri v. United States, 541 U.S. 600, 611 (2004):

I write further because I find questionable the scope the Court gives to the Necessary and Proper Clause as applied to Congress' authority to spend. In particular, the Court appears to hold that the Necessary and Proper Clause authorizes the exercise of any power that is no more than a "rational means" to effectuate one of Congress' enumerated powers. Ante, at 1946. This conclusion derives from the Court's characterization of the seminal case McCulloch v. Maryland, 4 Wheat. 316, 4 L.Ed. 579 (1819), as having established a "means-ends rationality" test, ante, at 1946, a characterization that I am not certain is correct.

81. In doing so, Justice Thomas emphasized that he found the statute within the commerce power based on precedent (citing *Perez*), but that he "continue[d] to doubt that we have correctly interpreted the Commerce Clause."

82. Bracketed material in original; quoting *McCulloch*.

83. Bracketed material supplied by the author.

84. Thus, it is not surprising that Justice Thomas referred approvingly to *Jinks* in his *Sabri* concurrence.

85. The requirement of legitimate ends also means that, to the extent that particular ends are themselves unconstitutional (for example, racial discrimination), some ends that might otherwise be within the scope of an enumerated power cannot form the basis for necessary and proper legislation. This limitation, while of obvious constitutional significance, is not of particular concern for the analysis in this book.

86. As discussed previously, there was some language in *Morgan* which might have been read as ascribing to Congress a role in affording content to Fourteenth Amendment rights, but *Boerne* squarely rejected any such role.

87. See United States v. Ptasynski, 462 U.S. 74 (1983) (uniform taxation); Railway Labor Executives' Ass'n v. Gibbons, 455 U.S. 457 (1982) (uniform bankruptcy laws).

88. See Feist Publications v. Rural Telephone Service Co., 499 U.S. 340 (1991) (holding that there is a constitutional requirement of originality for copyright).

89. See *supra* note 30 and accompanying text.

90. It is not entirely, clear, however, how this kind of power should be characterized. To the extent that the cases indicate that addressing the effects of war is a permissible "end," this would be a construction of the war power itself, because *McCulloch* requires ends within the enumerated powers. The cases, however, are also consistent with a reading that the conduct of the war is the "end" and addressing its effects is the "means," which would suggest that the source of the power to enact such measures is the Necessary and Proper Clause.

91. Article I, section 8, cl. 5.

92. Article I, section 8, cl. 7.

93. Article I, section 8, cl. 10.

94. Article I, section 8, cl. 3 (power to "regulate Commerce with foreign Nations, and among the several States, and with the Indian Tribes"); see also *id.* at cl. 5 (power to "coin Money, and regulate the value thereof"); *id.* at cl. 14 (power "to make Rules for the Government and Regulation of the land and naval Forces").

95. Article I, section 8, cl. 4.

96. Article I, section 8, cl. 1.

97. Article I, section 8, cl. 8.

98. One obvious possibility would be legislative history. Compare United States v. O'Brien, 391 U.S. 367 (1968) (refusing to strike down law prohibiting the destruction of draft cards on the basis of legislative history apparently showing purpose to suppress antiwar protests) with United States Dept. of Agriculture v. Moreno, 413 U.S. 528 (1973)

(relying on legislative history as evidence that statutory provisions was motivated by animus against "hippie communes"). Another possibility would be to use extremely poor fit as evidence that an asserted purpose is a pretext. See Romer v. Evans, 512 U.S. 374 (1996).

99. This problem is exacerbated by the form of the grant of authority in terms of a power to act in a certain way, for it is an odd question to ask whether the ends are within a power to act by particular means.

100. This language is from Katzenbach v. Morgan (1966). While City of Boerne v. Flores (1996) and subsequent cases employ a relatively restrictive congruence and proportionality test for means, there does not appear to be any correspondingly more rigorous review of Congress's characterization of the ends. Of course, under this elevated scrutiny of the fit between the means and the ends, it is much more difficult to defend a law as sufficiently related to purposes that are advanced to mask other motives. In this sense, scrutiny of means can be understood as a mechanism for ferreting out pretextual purposes, a point that will be addressed in greater detail below.

101. See United States v. Carolene Products, 304 U.S. 144, 152 (1938) ("regulatory legislation affecting ordinary commercial transactions is not to be pronounced unconstitutional unless in the light of the facts made known or generally assumed it is of such a character as to preclude the assumption that it rests upon some rational basis within the knowledge and experience of the legislators"). The rational basis test applies most deferentially in connection with due process and equal protection challenges to economic and social legislation that does not burden fundamental rights or employ suspect classifications.

102. When the power over a substantive field is not qualified by a specification of substantive ends, the possibility arises that the power may be used as a means to achieve an end unrelated to that power. For example, Congress may regulate commerce in order to achieve some other ends, such as improving working conditions in manufacture and production. This possibility complicates the characterization of the ends of a given statute.

103. See Hodel v. Virginia Surface Mining and Reclamation Ass'n, 452 U.S. 264 , 277 (1981) (stating that "when Congress has determined that an activity affects interstate commerce, the Court need inquire only whether the finding is rational"). Under some versions of the rational basis test, as applied in the due process and equal protection contexts, the Court presumes that there is a factual basis for legislative action, placing the burden on the party challenging it to disprove the facts to support every plausible purpose. See United States v. Carolene Products, 304 U.S. 144, 152 (1938). It is unclear whether this presumption applies to the Necessary and Proper Clause version of the rational basis test.

104. See Heart of Atlanta Motel v. United States, 379 U.S. 241 (1964) (upholding civil rights legislation based on commerce power to avoid addressing state action issue under the Fourteenth Amendment power).

105. Indeed, as will be discussed below in connection with means, one way to use the fit inquiry is to treat a bad fit as creating an inference that the asserted purpose is pretextual.

106. This analysis served to distinguish Katzenbach v. Morgan (1964), where the legislative record reflected the desire to prevent intentional discrimination by prohibiting the facially neutral literacy test for voting.

107. In this respect, the Court apparently used the congruence and proportionality test to conclude that the asserted ends of RFRA, which fell within the scope of the Fourteenth Amendment power, were a pretext for ends that did not.

108. The material in the first set of brackets was added by the author; the material in the second set of brackets is original.

109. Insofar as the means-ends analysis is sometimes used to determine the real ends of legislation, there is obviously a close connection between the first two components of the *McCulloch* test.

110. The Court reasoned further that even if the degree of necessity was the subject of dispute, it was up to Congress to make that determination.

111. See Hodel v. Virginia Surface Mining and Reclamation Ass'n, 452 U.S. 264 (1981); Perez v. United States, 402 U.S. 146 (1971); Katzenbach v. McClung, 379 U.S. 294 (1964); Heart of Atlanta Motel v. United States, 379 U.S. 241 (1964).

112. See United States v. Morrison, 529 U.S. 598 (2000); United States v. Lopez, 514 U.S. 549 (1995).

113. In this sense, *Lochner* was a power allocation case, even if it is commonly understood as an economic rights (liberty of contract) case. The power of the state to interfere with contracts depended on the characterization of the law as a health and safety measure within the police power.

114. 198 U.S. 45, 62–63 (1905) ("When assertions such as we have adverted to become necessary in order to give, if possible, a plausible foundation for the contention that the law is a 'health law,' it gives rise to at least a suspicion that there was some other motive dominating the legislature than the purpose to subserve the public health or welfare.")

115. A recent example of this approach is Romer v. Evans, 517 U.S. 620, 635 (1996), in which the Court reasoned that the "breadth" of a Colorado constitutional amendment prohibiting antidiscrimination laws protecting homosexuals was "so far removed" from the state's justifications for it, "we find it impossible to credit them."

116. Likewise, *Lopez* and *Morrison* might be read as inferring from the tenuous connection to interstate commerce that the true purpose of Congress was to regulate private noncommercial activity for police power ends that are not within the scope of federal authority.

117. See Cruzan v. Director, Missouri Dept. of Health, 497 U.S. 261, 279 (1990) (government interest in preserving life balanced against liberty interest in refusing unwanted medical treatment); Planned Parenthood of Southeastern Pennsylvania v. Casey, 505 U.S. 833, 874 (1992) (undue burden test for regulation of abortion).

118. In other words, the various levels of individual rights scrutiny can be understood as requiring correspondingly greater governmental interests to justify interference with fundamental rights, particularly insofar as the quality of the governmental interest (legitimate, important, or compelling) varies with the kind of right that is burdened. Greater scrutiny of fit also reflects a greater insistence that the government benefit actually be achieved.

119. The principle that state laws burdening interstate commerce are invalid originated as a power allocation principle—states were prohibited from regulating interstate commerce because the power vested in Congress to do so is exclusive. See Gibbons v. Ogden, 22 U.S. (9 Wheat.) 1 (1824). Although that rationale has figured less prominently in more recent cases, it remains relevant in some contexts. See Reeves v. Stake, 447 U.S. 429, 436–37 (1980) (state market participation cannot violate the commerce clause in part because it is not regulation).

120. See Pike v. Bruce Church, 397 U.S. 137, 142 (1970) ("Where the statute regulates even-handedly to effectuate a legitimate local public interest, and its effects on interstate commerce are only incidental, it will be upheld unless the burden imposed on such commerce is clearly excessive in relation to the putative local benefits."). For example, in Kassel v. Consolidated Freightways, 450 U.S. 662 (1981) (plurality opinion) and Southern Pac. Co. v. Arizona, 325 U.S. 761 (1945), the court invalidated state laws burdening interstate commerce because the safety benefits they would purportedly achieve were illusory.

121. Likewise, Justice Thomas's dissatisfaction with the rational basis formulation of the *McCulloch* test is, in effect, a call for higher levels of scrutiny in order to protect the values of federalism.

122. See *supra* notes 74–77 and accompanying text.

123. United States v. Morrison, 529 U.S. 598, 615–16 (2000) ("Petitioners' reasoning, moreover, will not limit Congress to regulating violence but may, as we suggested in *Lopez*, be applied equally as well to family law and other areas of traditional state regula-tion since the aggregate effect of marriage, divorce, and childrearing on the national econ-omy is undoubtedly significant."); United States v. Lopez, 514 U.S. 549, 564 (1995) ("Thus, if we were to accept the Government's arguments, we are hard pressed to posit any activity by an individual that Congress is without power to regulate.").

124. The key decisions in this regard were the *Slaughterhouse Cases*, 83 U.S. 36 (1873), and the *Civil Rights Cases*, 109 U.S. 3 (1883), which are discussed in Part I.

125. In refusing to reverse or reconsider the state action requirement under the Fourteenth Amendment, the Court in *Morrison* emphasized the need to preserve federalism and the reserved powers of states. See 529 U.S. at 620–22. For similar reasons, the Court's aggressive application of the congruence and proportionality test to preclude remedies for age discrimination in Board of Trustees of the University of Alabama v. Garrett, 531 U.S. 356 (2001), and disability discrimination in Kimel v. Florida Board of Regents, 528 U.S. 62 (2000) could reflect particular concerns for preserving state sovereign immunity.

126. Thus, for example, the *McCulloch*-based *Dole* test for conditions on the spending power uses the language of an "independent constitutional bar." South Dakota v. Dole, 483 U.S. 203, 200–211 (1987) ("[T]he 'independent constitutional bar' limitation on the spending power is not, as petitioner suggests, a prohibition on the indirect achievement of objectives which Congress is not empowered to achieve directly. Instead, we think that the language in our earlier opinions stands for the unexceptionable proposition that the power may not be used to induce the States to engage in activities that would themselves be unconstitutional.")

127. See Garcia v. San Antonio Metropolitan Transit Authority, 469 U.S. 528, 549 (1985).

128. For example, Randy E. Barnett, "Necessary and Proper," 44 *U.C.L.A. L. Rev.* 745 (1997); Gary Lawson & Patricia B. Granger, "The 'Proper' Scope of Federal Power: A Jurisdictional Interpretation of the Sweeping Clause," 43 *Duke L.J.* 267, 297 (1993).

129. See Tom Stacy, "What's Wrong with *Lopez*," 44 *U. Kan. L. Rev.* 243 (1996).

130. Randy Barnett appears to have taken this position. See *Restoring the Lost Constitution: The Presumption of Liberty* (2004).

131. See Stephen Gardbaum, "New Deal Constitutionalism and the Unshackling of the States," 64 *U. Chi. L. Rev.* 483 (1997) (arguing that the New Deal switch did as much or more to expand state regulatory authority as federal regulatory authority).

132. See George A. Bermann, "Taking Subsidiarity Seriously: Federalism in the European Community and the United States," 94 *Colum. L. Rev.* 331 (1994).

133. A subsidiarity requirement is expressly incorporated into the legislative power of the European Union, but its judicial enforcement remains controversial and its effective-ness remains unclear. See Ernest A. Young, "Protecting Member State Autonomy in the European Union: Some Cautionary Tales from American Federalism," 77 *N.Y.U. L. Rev.* 1612, 1677–1682 (2002).

134. The President's substantial independent foreign relations authority is an additional component of the executive power, the implications of which are not particularly relevant at this juncture.

135. See the Federalist Nos. 47 and 48 (Madison).

136. As Richard Stewart has observed, "Insofar as statutes do not effectively dictate agency actions, individual autonomy is vulnerable to the imposition of sanctions at the unruled will of executive officials. . . ." Richard B. Stewart, "The Reformation of American Administrative Law," 88 *Harv. L. Rev.* 1667, 1676 (1975).

137. See generally Sidney A. Shapiro and Richard E. Levy, "Government Benefits and the Rule of Law: Toward a Standards-Based Theory of Due Process," 57 *Admin L. Rev.* 107 (2005).

138. See Lichter v. United States, 334 U.S. 742, 778 (1948) (observing that "[a] constitutional power implies a power of delegation of authority under it sufficient to effect its purposes"); Sunshine Anthracite Coal Co. v. Adkins, 310 U.S. 381, 398 (1940) ("Delegation by Congress has long been recognized as necessary in order that the exertion of legislative power does not become a futility.")

139. See Chevron, U.S.A., Inc. v. Natural Resources Defense Council, 467 U.S. 837, 843-44 (1984):

If Congress has explicitly left a gap for the agency to fill, there is an express delegation of authority to the agency to elucidate a specific provision of the statute by regulation. Such legislative regulations are given controlling weight unless they are arbitrary, capricious, or manifestly contrary to the statute. Sometimes the legislative delegation to an agency on a particular question is implicit rather than explicit. In such a case, a court may not substitute its own construction of a statutory provision for a reasonable interpretation made by the administrator of an agency.

140. See, e.g., Charles N. Steele & Jeffrey H. Bowman, "The Constitutionality of Independent Regulatory Agencies under the Necessary and Proper Clause: The Case of the Federal Election Commission," 4 *Yale J. Reg.* 363 (1987) (arguing that the Necessary and Proper Clause provides a basis for the creation of independent agencies).

141. This basic principal was established by no less a decision than Marbury v. Madison, 5 U.S. (1 Cranch) 137 (1803). See Sidney A. Shapiro & Richard E. Levy, "Government Benefits and the Rule of Law: Toward a Standards-Based Theory of Due Process," 57 *Admin L. Rev.* 107 (2005).

142. See United States v. Mistretta, 488 U.S. 361 (1989); Wayman v. Southard, 23 U.S. 1 (1825). This kind of delegation presents particular issues concerning the nature and scope of the judicial power that are beyond the scope of this book.

143. This principle is captured in the Latin maxim "delegatus non potest delegare"— which translates as "a delegated power authority cannot be delegated." This maxim was applied to the legislative power by John Locke. See John Locke, *The Second Treatise of Government: An Essay Concerning the True Original, Extent, and End of Civil Government* 362 (Cambridge University Press, 1988); see also J.W. Hampton, Jr. & Co. v. U.S., 276 U.S. 394, 405 (1928). For the argument that the nondelegation principle should be understood as precluding only delegation of the power to vote on legislation, see Eric A. Posner & Adrian Vermeule, "Interring the Nondelegation Doctrine," 69 *U. Chi. L. Rev.* 1721 (2002).

144. See generally David Schoenbrod, *Power Without Responsibility: How Congress Abuses the People Through Delegation* (1993) (arguing that Congress uses broad delegations to escape political accountability).

145. In this respect, Clinton v. City of New York is similar to INS v. Chadha, 462 U.S. 919 (1983). Both focused on the violation of the constitutionally prescribed process for enacting, amending, or repealing legislation. In both, this conclusion rested on the premise

that the power being exercised was legislative in character. The corollary principle is that the legislative power could not be delegated to either the President or a single house of Congress.

146. For example, Marshall Field & Co. v. Clark, 143 U.S. 649 (1892); Brig Aurora v. United States, 11 U.S. (7 Cranch) 382 (1813).

147. For example, United States v. Grimaud, 220 U.S. 506 (1911).

148. Industrial Union Dept., AFL-CIO v. American Petroleum Institute (*Benzene*), 448 U.S. 607, 685–86 (1980).

149. While the Court at the time was typically sharply divided on federalism and substantive due process issues, in *Schechter Poultry* it was unanimous on the nondelegation issue, although Justice Cardozo wrote a concurring opinion joined by Justice Stone.

150. In the course of its reasoning, the Court also identified various functional considerations that weighed against the law—the lack of procedural safeguards, the fact that the delegated authority was exercised in part by private groups, and the imposition of criminal sanctions for violations of the code. These considerations will be discussed further below.

151. The only other Supreme Court decision to clearly rely on the nondelegation doctrine to invalidate legislation is Panama Refining Co. v. Ryan, 293 U.S. 388 (1935), another New Deal case involving a different provision of the same statute. A third New Deal case, Carter v. Carter Coal Co., 298 U.S. 238 (1936), also seems to rest in part on the nondelegation doctrine, but the Court invalidated the statute in question primarily on the ground that it exceeded the scope of the commerce power.

152. The Court rejected the argument that this power was confined to technical aspects of radio broadcasts and reasoned that the public interest in this context referred to the interests of listeners in the larger and more effective use of the radio, as prescribed in the statute. See National Broadcasting Co. v. United States, 319 U.S. 190, 215–18 (1943). This case has been characterized as "the single decision in which a majority of the Court approved a wholly open-ended and non-trivial grant of regulatory power to a federal agency." Alfred C. Aman, Jr. & William T. Mayton, *Administrative Law* 20 (2d ed., 2001).

153. The Court also treated the underlying statutory purpose of preventing inflation and the requirement that consideration be given to prevailing prices as providing additional constraints.

154. Whitman v. American Trucking Associations, 531 U.S. 457, 475 (2001).

155. See, e.g., David Schoenbrod, *Power Without Responsibility: How Congress Abuses the People Through Delegation* (1993); Gary Lawson, "Discretion as Delegation: the 'Proper' Understanding of the Nondelegation Doctrine," 73 *Geo. Wash. L. Rev.* 235 (2005); and Gary Lawson, "Delegation and Original Meaning," 88 *Va. L. Rev.* 327 (2002).

156. Justice Stevens wrote a concurring opinion in Whitman (joined by Justice Souter) suggesting that the Court frankly acknowledge that the power exercised by an agency when it promulgates binding regulations is legislative, but nonetheless permit such delegations provided there is an intelligible principle.

157. A few cases in the lower federal courts have found violations of the nondelegation doctrine, but these cases have not withstood review. See South Dakota v. United States Dep't of the Interior, 69 F.3d 878 (8th Cir. 1995), vacated and remanded, 519 U.S. 919 (1996) (remanding for further consideration by Secretary of the Interior), on appeal after remand, 423 F.3d 790 (8th Cir. 2005) (finding sufficient standards to satisfy nondelegation doctrine); United States v. Widdowson, 916 F.2d 587 (10th Cir. 1990), vacated and remanded for further consideration, 502 U.S. 801 (1991), reversed on reconsideration, 949 F.2d 1063 (10th Cir. 1991) .

158. See, e.g., Yakus v. United States, 321 U.S. at 423 (1944); American Power & Light Co. v. Securities and Exchange Commission, 329 U.S. 90 (1946) ("[T]hese standards need not be tested in isolation. They derive much meaningful content from the purpose of the Act, its factual background and the statutory context in which they appear.").

159. See, e.g., Zemel v. Rusk, 381 U.S. 1, 18 (1965); Fahey v. Mallonnee, 332 U.S. 245, 250 (1947).

160. See Whitman v. American Trucking Associations, 531 U.S. 457, 471 (2001) (refusing to apply the canon because "[n]o matter how severe the constitutional doubt, courts may choose only between reasonably available interpretations of a text").

161. The Independent Offices Appropriations Act of 1952, quoted in National Cable Television Association, Inc. v. United States, 415 U.S. 336, 337 (1974).

162. See Skinner v. Mid-America Pipeline Co., 490 U.S. 212 (1989), discussed below.

163. See Richard E. Levy & Robert L. Glicksman, "Judicial Activism and Restraint in the Supreme Court's Environmental Law Decisions," 42 *Vanderbilt L. Rev.* 343, 379–82 (1989).

164. It would certainly appear that the standards quoted above are at least as specific as other standards that have been upheld by the Court.

165. See Kenneth Culp Davis, "A New Approach to Delegation," 36 *U. Chi. L. Rev.* 713 (1969)

166. Amalgamated Meat Cutters v. Connally, 337 F.Supp. 737 (D.D.C. 1971) (three-judge district court).

167. American Trucking Associations v. EPA, 175 F.3d 1027 (D.C. Cir.), modified on denial of rehearing, 195 F.3d 4 (D.C. Cir. 1999); see also International Union, United Auto., Aerospace & Agr. Implement Workers of America, UAW v. Occupational Safety & Health Admin., 938 F.2d 1310 (D.C. Cir. 1991).

168. Some of the economic literature recognizes that delegating discretion to agencies under broad discretionary standards is a way that Congress avoids accountability for controversial decisions, a consideration that some critics of current doctrine rely on to support a stricter application of the nondelegation doctrine. See David Schoenbrod, *Power Without Responsibility: How Congress Abuses the People Through Delegation* (1993). For a more favorable economic analysis of legislative delegation, see David B. Spence & Frank Cross, "A Public Choice Case for the Administrative State," 89 *Geo. L.J.* 97 (2000).

169. The Court went on to offer an illustration: "While Congress need not provide any direction to the EPA regarding the manner in which it is to define 'country elevators,' which are to be exempt from new-stationary-source regulations governing grain elevators, see 42 U.S.C. § 7411(i), it must provide substantial guidance on setting air standards that affect the entire national economy."

170. The referenced discussion in *Loving* reasoned that delegation of power to the President to define aggravating factors in capital court-martial cases required less specific standards because of the President's independent authority as commander-in-chief. Loving v. United States, 517 U.S. 748, 772-773 (1996). The Court employed similar reasoning in *Mazurie* to support broad delegations to Indian tribes. United States v. Mazurie, 419 U.S. 544, 556–57 (1975). These decisions are discussed further below, in connection with the implications of who receives a legislative delegation.

171. See Alfred C. Aman, Jr. & William T. Mayton, *Administrative Law* 22 (2d ed., 2001) (concluding that "[o]utside of ratemaking or minor matters suited to administrative routine," NBC v. FCC is the only case upholding an open ended public interest standard).

172. In *Schechter Poultry* the power was to establish comprehensive codes of fair competition to govern industrial and commercial activities; in *Panama Refining* it was the

discretionary power to prohibit the transportation of "hot oil" among the states. Both of these powers were granted by provisions of the NIRA and in both cases the Court rejected the Act's explicit declaration of purposes as providing an insufficient standard because the purposes were so broad and contradictory that they did not substantially limit discretion. Under the *American Trucking* analysis, however, one would expect that even those standards might be sufficient in *Panama Refining* because the scope of the power delegated was so narrow.

173. This language is quoted above in the discussion of how the nondelegation doctrine may be used to narrowly construe statutory language.

174. Although not directly related to the nondelegation doctrine, this kind of reasoning may also explain the widespread assumption that Congress may authorize the President to make executive agreements. See Dames & Moore v. Regan, 453 U.S. 654 (1981).

175. Quoting United States v. Mazurie, 419 U.S. 544, 556–57 (1975).

176. See generally 16A Am. Jur. 2d Constitutional Law §§ 308–309.

177. See Kentucky Div., Horsemen's Benev. & Protective Ass'n, Inc. v. Turfway Park Racing Ass'n, Inc., 20 F.3d 1406, 1417 (6th Cir. 1994):

When Congress affords the States the option of regulating a particular activity, however, there is no danger that the federal legislative power will be exercised by the executive or judicial Branches of the federal government; instead, if the State accepts the invitation extended to it by Congress, the federal legislative power is not exercised at all. Thus, the separation of powers principle and, a fortiori, the nondelegation doctrine, simply are not implicated by Congress' "delegation" of power to the States. Rather than violate the separation of powers principle, such a delegation in fact furthers another core constitutional value—that of federalism.

178. See, e.g., Yakus v. United States, 321 U.S. 414, 424 (1944) ("The function of formulating the codes [in *Schechter Poultry*] was delegated, not to a public official responsible to Congress or the Executive, but to private individuals engaged in the industries to be regulated.").

179. But see Kentucky Div., Horsemen's Benev. & Protective Ass'n, Inc. v. Turfway Park Racing Ass'n, Inc., 20 F.3d 1406 (6th Cir 1994).

180. See Currin v. Wallace, 306 U.S. 1, 15 (1939); Alfred C. Aman, Jr. & William T. Mayton, *Administrative Law* 31–33 (2d ed., 2001); 16A Am. Jur. 2d Constitutional Law §§ 303–307.

181. See generally John F. Manning, "Textualism as a Nondelegation Doctrine," 97 *Colum. L. Rev.* 673 (1997) (arguing that textualists' rejection of legislative history as a tool of statutory construction can be understood as a special rule against delegating power to subunits of Congress).

182. See Bowsher v. Synar, 478 U.S. 714 (1986) (invalidating a statutory provision vesting executive power in officers subject to congressional control).

183. See Wayman v. Southard, 23 U.S. (10 Wheat.) 1, 43 (1825) ("The line has not been precisely drawn which separates those important subjects, which must be entirely regulated by the legislature itself, from those of less interest, in which a general provision may be made, and power given to those who are to act under such general provisions to fill up the details.").

184. See generally Ronald J. Krotoszynski, Jr., "Reconsidering the Nondelegation Doctrine: Universal Service, the Power to Tax, and the Ratification Doctrine," 80 *Ind. L.J.* 239 (2005).

185. For one such reading, see James O. Freedman, *Crisis and Legitimacy: The Administrative Process and American Government* 80–86 (1978).

186. Skinner v. Mid-America Pipeline Co., 490 U.S. 212, 222-23 (1989); see also *id.* at 223–34 (explaining that *National Cable Television* reflected a requirement that Congress clearly state its intention to delegate a taxing power).

187. See Doe v. Bush, 240 F. Supp. 2d 95 (D. Mass. 2002) (dismissing nondelegation challenge to Congress's October 2002 Iraq Resolution on political question grounds), aff'd, 323 F.3d 133 (1st Cir. 2003); see generally Curtis A. Bradley & Jack L. Goldsmith, "Congressional Authorization and the War on Terrorism," 118 *Harv. L. Rev.* 2047 (2005).

188. This kind of argument would be particularly powerful if the delegation concerned when the President could use force in self-defense, because it is generally understood that the commander-in-chief power includes the power to repel invasions and suppress rebellions without a formal declaration of war. See The Prize Cases, 67 U.S. 635 (1862).

189. Authorization for Use of Military Force Against Iraq Resolution of 2002, Public Law 107–243, Oct. 16, 2002, 116 Stat. 1498; see also Curtis A. Bradley & Jack L. Goldsmith, "Congressional Authorization and the War on Terrorism," 118 *Harv. L. Rev.* 2047 (2005) (analyzing prior authorization of force resolution in war on terror).

190. See Doe v. Bush, 240 F. Supp. 2d 95 (D. Mass. 2002) (dismissing nondelegation challenge to Congress's October 2002 Iraq Resolution on political question grounds), aff'd, 323 F.3d 133 (1st Cir. 2003).

191. See *Schechter Poultry*, 295 U.S. at 576 (1935).

192. See Lichter v. United States, 334 U.S. 742, 786–87 (1948); United States v. Rock Royal Co-op., 307 U.S. 533, 576 (1939).

193. See Sidney A. Shapiro & Richard E. Levy, "Government Benefits and the Rule of Law: Toward a Standards-Based Theory of Due Process," 57 *Admin. L. Rev.* 107 (2005).

194. Even *Rock Royal*, which relied in part on procedures to distinguish *Schechter Poultry* acknowledged this basic limitation. United States v. Rock Royal Co-op., 307 U.S. 533, 576 (1939).

195. See Fahey v. Mallonnee, 332 U.S. 245, 249 (1947).

196. This sort of reasoning has been followed in some states. See, e.g., Lincoln Dairy Co. v. Finigan, 170 Neb. 777, 104 N.W. 2d 227 (1960).

197. See generally Alfred C. Aman, Jr. & William T. Mayton, *Administrative Law* § 1.3.3 (2d ed., 2001).

198. A detailed timeline of the case with links to relevant documents can be found at http://www.miami.edu/ethics2/schiavo/timeline.htm.

199. The petition and related documents, including copies of the relevant subpoenas is posted at http://www.miami.edu/ethics2/schiavo/031805-USHousePetition%20SCt.pdf.

200. See http://jweb.flcourts.org/pls/docket/ds_docket?p_caseyear=2005&p_casenumber= 449.

201. On the same day the Florida Supreme Court rejected the emergency petition, the "PEG" tube providing nutrition to Ms. Schiavo was removed. Shortly thereafter, Congress passed legislation specifically conferring jurisdiction on the Federal District Court for the Middle District of Florida to review the case. The district court did so, but found no basis for overturning the judgment of the Florida courts or ordering reinsertion of the tube. Appeals to the federal circuit court and the Supreme Court were unsuccessful, and not long thereafter Ms. Schiavo died.

202. Recently, the Senate filibuster has come under attack, particularly as applied to judicial appointments. It has been suggested by opponents that the filibuster is antidemocratic because it permits a minority of legislators to block action and may be unconstitutional because it effectively requires a two-third's vote, rather than a majority, to approve a

bill or nomination. For general discussion of the filibuster, see Martin B. Gold & Dimple Gupta, "The Constitutional Option to Change Senate Rules and Procedures: A Majoritarian Means to Overcome the Filibuster," 28 *Harv. J.L. & Pub. Pol'y* 205 (2004).

203. Elizabeth Garrett, "Harnessing Politics: The Dynamics of Offset Requirements in the Tax Legislative Process," 65 *U. Chi. L. Rev.* 501, 503 (1998) (discussing implications of legislative processes for budgetary outcomes).

204. For purposes of this power, the "qualifications" that may be determined are the explicit standing requirements of age, citizenship, and residency; Congress has no authority to impose additional qualifications. See Powell v. McCormack, 395 U.S. 486 (1969).

205. This is one explanation of why the power to expel members is expressly granted and why it requires a two-third's vote.

206. See, e.g., Subcommittee on Privileges and Elections, Senate Committee on Rules and Administration, "Senate Election, Expulsion and Censure Cases from 1793–1972" (1972) (compiled by Richard D. Hupman).

207. Thus, as suggested by the Schiavo case, noncompliance with subpoenas is more likely to be prosecuted as a statutory violation than with a congressional contempt resolution. Likewise, the federal bribery statute is used to prosecute persons accused of bribing members of Congress.

208. *In re* Chapman, 166 U.S. 661, 671 (1897) (stating that statutory provision making it a misdemeanor to fail to comply with a congressional subpoena "was an act necessary and proper for carrying into execution the powers vested in congress and in each house thereof.")

209. This was Jefferson's position in his Manual of Parliamentary Practice in the Senate. Thomas Jefferson, *A Manual of Parliamentary Practice: For the Use of the Senate* (U.S. Government Printing Office, 1993) (1801). A number of statutory provisions that reflect the deliberative powers are now in place. The Schiavo Petition filed by the House, for example, cited 18 U.S.C. § 1505 (making obstruction of a congressional investigation a crime), 18 U.S.C. § 1512 (making it a crime to kill or attempt to kill a person to prevent their appearance or to prevent the production of documents), and 2 U.S.C. § 192 (making it a misdemeanor to fail to comply with a congressional subpoena).

210. See Kilbourn v. Thompson, 103 U.S. (13 Otto) 168, 183–89 (1880) (reviewing precedents to conclude that contempt power in Parliament derives from its judicial functions and reasoning that "the right of the House of Representatives to punish the citizen for a contempt of its authority or a breach of its privileges can derive no support from the precedents and practices of the English Parliament . . .").

211. McGrain v. Daugherty, 273 U.S. 135, 162 (1927).

212. Joseph Story, *Commentaries on the Constitution of the United States* § 1503 (1833). Justice Story made this point to explain his conclusion that the Presidential pardon power did not extend to pardoning those found to be in contempt of Congress. *Id.*

213. There is no statutory provision prohibiting libel of Congress. Such a statute would, of course, present First Amendment problems. But those problems are no less present— and are arguably more pronounced—when Congress acts without the benefit of statute, precisely because the participation of the other branches is not required. Indeed, the only case involving the exercise of the contempt power for alleged libel, Marshall v. Gordon (1917), concluded that there was insufficient basis for its exercise. See *infra* notes 240–42 and accompanying text (discussing Marshall).

214. 2 U.S.C. § 192 provides:

Every person who having been summoned as a witness by the authority of either House of Congress to give testimony or to produce papers upon any matter under inquiry before either House, or any joint committee established by a joint or concurrent resolution of the two Houses of Congress, or any committee of either House of Congress, willfully makes default, or who, having appeared, refuses to answer any question pertinent to the question under inquiry, shall be deemed guilty of a misdemeanor, punishable by a fine of not more than $1,000 nor less than $100 and imprisonment in a common jail for not less than one month nor more than twelve months.

The background of this statute is discussed further below.

215. See 18 U.S.C. § 201, which makes it a crime to corruptly give, offer, or promise anything of value to a public official to influence their official conduct, and defines public officials to include members of Congress.

216. *In re* Chapman, 166 U.S. 661, 671-72 (1897) (upholding 2 U.S.C. § 192); accord Jurney v. MacCracken, 294 U.S. 125, 151–52 (1935) (holding that contempt statute did not prevent either house of Congress from continuing to exercise that power).

217. Perhaps the most obvious example of this point is when Congress exercises the power to impeach and to try impeachments against executive branch officials or judges.

218. Marshall v. Gordon, 243 U.S. 521, 543 & n.3 (1917) (distinguishing these examples from contempt sanctions for libel).

219. To the extent that disruptive behavior by legislators themselves is involved, historical precedents rest on the explicit textual authority of either house to punish its members (including expulsions) and hence stand on different constitutional footing.

220. The petitioner was apparently protesting cuts in welfare programs and the occupation apparently lasted approximately twelve hours, from noon to midnight. See Groppi v. Leslie, 404 U.S. 496, 498 (1972).

221. Increased reliance on the bribery statute does not necessarily reflect congressional concern with adhering to separation of powers. Instead, because the contempt power is limited to the life of the session in which the bribery occurs, it often proved to be an ineffective sanction.

222. In contrast, compulsory testimony and production of documents is not inherently criminal in character.

223. See Marshall v. Gordon, 243 U.S. 521, 546 (1917) (concluding that reliance on allegedly libelous letter's effects "upon the public mind" and the "sense of indignation" it would arouse in members to support contempt sanction "demonstrate that the contempt relied on was not intrinsic to the right of the House to preserve the means of discharging its legislative duties").

224. To the extent that the Alien and Sedition Act would permit prosecution for libel of Congress, it might be understood as an exercise of the deliberative powers of Congress. Most observers, however, regard that statute as a clear violation of the First Amendment. See N.Y. Times Co. v. Sullivan, 376 U.S. 254, 276 (1964) (stating that "although the Sedition Act was never tested in this Court, the attack upon its validity has carried the day in the court of history" and citing sources); Larry Kramer, "Understanding Federalism," 47 *Vand. L. Rev.* 1485, 1519 (1994) (stating that the Alien and Sedition Acts were "about as clear an example of unconstitutional legislation as one could find").

225. The Court permitted recovery against the sergeant-at-arms and others who enforced the contempt order, but not against individual members of Congress, who were protected by legislative immunity. See Kilbourn v. Thompson, 103 U.S. (13 Otto) 168, 200–205 (1880).

226. The Court reasoned further that actions of the House of Representatives were particularly prone to abuse and should be "watched with vigilance" to prevent encroachments on the other branches or individuals.

227. As will be discussed further below, this statute was adopted in the 1850s in response to the limitations of the contempt power, which cannot be used to punish beyond the end of the legislative session, thus compromising its effectiveness in many cases. The statute was upheld in *In re* Chapman, 166 U.S. 661 (1897).

228. Gojack v. United States, 384 U.S. 702, 709 (1966) ("There is no basis for invoking criminal sanctions to punish a witness for refusal to cooperate in an inquiry which was never properly authorized."). Technically, this holding was based on the statute, in the sense that "a specific, properly authorized subject of inquiry is an essential element of the offense." *Id.* at 708.

229. See Russell v. United States, 369 U.S. 749 (1962) (holding that indictments under statute were inadequate because they did not identify the subject under inquiry at the time of failure to testify).

230. See Deutsch v. United States, 367 U.S. 456 (1961) (holding that questions concerning communist infiltration into educational institutions were not pertinent to subcommittee investigation regarding infiltration into organized labor).

231. See Watkins v. United States, 354 U.S. 178 (1957) (invalidating conviction on the ground that broad scope of inquiry provided insufficient basis for a witness to assess pertinency of questions); United States v. Rumely, 345 U.S. 41 (1953) (narrowly construing scope of investigation to avoid First Amendment difficulties). These cases will be discussed further below.

232. See, e.g., Gojack v. United States, 384 U.S. 702, 798 (1966) (reversing conviction because of failure to prove that subcommittee investigation was properly authorized); Russell v. United States, 369 U.S. 749 (1962) (holding that indictments under statute were inadequate because they did not identify the subject under inquiry at the time of failure to testify).

233. 2 U.S.C. § 192 (reproduced in full *supra* note 214).

234. Deutsch v. United States, 367 U.S. 456, 467–68 (1961).

235. See *id.* at 468–69.

236. See Eastland v. United States Serviceman's Fund, 421 U.S. 491 (1975) (refusing to enjoin subpoena to bank where subpoena related to and was in furtherance of a valid investigation); Sinclair v. United States, 279 U.S. 263 (1929) (upholding contempt convictions arising from investigation of certain military contracts).

237. See Groppi v. Leslie, 404 U.S. 496, 499–500 (1972) (stating that there is nothing in the Constitution to suggest that the contempt power of state legislatures is less than that of Congress); Tenney v. Brandlove, 341 U.S. 367 (1951) (deferring to state legislative determination of the need for testimony).

238. 18 U.S.C. § 201.

239. See Jurney v. MacCracken, 294 U.S. 125, 151–52 (1935) (holding that contempt statute did not prevent either house of Congress from continuing to exercise that power); *In re* Chapman, 166 U.S. 661, 671–72 (1897) ("We grant that congress could not devest [*sic*] itself, or either of its houses, of the essential and inherent power to punish for contempt, in cases to which the power of either house properly extended. . . .").

240. The investigation concerned an organization called Labor's National Peace Council, to which the member belonged.

241. Marshall v. Gordon, 243 U.S. 521, 545 (1917).

242. The Court continued: "But to state this situation is to demonstrate that the contempt relied upon was not intrinsic to the right of the House to preserve the means of discharging its legislative duties. . . ."

243. Jurney v. McCracken, 294 U.S. 125, 148–49 (1935).

244. In the omitted language from the above-quoted passage in *Anderson*, the Court stated that the contempt power "may, at first view, and from the history of the practice of our legislative bodies, be thought to extend to other inflictions. But every other will be found to be mere commutation for confinement; since commitment alone is the alternative where the individual proves contumacious." Anderson v. Dunn, 19 U.S. (6 Wheat.) 204, 231 (1821). In Jurney v. MacCracken, moreover, the Court cited early instances of contempt in which the individual was imprisoned but then released upon the payment of fees. See 294 U.S. at 148, nn. 4 & 5.

245. See Watkins v. United States, 354 U.S. 178, 206-07 (1957):

Since World War II, the Congress has practically abandoned its original practice of utilizing the coercive sanction of contempt proceedings at the bar of the House. The sanction there imposed is imprisonment by the House until the recalcitrant witness agrees to testify or disclose the matters sought, provided that the incarceration does not extend beyond adjournment. The Congress has instead invoked the aid of the federal judicial system in protecting itself against contumacious conduct. It has become customary to refer these matters to the United States Attorneys for prosecution under criminal law.

The last Supreme Court case involving contempt sanctions by either house appears to be Jurney v. MacCracken in 1935. The many McCarthy-era cases and those since that time involve criminal prosecutions pursuant to statute.

246. Jurney v. McCracken, 294 U.S. 125, 151-52 (1935); *In re* Chapman, 166 U.S. 661, 671–72 (1897) ("We grant that congress could not devest [*sic*] itself, or either of its houses, of the essential and inherent power to punish for contempt, in cases to which the power of either house properly extended. . . .")

247. See Groppi v. Leslie, 404 U.S. 496, 501 (1972) ("The past decisions of this Court strongly indicate that the panoply of procedural rights that are accorded a defendant in a criminal trial has never been thought necessary in legislative contempt proceedings.").

248. See *Ex parte* Terry, 128 U.S. 289 (1888).

249. Watkins v. United States, 354 U.S. 178, 208 (1957).

250. See Gojack v. United States, 384 U.S. 702 (1966); Deutsch v. United States, 367 U.S. 456, 467–68 (1961); Watkins v. United States, 354 U.S. 178 (1957).

251. See Yellin v. United States, 374 U.S. 109 (1963) (holding that failure of committee to follow its own rules concerning going into executive session so as to protect a witness's reputation excused his failure to respond to questions).

252. In this sense, the requirement is related to the void for vagueness doctrine and the prohibition of ex post facto laws.

253. See Deutsch v. United States, 367 U.S. 456, 467–68 (1961) (distinguishing between due process requirement that "the pertinency of the interrogation to the topic under the congressional committee's inquiry must be brought home to the witness at the time the questions are put to him" from the "prosecution's duty at trial to prove that the questions propounded by the congressional committee were in fact 'pertinent to the question under inquiry . . .' ").

254. Although *Groppi* involved the imposition of criminal contempt sanctions by a state legislature, it is instructive for similar actions by Congress.

255. Although these cases arose in the context of statutory prosecutions, they would seemingly apply to direct contempt proceedings by either house as well, because the privilege against self-incrimination applies at the time of questioning and justifies a refusal to answer a valid question.

256. In a later decision, however, the Court upheld the conviction of a witness who disclaimed reliance on the Fifth Amendment, because such reliance could be used to impeach his testimony in a state trial arising out of the events in question, rejecting his argument that forcing him to choose between incriminating testimony and incriminating reliance on the Fifth Amendment violated due process. Hutcheson v. United States, 369 U.S. 599 (1962).

257. Emspak v. United States, 349 U.S. 190, 195–98 (1955).

258. Bart v. United States, 349 U.S. 219, 221–22 (1955).

259. See, e.g., Quinn v. United States, 349 U.S. 155, 164 (1955) ("It is precisely at such times—when the privilege is under attack by those who wrongly conceive of it as merely a shield for the guilty—that governmental bodies must be most scrupulous in protecting its exercise."); see also Slochower v. Board of Education, 350 U.S. 551 (1956) (holding that a state could not dismiss a tenured college teacher for invoking the privilege in response to questions from a congressional committee concerning past membership in the Communist Party).

260. 18 U.S.C. § 6002. This statute applies to testimony before "either House of Congress, a joint committee of the two Houses, or a committee or a subcommittee of either House."

261. See United States v. North, 910 F.2d 843, modified in part on rehearing, 920 F.2d 940 (D.C. Cir. 1990), cert. denied 500 U.S. 941 (1991).

262. As discussed above, however, the court invalidated the contempt finding on other grounds.

263. Russell v. United States, 369 U.S. 749, 766–72 (1962).

264. Sinclair v. United States, 279 U.S. 263, 298–99 (1929).

265. See United States v. Gaudin, 515 U.S. 506, 519–21 (1995) (overruling *Sinclair* in the context of rejecting a stare decisis argument for permitting judicial determination of "materiality" in a perjury prosecution).

266. *Chapman* rejected a challenge to the statute by a defendant who had not been sanctioned through direct congressional sanction, reasoning that there was no double jeopardy because contempt and criminal prosecutions were distinct actions by different jurisdictions. See *In re* Chapman, 166 U.S. 661, 672 (1897). In light of subsequent decisions, it is unlikely that the Court would today uphold both a congressional contempt sanction and a criminal prosecution for the same offense. See United States v. Dixon, 509 U.S. 688 (1993) (holding that double jeopardy prohibited prosecution for conduct previously punished as criminal contempt of court).

267. Compare, for example, Galvan v. Press, 347 U.S. 522 (1954) (upholding deportation of a longtime resident based on communist affiliation); Dennis v. United States, 341 U.S. 494 (1951) (upholding conviction of Communist Party leaders under the Smith Act for advocating the overthrow of the government) with, for example, American Communications Associations v. Douds, 339 U.S. 382 (1950) (invalidating provisions of the Taft Hartley Act requiring union officers to swear that they were not members of the Communist Party). See generally David P. Currie, *The Constitution in the Supreme Court: The Second Century, 1888–1986*, at 353–58, 385–96 (1990).

268. See also Wilkinson v. United States, 365 U.S. 399 (1961) (following *Barenblatt* in the context of a witness who criticized the House Committee on Un-American Activities).

269. Baker v. Carr, 369 U.S. 186 (1962).

270. See generally Robert J. Reinstein & Harvey A. Silverglate, "Legislative Privilege and the Separation of Powers," 86 *Harv. L. Rev.* 1113 (1973).

271. See Gravel v. United States, 408 U.S. 606 (1972).

272. *Kilbourn*, however, held that the sergeant-at-arms who had enforced the contempt order was not immune. This conclusion is difficult to reconcile with more recent cases, such as *Gravel* and Doe v. McMillan, 412 U.S. 306 (1973) in which the Court extended immunity to legislative staff.

273. This actually parallels in significant ways the Court's treatment of the executive branch, in which the President is absolutely immune from suit for his or her conduct in office, Clinton v. Jones, 520 U.S. 681 (1997), Nixon v. Fitzgerald, 457 U.S. 731 (1982), but subordinate officials have only qualified immunity. Harlow v. Fitzgerald, 457 U.S. 800 (1982).

274. Doe v. McMillan, 412 U.S. 306, 313 (1973).

275. The suit was dismissed both as to the defendants who were members of Congress and as to the chief counsel for the committee issuing the subpoena.

276. Quoting Tenney v. Brandlove, 341 U.S. 367, 378 (1951).

Conclusion

The history and jurisprudence of the Necessary and Proper Clause, legislative delegations, and the deliberative powers of Congress reflect a common understanding of the federal legislative power. Although incompletely articulated, this common understanding draws on implicit assumptions about the operation of government as a form of collective action.

If government is a form of collective action, governmental authority is the power to make and enforce decisions concerning the collective. The structure of government facilitates beneficial collective action by reducing transaction costs that may prevent collective decisions from being made and enforced. To achieve these benefits, however, individual members of the collective must accept particular collective decisions that run contrary to their interests because the interests of the collective (or of those who control its decisions) are not aligned perfectly with those of its individual members. Individual members of the collective accept particular government decisions that impose net costs on them, because those costs are far outweighed by the collective benefits achieved through government. While individual members are better off as a result of government, they also have interests that diverge from those of the collective and therefore have incentives to resist or cheat on collective decisions. To some extent, these incentives are inherent in the nature of collective goods (the free rider problem and the prisoners' dilemma), but when individuals can be bound without their consent, those who are net losers from particular collective decisions have especially strong incentives to resist or cheat. Conversely, there are strong incentives to gain governmental power to use it for personal or special interests without regard to the interests of the collective as a whole.

The essential problem of government is how to empower collective institutions with the authority to govern efficiently and effectively without subjecting individual members to the oppressive exercise of collective authority. In a constitutional democracy such as our own, these difficulties are addressed through a representative government exercising authority pursuant to the rule of law. Under this kind of arrangement, collective decisions are made by politically accountable institutions through the medium of laws that bind all members of the collective. Political accountability helps to ensure that government decisions reflect the interest of the collective as a whole rather than of a smaller subset of individuals who hold positions of power. The rule of law reinforces political accountability because when the government acts by means of generally applicable antecedent rules (laws), unelected government officials are held accountable to rules adopted by politically accountable institutions. Conversely, the rule of law facilitates enforcement of collective decisions because the enactment and enforcement of laws is broadly accepted as a legitimate exercise of collective authority. A broad social norm of binding obligation to obey laws fosters reciprocal and mutually reinforcing expectations of voluntary compliance with collective decisions.

In the U.S. constitutional system, political accountability and the rule of law are bolstered by a system of divided governmental authority. Authority is divided vertically between the federal and state governments, and horizontally among the legislative, executive, and judicial branches of the federal and state governments. The federal legislative power is the portion of governmental authority allocated to the federal government that is legislative in character. Article I, section 1, vests that authority in Congress, which is empowered to make necessary and proper laws with respect to certain enumerated powers. It seems reasonably clear that the Framers understood the term "legislative power" to mean the same kind of governmental authority contemporaneously exercised by other legislative bodies, such as the British Parliament or state legislatures. Nonetheless, unlike those legislative bodies, whose authority encompassed all subjects within the province of government, the legislative authority to be exercised by Congress was limited to subjects for which the Framers considered collective action at a broader national scale to be essential. Nonetheless, the Framers also contemplated that the reserved authority of states would enhance both the voice and the exit opportunities of citizens.

The legislative power is the essential sovereign authority delegated by a people to their government; that is, the power to decide on behalf of the nation what collective goods to pursue and how to pursue them. Under the rule of law, sovereign authority operates by means of laws and the legislative power is the antecedent power to make those laws. These laws establish the "ends" and "means" of collective action. Laws act as both a source of authority for and a constraint upon executive and judicial action to implement and enforce them. Given the importance of the federal legislative power, it is poorly understood and has been subjected to surprisingly little extended analysis. It has been my goal in this book to begin to fill this gap by bringing together three topics that are integrally connected with the federal legislative power but typically treated as distinct problems. The conjunction of necessary and proper legislation, legislative delegation, and deliberative powers offers a more comprehensive picture of the federal legislative power.

The Necessary and Proper Clause, as interpreted and applied since McCulloch v. Maryland, expresses fundamental principles of the federal legislative power. It is the power to determine the public policy ends within the enumerated powers and to specify the "necessary and proper" means to achieve these ends. This power is plenary in the sense that Congress is subject to no limits on its exercise except those expressed in the Constitution itself. In practice, the application of the *McCulloch* test has been the focal point for the especially difficult task of reconciling this "plenary power" principle with the concept of enumerated powers. The ends-means analysis of the *McCulloch* test expresses an intrinsic constitutional limit on the legislative power: it must further a legitimate governmental end. *McCulloch's* requirement that legislative means may not be inconsistent with the letter or spirit of the Constitution incorporates external limits on the federal legislative power, including those based on states' or individual rights.

Intrinsically, if the legislative power is the power to determine the ends of government policy and the means to achieve them, then valid legislation must be sufficiently related to the attainment of ends that are within the authority of the government to pursue. In a unitary state, these ends include the entire field of government action; only the pursuit of impermissible or illegitimate ends would be beyond the scope of the legislative power. In practice, such an inquiry typically merges with external limitations imposed by individual rights. The impermissible or illegitimate ends are ends that violate individual rights, such as suppressing speech or religion, conferring benefits, or imposing burdens on account of race or other improper factors. The determination of impermissible ends is less concerned with the nature of legislative power than it is with the scope of the individual right at issue. In our federal system, however, the question of ends takes on added urgency and complexity because substantive legislative authority is divided between the federal government and the states. The enumeration of a finite set of ends that are the proper subject of the federal legislative power implies that the range of permissible means attached to them are likewise finite. But virtually any law can plausibly be justified as connected to one of the enumerated powers, and federalism would therefore seem to demand that the Court construct and enforce intrinsic limitations that confine the federal legislative power to its proper sphere.

While the *McCulloch* test provides a framework for such intrinsic limits, its interpretation and application over the years raise a number of fundamental questions that are largely unresolved. To begin with, the relationship between the Necessary and Proper Clause and the other enumerated powers of Congress remains ambiguous. Each enumerated power may represent a substantial source of legislative authority in its own right, with the Necessary and Proper Clause serving as a distinct additional source of authority, or the Necessary and Proper Clause could, in effect, define the legislative authority that is granted with respect to each power. This ambiguity has greater significance for the framework of analysis than for the ultimate answer to the question whether a particular law is within the scope of the federal legislative power.

A second source of uncertainty—one with much greater significance for the scope of the federal legislative power—is the "level of scrutiny" required under the *McCulloch* test. Every federal statute incorporates an implicit or explicit congressional judgment that the law is within the scope of the federal legislative power; that is, that it is a necessary and proper means to an end within the enumerated powers. Thus, judicial review of legislation under the *McCulloch* test is essentially a question of how much deference should be given to that congressional judgment. Respect for separation of powers and the representative character of Congress counsel strongly in favor of deference, whereas concern over federalism and the vulnerability of states counsel in favor of meaningful judicial review. In practice, the Court has, for the most part, opted in favor of deference, and the *McCulloch* test is usually understood as reflecting the highly deferential "rational basis test." But the language of *McCulloch* itself is not so clear on this point, and some Justices have recently argued that a more searching judicial inquiry is required. In addition to these overarching uncertainties, a number of particular issues arise when the Necessary and Proper Clause is linked with a specific enumerated power, as divergent tests have evolved for many of the most significant powers, including the commerce power, the spending power, and the power to enforce the Reconstruction Amendments.

To the extent that the Court has enforced limits on federal legislative power, those limits have generally been external rather than intrinsic. Cases holding that federal statutes exceed the scope of federal legislative power generally start with the premise that some aspect of state sovereignty is beyond the reach of the federal legislative power and invalidate the federal statute in question because it intrudes into this protected sphere. Cases involving sovereign immunity and the no-commandeering rule are the clearest examples of this sort of reasoning, even if the Court has attempted to characterize them as intrinsic limits by declaring that external restrictions based on state sovereignty are the mirror image of intrinsic limits on legislative means. Likewise, cases concluding that federal statutes exceed the substantive authority of Congress typically emphasize that these statutes intrude into fields of regulation that are constitutionally reserved to the states. This kind of reasoning was most formal and explicit during the pre–New Deal era, but has resurfaced as a factor under the *Lopez* framework.

In the final analysis, we are left with an ongoing struggle over whether the Court should more strictly scrutinize the ends-means connection, thereby constructing and enforcing intrinsic limits on federal legislative power. Some Justices have advocated such an approach, rejecting the rational basis test and arguing that *McCulloch* contemplates a more rigorous ends-means scrutiny in reviewing the exercise of the federal legislative power. Adopting such an approach, however, would carry complications of its own. Unless the Court is prepared to similarly scrutinize the exercise of state legislative powers, it would mean that the federal legislative power vested in Congress is not the same kind of legislative power exercised by the states, which is inconsistent with the original understanding of the Framers. Elevating scrutiny of ordinary state legislation to ensure that it is a proper exercise of legislative powers within the authority of states, however, would engage the federal courts in an aggressive review of state legislation that itself would constitute federal interference with the regulatory autonomy of states in areas of their traditional sovereign legislative authority.

Whatever the uncertainties surrounding the scope of congressional authority to enact necessary and proper laws, the common understanding remains that this power includes the power to determine public policy ends and the means to achieve them. The analysis of legislative delegation builds on this common understanding. The ends and means specified by legislation must be implemented somehow, and separation of powers means that the power to make the laws must be separate from the power to implement them. Thus, Congress itself cannot implement the laws, and the ends and means specified in legislation necessarily contemplate the delegation of executive and judicial power to the other branches of government. While Congress must inevitably delegate executive and judicial power, the Vesting Clause and separation of powers principles prohibit Congress from delegating the legislative power itself. To police the boundaries between permissible and impermissible legislative delegations, the Court has developed the nondelegation doctrine, under which legislation must contain an "intelligible principle," or standard, that guides and controls the exercise of delegated authority.

The intelligible principle test therefore expresses one essential aspect of the federal legislative power and must be integrated into our basic understanding of it. Put simply, necessary and proper legislation establishes legal standards that bind the general public and government officials. The adoption of standards reflects and embodies the ends of public policy. The means of achieving these ends is the exercise of delegated authority pursuant to those standards. So understood, the nondelegation doctrine and the intelligible principle test reinforce both the political accountability and rule of law functions of separation of powers. Congress is designed to be the most politically accountable branch of government, and the intelligible principle test ensures that Congress can be held accountable for the public policy ends it chooses and the means it adopts to achieve them. The adoption of standards also makes it possible for the rule of law to operate, because the exercise of delegated authority can be tested for compliance with these standards.

As a matter of historical and doctrinal analysis, the Court has consistently endorsed these principles, but "almost never" found a violation of the nondelegation doctrine. As a result, Congress may delegate broad government authority pursuant to open-ended general standards and a great many important policy decisions are made by administrative agencies or the courts in their interpretation and application of these standards. Critics of this state of affairs can argue with some force that this sort of delegation undermines political accountability, as Congress can effectively avoid accountability by delegating critical decisions to administrative agencies. Likewise, open-ended standards arguably do little to constrain the discretion of government officials and therefore undermine the rule of law functions of separation of powers. Nonetheless, there seems to be little support on the Court for strengthening or more aggressively applying the intelligible principle test.

Necessary and proper legislation and the nondelegation doctrine are mutually reinforcing principles that reflect a coherent concept of the federal legislative power, but the deliberative powers of Congress do not fit neatly into that concept. Congress may exercise the deliberative powers by enacting necessary and proper laws, but it may also exercise these powers directly, engaging in governmental action that neither follows bicameralism and presentment nor takes the form of legislation. Moreover, while some deliberative powers are express, others are not. These nontextual implicit deliberative powers include authority to reach beyond the internal operations of Congress to compel private persons to testify and produce documents or to remove obstructions to legislative deliberations by imposing sanctions for contempt. The historical and doctrinal justification for such deliberative powers has been the institutional necessities of Congress.

The deliberative powers of Congress are essential prerequisites to the exercise of the legislative power vested in Congress. In this sense, their exercise is justified only if it is connected to the enactment of necessary and proper laws (or other actions, such as impeachment, specifically vested in Congress). For this reason, the deliberative powers cases also tell us something about the federal legislative power, albeit indirectly. Most clearly, the early recognition of implicit deliberative powers tends to confirm the conclusion that Congress was expected to exercise the same kind of legislative power exercised by other such bodies at the time of the founding. In addition, the breadth of deliberative powers reflects the sense that the legislative power embodies the power to make the antecedent policy choice concerning the ends and means of collective action and the vesting of this power in a politically accountable body. The deliberative powers of Congress mean that Congress is not dependent on any other body for the information and security it needs to make those policy choices.

In this broader sense, the enactment of necessary and proper laws, legislative delegations, and deliberative powers represent a comprehensive framework for the exercise of the federal legislative power. Although collective action theory is a relatively recent development, the constitutional design reflects the Framers' intuitive understanding of the problems of collective action and their creative responses to those problems. The federal legislative power, in other words, is one more example of the remarkable ingenuity reflected in the design of the U.S. Constitution.

Bibliographic Essay

There is a massive body of literature addressing the federal legislative power from a variety of perspectives. This bibliographic essay cannot comprehensively review that literature and will therefore concentrate on the most useful and essential sources. For convenience, the review divides the literature into five substantive categories. The first category covers general sources on constitutional law, including historical and doctrinal treatments that address multiple topics covered in this book. The next three categories encompass each of the three main subjects analyzed in the book—necessary and proper legislation, legislative delegation, and deliberative powers. A concluding section discusses the literature on collective action with particular reference to interstate relations.

GENERAL SOURCES

There are a number of "standard" works on constitutional law that cover a wide range of subjects, including the federal legislative power. These works typically devote some attention to necessary and proper legislation, legislative delegation, and deliberative powers. The interpretation and application of the Necessary and Proper Clause, in particular, often receives extended treatment in general works on constitutional law, including both doctrinal treatises and historical accounts.

I have found two constitutional histories to be particularly helpful. The first is Professor David P. Currie's two-volume treatment of the Supreme Court's constitutional decisions: *The Constitution in the Supreme Court: The First Hundred Years 1789–1888* (1985) and *The Constitution in the Supreme Court: The Second Century, 1888–1986* (1990). Professor Currie offers a remarkably concise, yet complete and rich, analysis that focuses on the Supreme Court's reasoning in leading decisions and addresses most of the cases discussed in this book. Second, Alfred Kelly, Winfred Harbison, & Herman Belz, *The American Constitution: Its Origin and Development*, 2 vols. (7th ed., 1991) offers a lucid historical account of constitutional evolution that places judicial decisions and other developments in their political context. Another important historical and doctrinal analysis is

Bruce Ackerman's two-volume work, *We the People*, vol. 1, *Foundations* (1991) and *We the People*, vol. 2, *Transformations* (1998), in which Ackerman developed the idea that in addition to the founding, there are other critical "constitutional moments" in which societal consensus on constitutional principles was formed. These moments include reconstruction, the New Deal Crisis, and the civil rights movement, all of which Ackerman discusses in detail.

For readers interested in doctrinal analysis of constitutional issues, there are several treatises that may be useful. The standard constitutional law treatise is Ronald D. Rotunda & John E. Nowak, *Treatise on Constitutional Law: Substance & Procedure* (3d ed., 1999). This multivolume set contains a detailed analysis that is updated regularly and contains some discussion of all of the issues covered in this book. Other standard works include Laurence Tribe's treatise on constitutional law, *American Constitutional Law* (2d ed., 1988), which has been partially updated in what was originally intended to be a two-volume revision, Laurence H. Tribe, *American Constitutional Law* (3d ed., 2000). Although Professor Tribe has apparently decided not to complete the revision, the first volume of the third edition deals with structural issues, including separation of powers and federalism, and therefore covers most of the topics addressed in this book. Two shorter treatments of constitutional doctrine directed toward students are Erwin Chemerinsky, *Constitutional Law: Principles and Policies* (2d ed., 2002) and the "hornbook" version of Rotunda and Nowak's treatise, John E. Nowak & Ronald D. Rotunda, *Constitutional Law* (7th ed., 2004).

Historical treatments of constitutional doctrine and decisions also abound. The most ambitious of these is the Oliver Wendell Holmes Devise History of the Supreme Court of the United States, which remains incomplete but contains a number of published volumes that provide an in-depth treatment of historically significant cases and contain considerable information about the political context of the decisions. Published volumes include vol. 1, Julius Goebel, Jr., *Antecedents and Beginnings to 1801* (1971); vol. 2, George Lee Haskins & Herbert A. Johnson, *Foundations of Power: John Marshall, 1801–15* (1981); vols. 3–4, G. Edward White, *The Marshall Court and Cultural Change, 1815–35* (1988); vol. 5, Carl Brent Swisher, *The Taney Period, 1836–64* (1974); vols. 6–7, Charles Fairman, *Reconstruction and Reunion, 1864–88* (1971); vol. 8, Owen Fiss, *Troubled Beginnings of the Modern State, 1888–1910* (1993); and vol. 9, Alexander M. Bickel & Benno C. Schmidt, Jr., *The Judiciary and Responsible Government, 1910–21* (1984). Volumes 10–13 are apparently in process and may be available soon. While comprehensive, detailed, and often insightful, this work may be too large and cumbersome to be of much use to many readers.

Somewhat dated treatments of constitutional doctrine that are of analytical and historical interest include Joseph Story, *Commentaries on the Constitution of the United States*, 3 vols. (1833); Thomas M. Cooley, *A Treatise on the Constitutional Limitations Which Rest Upon the Legislative Power of the States of the American Union* (1868); Charles Ticknor Curtis, *Constitutional History of the United States from their Declaration of Independence to the Close of their*

Civil War, 2 vols. (1889); Charles Warren, *The Supreme Court in United States History*, 3 vols. (rev. ed., 1926); *American Constitutional History: Essays By Edward S. Corwin* (Mason & Garvey eds., 1964); and James Bradley Thayer, "The Origin and Scope of the American Doctrine of Constitutional Law," 7 *Harv. L. Rev.* 129 (1893).

Primary sources concerning the founding are compiled in Max Farrand, ed., *The Records of the Federal Convention of 1787*, 3 vols. (1937) (focusing on the Constitutional Convention) and 1–5 Jonathan Elliot, ed., *The Debates in the Several State Conventions on the Adoption of the Federal Constitution* (1836). Searchable online versions of both compilations, as well as other early documents concerning the constitution are available at the Library of Congress Web site, "A Century of Lawmaking for a New Nation: U.S. Congressional Documents and Debates, 1774–1785," available at lcweb2.loc.gov/ammem/amlaw/lawhome.html. A variety of documents concerning early constitutional history, including the Federalist Papers and documents relating to the national bank controversy, are available online on The Avalon Project at Yale Law School Web site, available at www.yale.edu/lawweb/avalon/avalon.htm. A link to the Federalist Papers is also available through the Library of Congress "Thomas" Web site, available at lcweb2.loc.gov/const/fed/fedpapers.html. The most complete source for primary materials on the ratification of the Constitution is John P. Kaminski & Gaspare J. Saladino, eds., *The Documentary History of the Ratification of the Constitution* (Madison: State Historical Society of Wisconsin (multiple volumes, published in various years), which includes volumes on the ratification debates generally, as well as volumes with materials organized by state. For anti-Federalist writings not available in other sources, see Herbert J. Storing, ed., *The Complete Anti-Federalist*, 7 vols. (1981). Two other compilations of founding documents may also be quite useful. First, Philip B. Kurland & Ralph Lerner, *The Founders' Constitution* (1986), is a five-volume set containing excerpts from the Constitutional Convention and ratification debates organized on the basis of the relevant constitutional provision. An online version can be found at press-pubs.uchicago.edu/founders/. A smaller, student-oriented collection is Daniel Farber & Suzanna Sherry, *A History of the American Constitution* (1990), which is also organized by topic.

There is a wealth of secondary literature addressing various periods in our constitutional history, of which a few are worth noting here. For secondary literature focusing on the founding, see Melvin E. Bradford, *Original Intentions: On the Making and Ratification of the United States Constitution* (1993); Gordon S. Wood, *The Creation of the American Republic 1776–1787* (1969); Bruce Ackerman, "Our Unconventional Founding," 62 *U. Chi. L. Rev.* 475 (1995); and Joseph M. Lynch, *Negotiating the Constitution: The Earliest Debates Over Original Intent* (1999). Professor Currie has also produced a unique and extremely useful constitutional analysis of early congressional activity that is particularly helpful in considering legislative precedents. To this point, there are four volumes in this analysis: David P. Currie, *The Constitution in Congress: The Federalist Period, 1789–1801* (1997); David P. Currie, *The Constitution in Congress: The Jeffersonians, 1801–1829*

(2001); David P. Currie, *The Constitution in Congress: Democrats and Whigs, 1829–1861* (2005); and David P. Currie, *The Constitution in Congress:Descent into the Maelstrom, 1829–1861* (2005). Finally, G. Edward White, *The Constitution and the New Deal* (2000), provides a comprehensive account of the New Deal constitutional crisis.

NECESSARY AND PROPER LEGISLATION

Most of the general works on constitutional law discussed above contain extended discussions of the Necessary and Proper Clause and McCulloch v. Maryland. Nonetheless, there is surprisingly little scholarship focused exclusively on the Clause itself. A few of the more prominent works include William W. Van Alstyne, "The Role of Congress in Determining Incidental Powers of the President and of the Federal Courts: A Comment on the Horizontal Effect of the Sweeping Clause," 40 *Law & Contemp. Probs.* 102 (1976); Eugene Gressman, "Some Thoughts on The Necessary and Proper Clause," 31 *Seton Hall L. Rev.* 37 (2000); Martin S. Flaherty, "John Marshall, McCullouch v. Maryland, and 'We the People': Revisions," 43 Wm. & Mary L. Rev. 1339 (2002); and J. Randy Beck, "The New Jurisprudence of the Necessary and Proper Clause," 2002 *U. Ill. L. Rev.* 581 (2002).

Some recent scholarship has focused on the history of the Necessary and Proper Clause as a basis for arguing in favor of restricting federal legislative power. Randy Barnett has written two articles arguing that the original meaning of the Clause was much narrower and that the term "proper" was meant to prevent legislative actions encroaching on individual liberties: Randy E. Barnett, "The Original Meaning of the Necessary and Proper Clause," 6 *U. Pa. J. Const. L.* 183 (2003); Randy E. Barnett, "Necessary and Proper," 44 *U.C.L.A. L. Rev.* 745 (1997). The substance of these articles eventually found its way into a book-length presentation of his libertarian view on the meaning of the Constitution: Randy E. Barnett, *Restoring the Lost Constitution* (2004). A similarly restrictive view of the Clause is advanced in Gary Lawson & Patricia B. Granger, "The 'Proper' Scope of Federal Power: A Jurisdictional Interpretation of the Sweeping Clause," 43 *Duke L.J.* 267, 297 (1993). Other articles in the same vein include David E. Engdahl, "The Necessary and Proper Clause as an Intrinsic Restraint on Federal Lawmaking Power," 22 *Harv. J. L. & Pub. Pol'y* 107 (1998); and H. Jefferson Powell, "Enumerated Means and Unlimited Ends," 94 *Mich. L. Rev.* 651 (1995). An alternative historical account concluding that the Clause derived from agency law and confirmed broad authority to implement the charge entrusted in Congress as well as Congress's fiduciary duty to the people is Robert G. Natelson, "The Agency Law Origins of the Necessary and Proper Clause," 55 *Case W. Res. L. Rev.* 243 (2004).

There is also a great deal of literature focusing on the early history of the Bank of the United States, which is rich in contextual detail for the decision in *McCulloch*. Historical documents are gathered in M. St. Clair Clarke & D.A.

Hall, eds., *Legislative and Documentary History of the Bank of the United States* (1832). A broad overview of the historical role of banks, including the Bank of the United States, can be found in Bray Hammond, *Banks and Politics in America from the Revolution to the Civil War* (1957). Historical works focusing on Jackson's opposition to the second Bank of the United States include Robert V. Remini, *Andrew Jackson and the Bank War* (1967); R. Cattrall, *The Second Bank of the United States* (1902); and Thomas P. Govan, *Nicholas Biddle: Nationalist and Public Banker* (1959).

Most of the literature addressing the Necessary and Proper Clause and *McCulloch* does so in the context of a discussion of other enumerated powers. As one might expect, much of this literature focuses on the commerce power. Some of the leading articles addressing necessary and proper legislation under the commerce power include Robert H. Bork & Daniel E. Troy, "Locating the Boundaries: The Scope of Congress's Power to Regulate Commerce," 25 *Harv. J. L. & Pub. Pol'y* 849 (2002); John T. Valauri, "The Clothes Have No Emperor, Or, Cabining the Commerce Clause," 41 *San Diego L. Rev.* 405 (2004); Donald H. Regan, "How to Think About the Federal Commerce Power and Incidentally Rewrite United States v. Lopez," 94 *Mich. L. Rev.* 554 (1995); David G. Wille, "The Commerce Clause: A Time for Reevaluation," 70 *Tulane L. Rev.* 1069 (1996); Martin H. Redish, "Doing It With Mirrors: New York v. United States and Constitutional Limitations on Federal Power to Require State Legislation," 21 *Hastings Const. L. Q.* 593 (1994); Lawrence Lessig, "Translating Federalism: United States v. Lopez," 1995 *Sup. Ct. Rev.* 125 (1995); and Grant S. Nelson & Robert J. Pushaw, Jr., "Rethinking the Commerce Clause: Applying First Principles to Uphold Federal Commercial Regulations But Preserve State Control Over Social Issues," 85 *Iowa L. Rev.* 1 (1999). For a comprehensive review of recent commerce power scholarship, see Arthur B. Mark, III, "Currents in Commerce Clause Scholarship since Lopez: A Survey," 32 *Cap. U. L. Rev.* 671 (2004).

The literature on other federal legislative powers is less voluminous, but there is nonetheless some useful scholarship addressing the relationship between those powers and the Necessary and Proper Clause. For discussion of the spending power, see David E. Engdahl, "The Spending Power," 44 *Duke L.J.* 1 (1994); Gary Lawson, "Making a Federal Case Out of It: Sabri v. United States and the Constitution of Leviathan," 2004 *Cato Sup. Ct. Rev.* 119 (2004); and Richard W. Garnett, "The New Federalism, the Spending Power, and Federal Criminal Law," 89 *Cornell L. Rev.* 1 (2003). The Court's recent cases involving the power to enforce the Fourteenth Amendment have provoked a number of articles, many of which are critical: Robert J. Kaczorowski, "The Supreme Court and Congress's Power to Enforce Constitutional Rights: An Overlooked Moral Anomaly," 73 *Fordham L. Rev.* 153 (2004); Robert J. Kaczorowski, "Congress's Power to Enforce Fourteenth Amendment Rights: Lessons from Federal Remedies the Framers Enacted," 42 *Harv. J. Legis.* 187 (2005); John T. Valauri, "McCulloch and the Fourteenth Amendment," 13 *Temp. Pol. & Civ. Rts. L. Rev.* 857 (2004); and Evan H. Caminker, "'Appropriate' Means-ends Constraints on Section 5 Powers,"

53 *Stan. L. Rev.* 1127 (2001). There are also a number of useful articles discussing foreign relations powers. The war power is addressed in John C. Yoo, "The Continuation of Politics By Other Means: The Original Understanding of War Powers," 84 *Cal. L. Rev.* 167 (1996); Michael Stokes Paulsen, "The Constitution of Necessity," 79 *Notre Dame L. Rev.* 1257 (2004); and Michael Stokes Paulsen, "Youngstown Goes to War," 19 *Const. Comment.* 215 (2002). A recent comprehensive treatment of the treaty power is Nicholas Q. Rosenkranz, "Executing the Treaty Power," 118 *Harv. L. Rev.* 1867 (2005).

LEGISLATIVE DELEGATION AND THE NONDELEGATION DOCTRINE

There is a wealth of literature addressing legislative delegation and the nondelegation doctrine. A classic book-length treatment of these issues and the birth of the administrative state is Leonard D. White, *The Federalists: A Study in Administrative History* (Macmillan Co., 1948). Standard treatments of the nondelegation doctrine include Patrick W. Duff & Horace E. Whiteside, "Delegata Potestas Non Potest Delegari: A Maxim of American Constitutional Law," 14 *Cornell L. Q.* 168 (1928); Kenneth Culp Davis, "A New Approach to Delegation," 36 *U. Chi. L. Rev.* 713 (1969); and Carl McGowan, "Congress, Court and Control of Delegated Power," 77 *Colum. L. Rev.* 1119 (1977). Peter H. Aranson, Ernest Gellhorn, & Glen O. Robinson, "A Theory of Legislative Delegation," 68 *Cornell L. Rev.* 1 (1982), provides an influential and sophisticated economic analysis of delegations. More recent economic treatments of the doctrine drawing on public choice theory include Jerry Mashaw, *Greed, Chaos, and Governance: Using Public Choice to Improve Public Law* (1997), and David B. Spence & Frank Cross, "A Public Choice Case for the Administrative State," 89 *Geo. L. J.* 97 (2000). Other extended analyses of the doctrine include Thomas W. Merrill, "Rethinking Article I, Section 1: From Nondelegation to Exclusive Delegation," 104 *Colum. L. Rev.* 2097 (2004); Lisa Schultz Bressman, "Schechter Poultry at the Millennium: A Delegation Doctrine for the Administrative State," 109 *Yale L. J.* 1399 (2000); and Ronald J. Krotoszynski, Jr., "Reconsidering the Nondelegation Doctrine: Universal Service, the Power to Tax, and the Ratification Doctrine," 80 *Ind. L. J.* 239 (2005).

Periodically, debate over the nondelegation doctrine flares up, as leading scholars either propose reinvigorating the doctrine or dispensing with it altogether. A prominent proponent of a strong nondelegation doctrine is David Schoenbrod, whose ongoing efforts to reinvigorate limits on legislative delegations ultimately culminated in a book-length treatment in which he argued that congressional abuse of legislative delegations undermines democracy by allowing legislators to shirk responsibility: David Schoenbrod, *Power without Responsibility: How Congress Abuses the People Through Delegation* (1993). For critical reaction, see Harold J. Krent, "Delegation and Its Discontents," 94 *Colum L. Rev.* 710 (1994); and Peter Schuck, "Delegation and Democracy: Comments on David Schoenbrod," 20 *Cardozo L. Rev.* 775 (1999). For Professor Schoenbrod's response, see David

Schoenbrod, "Delegation and Democracy: A Reply to My Critics," 20 *Cardozo L. Rev.* 731 (1999).

Professor Gary Lawson has also argued for a reinvigoration of the doctrine based on his view that excessive delegations are not "necessary and proper laws" for carrying into effect the enumerated powers. See Gary Lawson, "Delegation and Original Meaning," 88 *Va. L. Rev.* 327 (2002); and Gary Lawson, "Discretion as Delegation: the "Proper" Understanding of the Nondelegation Doctrine," 73 *Geo. Wash. L. Rev.* 235 (2005). Although I do not agree with all of his conclusions, I find this approach to be of particular interest in the context of this book, because it links the Necessary and Proper Clause and the problem of legislative delegation together as part of a larger theory of the legislative power.

On the other side of the coin, Professors Eric Posner and Adrian Vermeule have created something of a stir by arguing that there is no such thing as the nondelegation doctrine as conventionally understood and reinterpreting John Locke's rule against delegation of the legislative power as limited to the premise that the power to vote on legislation may not be delegated. Eric A. Posner & Adrian Vermeule, "Interring the Nondelegation Doctrine," 69 *U. Chi. L. Rev.* 1721 (2002). This argument prompted a critical response, see Larry Alexander & Saikrishna Prakash, "Reports of the Nondelegation Doctrine's Death Are Greatly Exaggerated," 70 *U. Chi. L. Rev.* 1297 (2003), to which Professors Posner and Vermeule replied in Eric A. Posner & Adrian Vermeule, "Nondelegation: A Post-Mortem," 70 *U. Chi. L. Rev.* 1331 (2003).

DELIBERATIVE POWERS

Although the deliberative powers of Congress have received less attention in the scholarly literature than other aspects of the legislative power, there are nonetheless a number of excellent resources on this topic. A number of sources gather information about the historical use of deliberative powers. These sources are particularly useful because many historical precedents are not otherwise easily identified or discovered. A comprehensive account of Senate disciplinary actions, including use of the contempt power, prepared for the Senate itself, is Richard D. Hupman, ed., *Senate Election, Expulsion and Censure Cases from 1793 to 1972*, S. Doc. No. 7, 92d Cong., 1st Sess. (1972). Somewhat dated yet very useful law review accounts of the use of the deliberative powers are James M. Landis, "Constitutional Limitations on the Congressional Power of Investigation," 40 *Harv. L. Rev.* 153 (1926); and C.S. Potts, "Power of Legislative Bodies to Punish for Contempt, Part I," 74 *U. Pa. L. Rev.* 691 (1926). The McCarthy hearings also prompted some contemporaneous analysis of the investigatory and contempt powers. Telford Taylor, *The Grand Inquest: The Story of Congressional Investigations* (1955) offers an extended treatment of congressional investigations, emphasizing the danger that the investigatory power may be abused as a means of enforcing political orthodoxy. Miriam Lashley, "The Investigating Power of Congress: Its Scope and Limitations," 40 *A.B.A.J.* 763 (1954), winner of the 1954 Ross Essay Contest, undertakes a more objective analysis of the investigatory powers. See also Note, "The Power of Congress to Investigate and to Compel Testimony," 70 *Harv. L. Rev.* 671 (1957). Documents relating to the McCarthy hearings can be found online, with each year's executive sessions of the Permanent Subcommittee on investigations posted as one of five separate PDF documents. For example, the 1953 executive sessions are available at news.find-law.com/hdocs/docs/mccarthy/hearingsvol1.pdf. For subsequent years, the volume number on the URL must be changed.

Several more recent works consider particular components of the deliberative powers. For a concise overview of the constitutional and statutory doctrine concerning contempt, see Jay R. Shampansky, *Congress' Contempt Power* (2003) Other general treatments of deliberative powers include Roberto Iraola, "Congressional Oversight, Executive Oversight, and Requests for Information Relating to Federal Criminal Investigations and Prosecutions," 87 *Iowa L. Rev.* 1559 (2002); Allen B. Moreland, "Congressional Investigations and Private Persons," 40 *S. Cal. L. Rev.* 189 (1966); and Sam Nunn, "The Impact of the Senate Permanent Subcommittee on Investigations on Federal Policy," 21 *Ga. L. Rev.* 17 (1986) . For analysis focusing on internal self-policing by Congress, see Theresa A. Gabaldon, "The Self-Regulation of Congressional Ethics: Substance and Structure," 48 *Admin. L. Rev.* 39 (1996). Peter M. Shane, "Presidents, Pardons, and Prosecutors: Legal Accountability and the Separation of Powers," 11 *Yale L. & Pol'y Rev.* 361 (1993), provides a more general examination of separation of powers relating to investigations and prosecutions that touches on the deliberative powers of Congress.

Considerable attention has been devoted to the particular problem of congressional investigations into the executive branch, either generally or in connection with an impeachment inquiry. Several articles consider these issues in general terms. See Stanley M. Brand & Sean Connelly, "Constitutional Confrontations: Preserving a Prompt and Orderly Means By Which Congress May Enforce Investigative Demands Against Executive Branch Officials," 36 *Cath. U. L. Rev.* 71 (1986); Todd D. Peterson, "Prosecuting Executive Branch Officials for Contempt of Congress," 66 *N.Y.U.L. Rev.* 563 (1991); Project, "An Overview of Congressional Investigation of the Executive: Procedures, Devices, and Limitations of Congressional Investigative Power," 1 *Syracuse J. Legis. & Pol'y* 1 (1995); and Michael B. Rappaport, "Replacing Independent Counsels with Congressional Investigations," 148 *U. Pa. L. Rev.* 1595 (2000). For discussion that focuses on the congressional role in impeachments, see Frank O. Bowman & Stephen L. Sepinuck, "High Crimes and Misdemeanors: Defining the Constitutional Limits on Presidential Impeachment," 72 *S. Cal. L. Rev.* 1517 (1999), and Jonathan Turley, "Senate Trials and Factional Disputes: Impeachment as a Madisonian Device," 49 *Duke L.J.* 1 (1999). See also Jack Chaney, "The Constitutionality of Censuring the President," 61 *Ohio St. L. J.* 979 (2000) (arguing against a congressional power to censure the president).

Several works focus on particular congressional investigations or impeachments relating to the executive branch. The classic treatment of the Watergate prosecution, written by the special prosecutor himself, is Leon Jaworski, *The Right and the Power: The Prosecution of Watergate* (1976). See also Mark J. Rozell, "Executive Privilege and the Modern Presidents: In Nixon's Shadow," 83 *Minn. L. Rev.* 1069 (1999). Discussions of the Iran-Contra investigations include R.S. Ghio, "The Iran-Contra Prosecutions and the Failure of Use Immunity," 45 *Stan. L. Rev.* 229 (1992), and Robert F. Turner, "The Constitution and the Iran-Contra Affair: Was Congress the Real Lawbreaker?" 11 *Hous. J. Int'l L.* 83 (1988). Of course, the literature on the Clinton impeachment abounds, most of it focusing on issues such as the constitutional standard for impeachment or the role of the independent counsel, neither of which are particularly relevant to the issues addressed in this book. Three works that afford some attention to the processes within the House and Senate are Richard A. Posner, *An Affair of State: The Investigation, Impeachment, and Trial of President Clinton* (1999); Susan Low Bloch, "A Report Card on the Impeachment: Judging the Institutions That Judged President Clinton," 63 *Law & Contemp. Probs.* 143 (2000); and Charles Tiefer, "The Senate Impeachment Trial for President Clinton," 28 *Hofstra L. Rev.* 407 (1999).

Finally, a number of works examine the external limits on the contempt and investigatory powers of Congress. For discussion of the Fifth Amendment privilege against self-incrimination in the context of congressional investigations, see Michael Edmund O'Neill, "The Fifth Amendment in Congress: Revisiting the Privilege Against Compelled Self-Incrimination," 90 *Geo. L.J.* 2445 (2002), and Roberto Iraola, "Self-Incrimination and Congressional Hearings," 54 *Mercer L. Rev.* 939 (2005). The avoidance of Fifth Amendment issues through the grant of immunity by congressional committees and the implications of immunity for other investigations are explored in Howard R. Sklamberg, "Investigation versus Prosecution: The Constitutional Limits on Congress's Power to Immunize Witnesses," 78 *N.C. L. Rev.* 153 (1999), and John von Loben Sels, Note, "From Watergate to Whitewater: Congressional Use Immunity and its Impact on the Independent Counsel," 83 *Geo. L.J.* 2385 (1995). The First Amendment implications of congressional investigations are discussed in James J. Mangan, "Contempt for the Fourth Estate: No Reporter's Privilege Before a Congressional Investigation," 83 *Geo. L.J.* 129 (1994). Several of these articles generally address the investigatory power in order to provide background for their analysis of particular constitutional limits.

COLLECTIVE ACTION AND INTERSTATE RELATIONS

Since Mancur Olson's seminal work, *The Logic of Collective Action* (1965), there has been considerable development in the theory of collective action, which has made its way into the legal literature and is increasingly applied in the context of interstate relations. Some works directed toward collective action generally include James S. Coleman, *Individual Interests and Collective Action* (1986); Michael Hechter, *Principles of Group Solidarity* (1987); Mancur Olson, *The Rise and Decline of Nations* (1982); David Reisman, *Theories of Collective Action*

(1990); Todd Sandler, *Collective Action: Theory and Applications* (1992); and Thomas Schwartz, *The Logic of Collective Choice* (1986). Other research has emerged to challenge the accuracy of Olson's analysis. An overview of this research can be found in Dan M. Kahan, "The Logic of Reciprocity: Trust, Collective Action, and Law," 102 *Mich. L. Rev.* 71 (2003).

The application of collective action theory to interstate relations, including federalism, is of relatively recent origin. For general discussion of collective action theory and federalism, see William W. Buzbee, "Recognizing the Regulatory Commons: A Theory of Regulatory Gaps," 89 *Iowa L. Rev.* 1 (2003); Clayton P. Gillette, "The Exercise of Trumps by Decentralized Governments," 83 *Va. L. Rev.* 1347 (1997); Ken Killman, John H. Miller, & Scott E. Page, "Decentralization and the Search for Policy Solutions," 16 *J. L. Econ. & Org.* 102 (2000); and Richard E. Levy, "Federalism and Collective Action," 45 *U. Kan. L. Rev.* 1241 (1997).

A great deal of recent literature addresses the problem of interjurisdictional competition in federal systems using economic theory to address the question whether this sort of competition is beneficial or leads to a "race to the bottom." The debate originated in the field of corporate law, where critics argued that regulation of corporate governance and structure had become too lax as a result of competition for corporate charters. See William L. Cary, "Federalism and Corporate Law: Reflections upon Delaware," 83 *Yale L.J.* 663 (1974). For a more recent exposition of this critique, see Lucian Arye Bebchuk, "Federalism and the Corporation: The Desirable Limits on State Competition in Corporate Law," 105 *Harv. L. Rev.* 1435, 1441 (1992). The race-to-the-bottom argument was challenged by critics from the law and economics movement who argued that competition for corporations led to more efficient legal rules concerning corporate governance. See, for example, Daniel R. Fischel, "The 'Race to the Bottom' Revisited: Reflections on Recent Developments in Delaware's Corporation Law," 76 *Nw. L. Rev.* 913 (1982); Roberta Romano, "Law as a Product: Some Pieces of the Incorporation Puzzle," 1 *J.L. Econ. & Org.* 225 (1985); and Ralph K. Winter, "State Law, Shareholder Protection, and the Theory of the Corporation," 6 *J. Legal Stud.* 251 (1977). Some, however, have challenged the notion that there is competition for corporate charters (as opposed to the actual location of businesses) at all. Marcel Kahan & Ehud Kamar, "The Myth of State Competition in Corporate Law," 55 *Stan. L. Rev.* 679 (2002).

The race-to-the-bottom metaphor has spilled over into other areas as well. There is, for example, a spirited debate regarding the existence of a race to the bottom in environmental law. See Daniel C. Esty, "Revitalizing Environmental Federalism," 95 *Mich. L. Rev.* 570 (1996); Richard L. Revesz, "Rehabilitating Interstate Competition: Rethinking the "Race-to-the-Bottom" Rationale for Federal Environmental Regulation," 67 *N.Y.U. L. Rev.* 1210 (1992); and Peter P. Swire, "The Race to Laxity and the Race to Undesirability: Explaining Failures in Competition Among Jurisdictions in Environmental Law," 14 *Yale J. Reg.* 67 (1996). Similarly, scholars have used the prisoners' dilemma and race-to-the-bottom analysis in analyzing state and local tax incentives to influence business location decisions. See Peter D. Enrich, "Saving the States from Themselves: Commerce Clause Constraints on State Tax Incentives for Business," 110 *Harv. L. Rev.* 377 (1996); Daniel P. Petrov, Note, "Prisoners No More: State Investment Relocation Incentives and The Prisoners' Dilemma," 33 *Case W. Res. J. Int'l L.* 71 (2001); and Maxwell L. Stearns, "A Beautiful Mend: A Game Theoretical Analysis of the Dormant Commerce Clause Doctrine," 45 *Wm. & Mary L. Rev.* 1 (2003); see also Christopher R. Drahozal, "On Tariffs v. Subsidies in Interstate Trade: A Legal and Economic Analysis," 74 *Wash. U. L.Q.* 1127 (1996). Collective action theory has also been used to analyze the unification of state laws. See Edward J. Janger, "Predicting When the Uniform Law Process Will Fail: Article 9, Capture, and the Race to the Bottom," 83 *Iowa L. Rev.* 569 (1998); and John Linarelli, "The Economics of Uniform Laws and Uniform Lawmaking," 48 *Wayne L. Rev.* 1387 (2003).

Federalism is just one approach to cooperation among states, and the collective action issues confronting federal systems are also present in international relations. For discussion of collective action theory and international relations, see Anne-Marie Slaughter, Andrew S. Tulumello, & Stephen Wood, "International Law and International Relations Theory: A New Generation of Interdisciplinary Scholarship," 92 *Am. J. Int'l L.* 367 (1998); and Jeffrey L. Dunoff & Joel P. Trachtman, "Economic Analysis of International Law," 24 *Yale J. Int'l Law* 1 (1999). See also Anne-Marie Slaughter Burley, "International Law and International Relations Theory: A Dual Agenda," 97 *Am. J. Int'l L.* 205 (1993). Like the federalism literature, the international law literature applies economic and collective-action theory and focuses a great deal of attention on interjurisdictional competition and its implications. See Bruno S. Frey & Reiner Eichenberger, "FOCJ: Competitive Governments for Europe," 16 *Int'l Rev. L. & Econ.* 315 (1996); Joel P. Trachtman, "Economic Analysis of Prescriptive Jurisdiction," 42 *Va. J. Int'l L.* 1 (2001); Horatia Muir Watt, "Choice of Law in Integrated and Interconnected Markets: A Matter of Political Economy," 9 *Colum. J. Eur. L.* 383 (2003); and Robert van den Bergh, Michael Faure, & Jurgen Lefevere, *The Subsidiarity Principle in European Environmental Law: An Economic Analysis, in Law and Economics of the Environment* (Eide & van den Bergh eds., 1996).

Table of Cases

Index

Adams, John Quincy, 40
administrative agencies, 26, 60, 96, 131, 135–38, 141, 146, 174n136, 174nn139–40, 175n152, 189; adjudicatory hearings, 124; the administrative or regulatory state, 57, 62–65, 74, 124, 176n168; administrative rules and regulations, 30, 51–53, 74–76, 124, 127–28, 130, 174n139, 175n156, 175n160
Age Discrimination in Employment Act, 68, 73
agency costs, 84–88, 138–39, 144–45, 162n5
agency law, 16, 77n4, 78n7. *See also* Necessary and Proper Clause
aggregate effects. *See* cumulative effects doctrine
Agricultural Adjustment Act, 57
A.L.A. Schechter Poultry Co. v. United States, 57–62, 74, 127–37, 175–78
Alden v. Maine, 8n10, 73, 94–95, 119
Alien and Sedition Acts, 19, 180n224
Alito, Justice Samuel, 77, 121
American Communications Associations v. Douds, 183n267
American Power & Light Co. v. Securities and Exchange Commission, 62, 128, 131, 176n158
American Revolution, 13
Americans with Disabilities Act, 8, 68, 69, 73, 100

American Textile Manufacturers Institute, Inc., v. Donovan, 74
Anderson v. Dunn, 9nn17–18, 33–34, 40, 53–54, 144, 151, 153, 166n50, 182n244
antebellum era, 12, 35–41
anti-Federalists, 17–19, 21, 33, 35
Article I: bicameralism and presentment provisions, 4, 8n13, 30, 134; transformation of Congress by, 13, 15–16; Vesting Clause, 4, 94, 125, 186, 189. *See also* bicameralism and presentment; Necessary and Proper Clause; *specific enumerated powers*
Article II, 3. *See also* executive power
Article III, 70, 75, 101, 110, 124, 125, 167n59
Article IV, 39
Articles of Confederation: application of collective action theory, 87–89, 163n13; compared to the Constitution, 12–16, 23; debts under, 19; foreign affairs under, 49; treaties made under, 80n51
asylum, 5–6
attorney general, 5–6, 20, 26, 55, 132, 137, 149

Bailey v. Drexel Furniture Co. (Child Labor Tax Case), 48–49, 96, 113, 164n30, 165n32
Bank of the United States. *See* national bank

interstate commerce. *See* commerce power
Interstate Commerce Commission, 7n7,
48, 51
investigatory power: collective action
theory and, 145; deliberative process,
142–44; external limits on, 156–57;
historical precedents, 31–35, 39–41,
53–56, 64–65; intrinsic limits on,
149–51, 154; subpoena power, 1–9,
31–32, 40–41, 53, 64, 139–40, 149–54,
160–61, 178n199, 179nn207–9,
181n236, 184n275; use immunity, 156,
160–61
Iran-Contra Arms for Hostages
investigation, 156
Iraq, delegation of war power and, 136,
178n187, 178nn189–90

Jackson, Andrew, 35–36, 40, 46, 79n38
Jefferson, Thomas, 20–21, 25, 33, 46,
78n10, 78n15, 78nn18–19, 79n37,
179n209
Jinks v. Richland County, S.C., 70, 101,
110, 114, 167n59, 170n84
Johnson, Andrew, 42–43
Johnson, Justice William, 28, 33–34
judicial review, 6, 75, 77, 101, 130–31,
148, 158–61, 162n9, 188
Judiciary Act of 1789, 19, 28
jurisdictional nexus. *See* United States v.
Lopez
Jurney v. MacCracken, 55, 154, 180n216,
181n239, 182nn243–46
J. W. Hampton, Jr. & Co. v. United States,
52, 126, 129, 174n143

Kassel v. Consolidated Freightways,
172n20
Katzenbach v. McClung, 63, 169n73,
169n76, 172n111
Katzenbach v. Morgan, 8n8, 62, 68, 70,
97, 106, 171n100, 171n106
Kennedy, Justice Anthony, 11
Kentucky Div., Horsemen's Benev. &
Protective Ass'n, Inc. v. Turfway
Park Racing Ass'n, Inc., 177n177,
177n179
Kentucky v. Dennison, 38, 70

Kent v. Dulles, 137
Kilbourn v. Thompson, 9n18, 53–56,
64–65, 79n34, 80n57, 149, 154,
160–61, 179n210, 180n225, 184n272
Kimel v. Florida Board of Regents, 8n8,
68, 73, 99, 173n125
Korean War, 2
Ku Klux Klan Act of 1871, 44

laissez faire constitutionalism, 13, 46,
50–53, 56–57, 60, 69
Lassiter v. Northampton County Bd. of
Elections, 63, 98
least power concept, 34, 101, 149, 153–54
Legal Tender Cases, 165n31
legislative agencies, 142
legislative immunity, 15, 148, 160–61,
180n225
legislative veto, 4–6, 75, 134
letters of marque and reprisal, 14
Leventhal, Judge Harold, 130
libel, 9n18, 31–32, 146–48, 151–52, 154,
156, 179n213, 180n218, 180nn223–24
liberties, 11, 17, 101, 120, 137
liberty of contract, freedom of contract,
50–51, 172n113
Library of Congress, 142
License Cases, 37
Lichter v. United States, 62, 174n138,
178n192
Lincoln, Abraham, 42
Line Item Veto Act, 9n21, 74, 76, 125
literacy requirements, equal protection
and, 63, 98, 171n106
Lochner v. State of New York, 50–51, 57,
62, 81n62, 116, 172n113
Lottery Case (Champion v. Ames), 48
Loving v. United States, 131–33, 176n170
Luther v. Borden, 44

Madison, James: construction of
Necessary and Proper Clause, 20–21,
36, 46; construction of spending power,
95; defense of Necessary and Proper
Clause, 1–2, 7n5, 17–18, 109, 168n63;
investigatory powers and, 32, 95; view
of factions, 123
Mann Act, 48